KU-734-965

CHRIST CHURCH
COLLEGE
CANTERBURY

AUTHOR. SWIATECKA, M.J.

TITLE. The idea of the symbol

CLASS NO. 820.8   COPY   B

THE IDEA OF THE SYMBOL

THE IDEA
OF THE SYMBOL

SOME NINETEENTH CENTURY
COMPARISONS WITH COLERIDGE

M. Jadwiga Swiatecka O.P.

CAMBRIDGE UNIVERSITY PRESS

CAMBRIDGE

LONDON   NEW YORK   NEW ROCHELLE

MELBOURNE   SYDNEY

Published by the Press Syndicate of the University of Cambridge
The Pitt Building, Trumpington Street, Cambridge CB2 1RP
32 East 57th Street, New York, NY 10022, USA
296 Beaconsfield Parade, Middle Park, Melbourne 3206, Australia

© Cambridge University Press 1980

First published 1980

Phototypeset in V.I.P. Baskerville by
Western Printing Services Ltd, Bristol
Printed in Great Britain at the
University Press, Cambridge

Library of Congress Cataloguing in Publication Data

Swiatecka, M Jadwiga.
The idea of the symbol.

Bibliography: p.
1. Symbolism – History. 2. Symbolism in literature.
3. Coleridge, Samuel Taylor, 1772–1834 – Allegory and symbolism.
4. Coleridge, Samuel Taylor, 1772–1834 – Influence. 5. English
literature – 19th century – History and criticism.
I. Title.
BV150.S89   201'.4   79–19802
ISBN 0 521 22362 8

171428

CONTENTS

Contents

PREFACE

I should like to acknowledge here my indebtedness to all those –
too many to name – who, by the help of their interest, encour-
agement, friendship or service, have made the writing of this
book possible. I should particularly like to thank the superiors
of my branch of the Dominican Order, The English Congregation of St Catherine of Siena, for allowing me the time for the
research involved, and to my own community, first at
Portobello Road, London, and later at Ealing, for its support
throughout.

My thanks are also due to Drs G. T. Cavaliero, J. W. Goetz,
D. M. Thompson and P. J. Sherry, and to Professors Dorothy
Emmet and N. L. A. Lash for discussing with me certain
aspects of the book during its early stages; and to Professor
D. M. McKinnon and Dr Stephen Prickett for their encouraging
reception of the completed manuscript. To all these I am
indebted for many helpful criticisms and suggestions.

Most of all, however, my thanks are due to Professor W. B.
Gallie, without whose interest and friendship this book would
neither have been begun nor ended. The stimulus to thought
provided first by his teaching, and then by correspondence and
conversations over many years has been largely instrumental in
the book's genesis, while his constant readiness to discuss with me
the problems involved was indispensable to its progress. Without this help, which invariably gave me fresh insight into the questions tackled, this book would have been by much the poorer.

Ealing   MJS, O.P.
Feast of St Catherine of Siena
April 1978

A NOTE ON NOTES

Whenever it has been possible to do so briefly, I have given the reference to both longer and shorter quotations in brackets within the text, rather than as footnotes. For this purpose I have used abbreviations for those titles which recur frequently. A key to these will be found at the beginning of the notes to the chapter in which they first, and most often, occur. Full details of editions used will be found in the Bibliography.

INTRODUCTION

There is a story told of an au pair girl who, on attending a Christmas service with her English employers, was puzzled by the phrase 'Mary was great with child'. This was easily and satisfactorily explained to her, but the explanation served only to add to her bewilderment when at a subsequent party she heard the father of the family described as 'great with children'.

I find myself in the same predicament of puzzled incomprehension with respect to the term 'symbol' and its cognates. Just when I think I know what the term means, I come across it in a context which destroys my confidence. I used to think that this was because, like the au pair girl, I had not really grasped the idiom. While this may still be true, I now think that the fault lies at least as much in the imprecisions with which the terms are used, and in the confusions which surround the concept. This book is an attempt to indicate what some, at least, of these imprecisions and confusions are, and why it is important that they should not be overlooked. It is therefore also a plea that, in the age of semiotics which seems to be upon us, more careful attention should be paid to the way these terms are used for, I submit, at present they are too often "full of sound and fury, signifying nothing".

What these confusions and imprecisions are in general I indicate in the next chapter. But my more particular examples I choose from the fields of literature and theology in the nineteenth century. For it was, roughly, at the beginning of that century that the effects of historical and scientific research began to throw serious doubts on the literal understanding of Scripture (and hence, also, on theological statements). One consequence of this was that the language of Scripture, and theology, began to be more widely regarded not as scientific or historical, but as a form of poetry. At the same time, however, with the rise of the 'Romantic' movement, Aristotle's theory of art as 'imitation' was being extended and replaced in such a way that poetry could no longer be regarded as a mirror held up to nature.[1] The question, then, of how, if not literally, or as faithful copies, any theological or literary language forms represented the truths which they attempted to convey became of increasingly greater moment. By the end of the century, the growing dissatisfaction with the 'copy' theory of knowledge, in view of the realization that *all* that we know is known, and therefore conveyed, from a particular standpoint, led to the suspicion that even scientific language was not literal. As a consequence, today we are prone to say – too easily – that all language and all knowledge is 'symbolic'. But unless we know what we mean by this term, we have said no more than that language is somehow not literal. To determine more precisely what this 'somehow' means, attention to the use of the term 'symbol' and its cognates by those who were beginning to grapple with these problems is instructive. In any case, an attempted analysis of twentieth century usages would have been too diffuse to be valuable, such is the proliferation of these terms.

One misconception about the use of the term 'symbol' in the nineteenth century must be cleared up at the outset. Because of our own, twentieth century, inclination to use the terms associated with it so profusely, writers on nineteenth century authors too often give the impression that these terms were equally prominent in the works which they review. Thus, for instance, W. A. Madden, in his doctoral dissertation on 'The Religious and Aesthetic Ideas of Matthew Arnold' writes that

Arnold has successfully made a transition from the old world of religious faith in an absolute, to the new world of scientific relativism. Arnold has managed to accept the historical dialectic without losing a centre, a point of rest, from which to master the outer spectacle and to control the inner dialogue which this dialectic uncovers. The centre, the point of rest, is the symbol – the poetic incarnation of the moment seen in the light of the imaginative ideal of beauty. (p. 115.)

And again,

Rational ideas as 'notions' under the dominion of the Time-spirit, relative and changing, are transformed by the imagination into symbols, which are historical variations on the permanent, the eternal human emotions. (p. 116.)

From such statements it would seem that the term 'symbol', and with the meaning ascribed to it here, must be a significant one in Arnold's works. But it is not. Arnold uses the word and its cognates hardly at all, and in those few (perhaps half a dozen) instances, only in passing. In these instances, moreover, the term 'symbol' for him means nothing like "the poetic incarnation of the moment seen in the light of imaginative beauty". This is disappointing, and it is a disappointment many times repeated in reading through both nineteenth century literary criticism and the documents of religious controversy, if one is interested in discovering what the terms when actually used meant to those who used them, rather than in designating as 'symbolic' some notion of language which the writers themselves described in quite other terms. For such, often improper, attribution is itself the cause of much current confusion.

The disappointment has, however, this advantage. It has meant that in the pursuit in which I have been engaged, which is – I must repeat – to discover what the term 'symbol' and its cognates meant when actually used in the contexts I have suggested, the cases for study have largely selected themselves. Coleridge, Carlyle, Newman, Inge, Tyrrell and MacDonald are here firstly because they use the terms significantly (though sometimes ambiguously) in relation to the way in which language functions in conveying truth or truths in literature and, or, theology. Omissions, as in the case of Arnold, but also of, for instance, F. D. Maurice, have been dictated by the fact that the terms under scrutiny do not appear significantly in their work, however surprising this may seem to us.

The choice, however, is not quite as fortuitous as this might make it seem. The inclusion of Coleridge needs no justification, not only because of his stature as poet and writer, but also because he is said to have 'popularized' the term 'symbol'[2] and because it has been asserted that in any consideration of symbolism, all roads lead back to him.[3] These statements themselves are questionable, as I shall show, but they indicate why he must be taken as a starting point. Carlyle and Newman, like

Coleridge, are sufficiently important nineteenth century writers to deserve inclusion if their uses of the relevant terms warrant this, as Carlyle's certainly does. Additionally, there is at least some question of how far the ideas of either might have been influenced by their older contemporary, Coleridge, and this has been a further motive for including Newman who, important as he is, does not use the term 'symbol' as often as might be thought. Moreover, recent distinction and conflation between his use of the term 'symbol' and that of Coleridge[4] illustrates neatly the kinds of confusions which must be avoided if the concept is to be helpful in contemporary discussions which involve such comparisons. George MacDonald, far removed as he is from the importance of either a Newman or a Carlyle, is included also because of his – in this case acknowledged – indebtedness to Coleridge, and also because his two 'fantasies for grown ups', *Lilith* and *Phantastes*, are now being seen as conscious attempts to embody in literary form (in some sense, therefore, in 'symbol') a theological content, and even, perhaps, to create through such embodiment new theological insights.[5] Inge and Tyrrell fall outside this link of indebtedness to Coleridge; it is doubtful if Tyrrell ever read him, and while Inge certainly did, he was equally certainly suspicious of his thought. They both belong, moreover, more purely to the theological rather than the literary sphere, and are probably not familiar to those who may have a wide acquaintance with the other authors mentioned. But Tyrrell's connection is with Newman, whom he cited as a progenitor of ideas for the development of which he was suspected of heresy, and in which the vocabulary of symbolization played no small part. Inge, while he distrusted the movement to which Tyrrell belonged, himself made use of the terms at about the same time, so that a comparison is interesting in any case; but also, while on the whole repudiating Coleridge, he wrote in the same Platonist tradition, which itself is capable of various interpretations. All six authors are therefore linked more or less directly, and the meanings with which each uses the terms in question are brought into sharper relief when juxtaposed with each other, and when seen more particularly in relation to those of Coleridge, which I use as the basis of comparison. His concept of 'symbol' is central to his philosophy and, in spite of its shortcomings, emerges as by far the most consistently used, the

4

most thoroughly thought through, and the most challenging because capable of further development. This view may not be surprising, but the analysis serves to show clearly where even present day thinking on the whole topic of symbolization needs to be extended, deepened and clarified.

Because, for the purpose of this investigation, I have wanted to make comparisons between more than two or three authors, and between closely inspected uses of the term 'symbol' and its cognates, particularly in relation to Coleridge, who therefore – as indeed he deserves – receives the closest and most extended attention, I have not been able to pursue all possible lines of investigation. As far as the authors treated in this book are concerned, I may seem, for instance, not to have paid due attention to all the changes in Newman's thought, and to have underplayed his Aristotelianism and his indebtedness to Butler. To do full justice to his thinking – which, as Charles Kingsley discovered to his cost, often prompts the question "What then did Newman mean?" – would have needed a different kind of book, and the subject has, in any case, received recent attention.[6] I have deliberately taken note only of that context which is directly relevant to his (as I have said) infrequent use of the term 'symbol', and I think sufficiently so to show significant ambiguities. It could be that further enquiry would show other divergent – or convergent – aspects of meaning, but this would not, I think, affect the argument. I regret, however, that I have not been able to pursue some comparison between Newman and another disciple of Bishop Butler, H. L. Mansel, who became Dean of St Paul's (1861–1871), and of whom, somewhat surprisingly perhaps, Newman approved. But even here I hope that I have given sufficient indication of the important consequences of imprecision.

There are, of course, very many other areas of interest relevant to the meanings of the term 'symbol' which I have scarcely touched, or not touched at all. One obvious one is the functioning of the term in the aesthetic theories of the French 'Symboliste' poets; another is its use by Emerson and his American contemporaries; a third is a comparison between Goethe and both Coleridge and Carlyle. The first and last of these would require an expertise in French and German greater than I possess; and like these, the American scene might deserve a study of its own. What I have attempted is necessarily limited since its purpose is to examine detail. Like archaeological digs the pursuit is at times exacting, appearing to concentrate only on minutiae, and one may often be tempted to raise one's eyes from one's own patch of ground to wider and more enticing scenery round about. But the sherds that are unearthed are often exciting and revealing. If my task here has been only to uncover a general outline of the foundations which underlie the complex structure of meanings attendant on the vocabulary of symbolization, and to have cleared one corner from its tangle of thorny growth, such preliminaries are necessary and can prove rewarding.

1

THE CONCEPT OF 'SYMBOL'

Our Present Discontents

"The word 'symbol'," wrote C. S. Peirce at the turn of the century, "has so many meanings that it would be an injury to language to add a new one."[1]

Since then the word has acquired such popularity, both in everyday speech and as a field of philosophical enquiry, that it is hardly possible to suppose that such injury has been avoided. Indeed, a number of writers have remarked upon the term's ubiquity, its practically indefinite extension, and the bewilderment to which such width of applicability can give rise. Martin Foss, H. H. Price, S. K. Langer, Brand Blanshard, F. W. Dillistone[2] have all, in various ways, indicated the term's diffusion and consequent diffuseness. Nevertheless, few of those who use the term 'symbol' or its cognates, even as central to the content of their exposition of a given subject, make any attempt to indicate the meaning they attach to them. One of the editors of the papers for the 13th Symposium of the Conference on Science, Philosophy and Religion, held in New York in 1952, whose general topic was *Symbols and Values: an Initial Study*, had occasion to remark in his introductory chapter that, out of forty-five papers submitted, only four undertook seriously to say anything about the nature of symbols and their use;[3] and if one glances through any collection of papers on symbols or symbolism the same lack of definition is soon evident.

Yet the implied assumption of univocity of the terms in question seems open to challenge on all sides. For one meets the term 'symbol', for instance, as a designation of widely heterogeneous entities; from hunger-cramps to Christ; from letters of the alphabet to 'the universe'; from dreams to mathematical formulae and their components; from the coloured shapes which compose our perception, to creeds and *King Lear*; – a variety which includes actual objects, language constructs, historical events, and indeed everything and anything. And this range of references makes it difficult to give clear focus to the other connected terms, such as 'symbolism', 'symbolization', 'symbolical' (even 'symbolific') when no indication of their particular use is given.

Sometimes, of course, the context is itself an indication of the author's general meaning, or of the class of things to which his use applies. At other times a definition is given which delimits that use for the purpose in view. Thus D. G. James's categorical statement that

The symbol is not something which stands for another thing: it is the way the object is given precision to our minds . . . it is a way of seeing the object which comes to clarity for us only in the form of symbol (*Matthew Arnold and the Decline of English Romanticism*, p. 46),

can be taken to apply to literary symbols only; whilst Ernest Nagel is careful to couch his definition thus:

By a symbol I understand any occurrence (or type of occurrence) usually linguistic in status, which is taken to signify something else by way of tacit or explicit conventions or rules of usage. ('Symbolism and Science', in *Symbols and Values: an Initial Study*, p. 44.)

Frequently, however, such delimitations are not made and are impossible to arrive at from a given context. Thus, to the same collection as Nagel's article, Dorothy D. Lee contributes an essay[4] whose thesis is that "the symbol is *in fact* a part of a whole" (p. 73, my italics) and it is not clear that she means to limit this in any specific way. Moreover, some definitions tend to create puzzling anomalies. Thus Nagel's definition compels him to speak, somewhat curiously, of the world 'bald' as a symbol of the class of those who are bald: while it excludes a large number of things which are normally designated 'symbols'; and definitions like Jung's, that a symbol is

the expression of an intuitive perception which can as yet neither be apprehended better nor expressed differently (*Contributions to Analytic Psychology*, p. 232),

exclude the signs of mathematics and logic to which the term 'symbol' is equally firmly attached.

Anomalous as this might be, it would not be confusing if there were some agreement that there are at least two more or less equivocal uses of the term 'symbol'. Instead, there are repeated attempts to produce a definition which will cover all cases. Even Alfred Schutz, who notes the heterogeneity of the term 'symbol' and 'symbolization', eventually says

If we try to find the common denominator of the various theories on significative and symbolic relations . . . we may say that the object, fact, or event called sign or symbol refers to something other than itself. ('Symbol, Reality and Society' in *Symbols and Society*, ed. Bryson, p. 143.)

This 'over-all' definition appears to exclude the kinds of symbols James was attempting to specify, as well as the symbols which pure mathematicians manipulate. And the same may be said of Blanshard's

the symbol is a means or vehicle that helps us fix our thought on something beyond it. ('Symbolism' in *Religious Experience and Truth: a Symposium*, p. 48.)

The same criticism of a failure to be as inclusive as is intended can be levelled at S. K. Langer's definition of symbol as "any device whereby we are led to make an abstraction";[5] similar but more serious here, since her central concern is an all-inclusive definition, and she offers this as a consequence of comparing the symbolic relation in logic and in art. It is difficult to see how this definition can make sense of the term 'symbol' as applied to *King Lear* or *The Tempest* without stretching the words "device" and "abstraction" beyond warrantable limits. Her later, more tentative, reformulation of this to

Any device whereby we make an abstraction is a symbolic element, and all abstraction involves symbolization (*Philosophical Sketches*, p. 63),

is not much more illuminating in this respect. For she has to admit that "there may be many ways of making abstractions and therefore many kinds of symbols", which leaves us with the original puzzle. Besides which she reveals herself wedded to Nagel's definition as the one which designates "genuine symbols", and she thus relegates works of art to the second-class citizenship of "quasi-symbols".

Unfortunately there are a number of writers who take precisely the opposite view, of whom E. I. Watkin may serve as an example since he, like Mrs Langer, is concerned with the "philosophy of form".[6] For him it is the conventional symbol which is not a true symbol, and a genuine symbol is a significant form expressive of an ideal or spiritual being whose reflection it is on the physical plane.

This may be thought odd, but to think it is an illicit departure from central, formal, well-established use is to ignore history. And Mrs Langer's "poor epistemologist" can hardly complain about what seems to him an encroachment of the jungle upon his tidy garden, since he himself is responsible for many of the seeds from which that jungle has sprung. It is disingenuous of H. H. Price to think that the "stretched" sense of the word 'symbol' as used in the Symbolist Theory (of thinking) is not potentially confusing, and that "when someone is told for the first time that thinking is symbolic cognition he knows at once what kind of theory he is being asked to accept . . ." (*Thinking and Experience*, p. 147.) To excuse the philosopher for distending words on the grounds that such distension occurs in barrack-room and bar is to make him more than usually redundant.

In view of the difficulties of arriving at a satisfactory definition to cover all cases of prescribed or actual usage, without having recourse to qualifying adjectives like 'illicit' or 'quasi-' which serve only to hide an inbuilt exclusiveness; and considering the hesitation to admit that the term 'symbol' is simply equivocal, it is surprising that none of those who have tried to deal with the problem have considered this chameleon word with explicit reference to Wittgenstein's notion of family resemblances, i.e. the idea that any set of things may share a group of common characteristics, though there may be no one trait which is common to all. However, those, like Philip Wheelwright,[7] who, while beginning with some very general statement about the nature of all symbols, concentrate rather on indicating the differences which such an initial description covers, might be considered as applying such a principle in effect.

But even then difficulties arise. There is the tendency, first, to give the name 'symbol' to the whole class designated by the original wide statement, using it, as it were, as the surname of the whole clan, and then to apply it exclusively to some groups within that clan. Thus Wheelwright's first definition is that symbols are "more in intention than they are in existence" (p. 7), that is to say that all symbols mean something; but his initial examples of "standing for" (which he quotes approvingly from Mary Anita Ewer, (p. 6)) suggest that symbols 'mean' in a very wide variety of ways. Moreover, it soon becomes evident that he excludes certain cases of meaning from the category of 'symbol'. This suggests that there is a more general, and a more particular, use of the term, and the two need to be more clearly distinguished. Failure to do so is of no real consequence in a careful exposition such as Wheelwright's, but it can be puzzling in other contexts where a writer may pass from one use to another inadvertently, or where it is not clear which use he has in mind.

The lack of distinction between a more general and a more particular use of the term 'symbol' is especially confusing when considered in relation to that other semiotic term 'sign'. For sometimes the words 'sign' and 'symbol' are used synonymously, whilst at other times the two are sharply, though often differently, distinguished. Thus Schutz, as quoted, uses the terms interchangeably; Peirce places symbols very firmly as a sub-group of signs: symbols are natural or conventional signs; David Cox, at one with Peirce in thinking symbols a special kind of sign, wishes to distinguish them also from both natural and conventional signs, saying that their particular characteristic is to be "part of the thing they signify";[8] whilst Jung attempts to drive a total division between signs and symbols, holding that "symbolic and semiotic meanings are entirely different things".[9]

Moreover, in attempts to break up the large clan of semiotic terms into smaller groups, we find but little attempt either to create or to maintain unity of nomenclature. There are intrinsic and extrinsic symbols, insight symbols, conventional symbols, expressive, organic and stipulative symbols, and though, within a given work, a chosen number of such terms may be used consistently and informatively, the choice and the definitions may overlap but not coincide with those elsewhere – as if the Smith family in Birmingham were called Jones in Liverpool and Brown in London, and in one place included second cousins, whilst in another only siblings, some of whom might there appear with wigs or wearing false noses, to accentuate their forbears in Farnborough, or distinguish them from the relatives in Ryde.

Even when we consider the term 'symbol' and its cognates as used within the narrower compass of a given discipline, the same lack of distinctness between a general and a particular use, and the same shifts in particular distinctions, are soon apparent. In literary criticism, for instance, the terms are sometimes used of the whole range of figurative speech – which includes metaphor, allegory, synecdoche; whilst at other times a symbol is distinguished from both metaphor and allegory, or from one rather than from another. And in theology there is the same uncertain relationship between the cluster of terms deriving from 'analogy' and derivatives of 'symbol'.

All these areas of potential perplexity and obscurity: the heterogeneity of things called 'symbols'; the variety of relationships designated 'symbolic'; the lack of definition, or the differences between definitions given, may often be of little significance. Often, but not always. For sometimes they may hide important differences of outlook; sometimes lead to unnecessary wrangling; sometimes obscure the real issues of a controversy. E. A. Bennet has already pointed out that the differences between Jung and Freud in their definition of 'symbol' and understanding of 'symbolism' was "more than a confusion of terminology – it indicates diametrically opposed attitudes. It would be true to say that Jung's concept of symbolism, and all that this implied, was an important element in the breakdown of collaboration with Freud." (*C. G. Jung*, p. 137.) Enough, perhaps, has been written about the ensuing differences of these two founding fathers of modern psychological theories. Not so much attention has, however, been paid to no less important dichotomies in literature and theology. A. G. Lehmann, who holds that the philosophers' and the literary critics' uses of the term 'symbol' are incompatible (and are linked to two different views of language) maintains that "far from being a source of pregnant insight into the poetry . . . [of the Symbolist Movement] . . . this confusion of terms has again and again misled critics and historians of literature". (*The Symbolist Aesthetic in France 1885–1895*, p. 129n.) And Dorothy D. Lee rightly remarks that "In Western civilization the difference in the conception of the symbol as representing or as participating, constitutes one of the main differences of doctrine between the Catholic Church and most of the Protestant sects. The question at issue is whether, at communion, the bread *represents* the flesh of Christ, or *is* the flesh of Christ." (*Symbols and Values*, p. 80.)

In both these fields, of literature and of theology, where discussions often overlap just where the use of the term 'symbol' seems both relevant and inescapable, the confusions which occur deserve more specific consideration.

Some Examples from Literature and their Theological Relevance

As Lehmann suggests, the richest source of confusions is to be found in the aesthetic theories of the French 'Symboliste' poets, from Mallarmé onwards. The meanings with which they endow the term 'symbol' and its cognates deserves a study of its own, for which the source book could well be Michaud's *La Doctrine Symboliste*. But there is, in fact, no need to stray into the realms of French literature itself to find literary examples of this same confusion. In 1899 Arthur Symons, friend of Yeats and English exponent of the French movement, published his best-known book, *The Symbolist Movement in Literature*, in which he attempted to deal with the aesthetic of several of the prominent writers of this period. Whilst six years previously he had rejected the label 'symbolism' as of no consequence, in this work, as Richard Ellmann points out in his introduction to the 1958 edition, Symons "fastened on the word 'symbolism'" and in so doing "gave a name to the preoccupations with modes of half-uttered or half-glimpsed meaning which . . . was a principal direction in modern thought." (p. vii.) But this 'unseen reality', the referent of the symbolic expression, was conceived of in a variety of ways. Sometimes in the book it seems to be a reality which is opposed to the world of appearance; sometimes a reality which is beyond the appearance but nevertheless not opposed to it; sometimes – somewhat differently – it is the world of appearance itself, but as seen with a visionary intensity; sometimes, again, the world of appearance apprehended as an organic unity. It is evident that, while Symons is using the term in a literary context, these various interpretations of the 'unseen reality' which is the referent of the literary symbolic expression do carry with them differing ontological assumptions and implications. Symbolism, as thus used, is, then, consonant with, or expressive of, attitudes to this world, our perception of it, and its relation to some other world. These attitudes differ in what clearly may be – and I shall argue are – theologically significant ways. Symons, however (and not Symons alone), is oblivious of these differences. Nor is he any more conscious of the fact that the relationship he posits between this – unspecified – referent, and the literary expression which is its symbol is left equally imprecise. For 'approximation' is a very vague term; and if, in the above instance, Symons seems to opt for a relationship between referent and symbol which is arbitrary and conventional rather than real, he blurs even this by stating, a little further on, that "It is sometimes permitted us to hope that our convention is indeed the reflection rather than merely the sign of that unseen reality." (p. 1.) Nor is his hesitant suggestion that

a symbol might be defined as a representation which is not a reproduction (*ibid.*)

any more helpful in definition, since he makes no attempt to specify what kind of representation (a crucial term in much literary criticism) is envisaged.

A further imprecision, again of some potential theological importance, is to be found in Symons' chapter on Huysmans. Here Symons writes that, in his novels, Huysmans shows "how inert matter, the art of stones, the growth of plants, the unconscious life of beasts, may be brought under the same law of the soul, may *obtain* through a symbol, a spiritual existence" (p. 80, italics mine), and that symbolism is

an *establishing* of the links which hold the world together (*ibid.*, italics mine).

It may be that in writing thus Symons did not intend his readers to think that symbolism had the power of *creating* links rather than of, more simply, exhibiting them, yet his phraseology does carry at least the possibility of such a meaning. Whatever his intention, this use indicates one element which the term 'symbolism' now often suggests: its reference to a world created by man, which is not necessarily the reflection (or representation) of the world created by God; the emphasis here is on 'symbolism' as a term designating the representation

of the way man sees things, without the implication that this is
also the way things are: it is a means whereby we underline the
subjectivity of all perception. In Symons' terminology, then,
since the relationship between the "unseen reality" and that
perceived is considered to be arbitrary, 'symbols' and 'symbolism' acquire a purely subjective character, and thus, the
"spiritual existence" which beasts and inanimate things can
"obtain" through symbols is theologically highly suspect, since
it appears to be a "spiritual existence" wholly dependent on
man. Thus, again, the literary concept carries with it both
philosophical and theological implications of some importance.

A similar tendency – to speak of symbols as relating to man's
perception of things, rather than as exhibiting the state of
things 'as they really are' – can be found in what is said of
symbols and symbolism by Symons' more famous contemporary, Yeats, who himself influenced and was influenced by
Symons. Certainly it is true that Yeats, more surely than
Symons in the book discussed, thought that there were
'ontological' (and not only conventionally established) links,
correspondences, between man's apprehension of the world,
his response to that world, and the way he could convey that
response and apprehension on the one hand, and the world of
nature, and indeed 'supernature' which existed independently
of him, on the other. 'Symbolism', for Yeats, is, then, an exhibi-
tion of these links, and a 'play' upon them, by which man is
made aware of their existence, and by which he is therefore also
brought into a relationship with the world outside him.
Moreover, since both the apprehension and the creation of the
symbols needs the response or the involvement of the whole
man, intellective and affective, in 'symbolism' man is helped to
achieve his own inner integration. But the way that Yeats
speaks of symbols often suggests that the referent of the symbol
is not an otherwise imperceptible but none-the-less independently existing idea, or state of things, or being, but rather
(again) a subjective response engendered by those things which
are symbols; subjective, even though it should be a response
common to all men. Thus, in the essay 'The Symbolism of
Poetry', Yeats speaks of symbols "evoking" either emotions or
ideas, adding that "in this sense all alluring or hateful things
are symbols" (p. 160); a stress which not only makes symbols
ubiquitous, but which also defines them primarily by their

effects upon us and not primarily because they are things of a particular kind, constituted or created in a particular way. Even more revealing of this tendency towards subjectivism is an earlier statement, in Yeats' edition of Blake, where he wrote:

Sometimes the mystical student . . . forgets for a moment that the history of moods is the history of the universe, and asks where is the final statement – the complete doctrine. The universe is itself that doctrine and statement. All others are partial, for it alone is the symbol of the infinite thought which is in turn symbolic of the universal mood we name God.[10]

Even if it is true that "mood" for Yeats did not mean a 'fleeting emotion' but rather a 'state of mind' in which the whole of man was engaged, the referent of the symbol, though possibly bearing the name of 'God', and so seeming to have some transcendent and independent being, turns out to be rather an aspect of man's psyche. And if God is an aspect of the human psyche, then he isn't God in the traditional Christian sense. And even if, in Yeats' more developed theory of symbolism there is a search for, and an affirmation of, a supernatural world which exists apart from man, and which man can discover in symbols, this transcendent world has, nevertheless, little relation to the traditional Christian cosmos.

Symbolism as a concept, then, as it emerged into literary prominence at the end of the nineteenth century did so with overtones which were theologically suspect. It seemed either to imply – as in Symons – a subjectivism which was not – then – easily compatible with theological affirmations about the nature of the world and our knowledge of it; or to belong – as in the later Yeats – to the realm of the occult and the magical. The lack of proper definition may be then, as I have suggested, a matter of more than merely semantic concern.

Some Confusions in Theology

That inattention to the potential ambiguities of the term 'symbol' and its cognates can indeed have resounding consequences can be seen in a study of the Modernist controversy, which, like the Symbolist movement in literature, developed in the closing decades of the last century, came to a head at the beginning of this, and, if one is to judge by some of the issues moved in current theological journals, and more particularly the Roman Catholic press, can still lead to acrimonious argument. There is no lack of documentation of the history of the Modernist movement – if it can, indeed, be called a 'movement' – and the people involved in it, most notably, perhaps, the French scripture scholar, Abbé Loisy, so that only a resumé need be given here.[11]

Briefly, Modernism (so called for the first time by the papal encyclical *Pascendi Gregis* of July 1907, in which it was condemned as a heresy) was a response by Roman Catholic thinkers, theologians, scripture scholars and those whose interests were more social than philosophical, to the recent developments in scientific, social and philosophical thinking. During the preceding decades, such developments seemed to pose a challenge to some of the tenets of Catholicism, especially perhaps those which concerned the nature of biblical truth. The challenge of "higher criticism", on the basis of archaeological findings and a new awareness of the cultural bias of all languages, had put a large question mark against the possibility that biblical statements – of the new as well as the old testaments – could be literally true. The Modernist response to such a challenge was made possible by the greater apparent liberalism towards scholarship evinced by Leo XIII, who followed Pius IX to the papal chair in 1878. Whether rightly or wrongly, with the accession of Pius X in 1903 the developments in biblical scholarship, as well as those in other areas of Catholic thought, fell under suspicion, and an amalgam of the principles supposedly involved, which, however, no individual Modernist ever acknowledged as his own, was condemned as a malicious fabrication of evil-purposed men. Though the condemnation affected directly only those within the Pope's jurisdiction, the issues involved were not purely internal to the Roman Catholic Church and its theology, as discussions then and now amply testify. One of the central points is the question of the symbolical nature of biblical or theological statements, and perhaps not the least curious phenomenon of the whole controversy is that no note has been taken of the different explanations given for the suspicion attaching to symbolism as a theological term. Curious, not only because these explanations give the terms 'symbol', 'symbolical' and 'symbolism' a variety of meanings, but also because they sometimes seem to find the terms suspect for precisely opposite reasons. A survey of these interpretations will serve to point the theologically significant confusions inherent in the terms when imprecisely used.

1. One such interpretation is given by M. L. Cozens in *A Handbook of Heresies*[12] and is subsequently appealed to by Maisie Ward in the life of her father, editor of *The Dublin Review* at the time of the controversy.[13] The reason for the condemnation here given is that by their use of phrases such as "dogmas are symbols", the Modernists denied that dogmas were true. They forgot, says Cozens, that a symbol "must be true or it does not symbolise". According to him their mistake lay in confusing "true" with "adequate", so that by saying that religious language is symbolical, they meant not only that it is inadequate (a point granted by all) but also that religious affirmations are not true.

'Truth' is, of course, a concept and a term as open to misunderstanding and misapplication as the word 'symbol'. It may well be doubted if the two can ever properly be linked; and it is equally doubtful if the way Cozens then uses the term (speaking of a map as a true representation of a country) does anything but confuse the issues. Nevertheless, he is certainly correct in pin-pointing *a* source of malaise: that to call dogmas 'symbols' somehow or other seems to impugn their truth. And it has always seemed important to a large majority of Christians that the claims Christianity makes should be true. Lionel Trilling, himself an agnostic, realizes this when he questions Matthew Arnold's Christianity by saying: "That Christianity is true: that is, after all, the one thing that Arnold cannot really say. That Christianity contains the highest moral law, that Christianity is natural, that Christianity is lovely, that Christianity provides a poetry serving the highest good, that Christianity *contains* the truth – anything but that *Christianity is true*." (*Matthew Arnold*, p. 364.) Does the use of the term 'symbolical' with reference to religious language, calling a dogma a 'symbol', imply this kind of attitude?

That the terms 'symbols' and 'symbolical' are sometimes used in ways which suggest their antithesis to 'truth' and 'true' – for instance in the sense of 'not true', 'fictitious' – cannot be denied. Thus D. G. James has written: "If we are willing to view any part of the life of Christ as symbolic merely, there is no overwhelming reason why we should not be prepared to view Christ himself as a symbol, one of unusual power and expressiveness, but only a fictitious creation." (*Scepticism and Poetry*, p. 246.) On the other hand the terms 'symbol' and 'true' are not always used as opposites, to which, surprisingly perhaps, D. G. James can also stand as witness. Speaking of Coleridge and Newman he says that for both "Christian dogma . . . is symbol"[14] but he does not think this is derogatory to their Christianity, as the earlier remarks in *Scepticism and Poetry* might lead us to think. No; for in this case "the symbol is truth so far as it is communicable to us".[15] Evidently, therefore, it is important to establish what relationship to 'truth' and 'fiction' a given use of the term 'symbol' is intended to have if we are to determine, for instance, whether such a criticism as that of Cozens is applicable, since the use of the term 'symbolic' in this guise does not necessarily mean to deny that Christianity is also true.

2. Related to the claim that Christianity is true is its claim that at least some of its credal statements are records of historical events. The questions 'What is history?' or 'What is a historical event?' are, of course, as fraught with difficulties as the question 'What is truth?' But in his Gifford Lectures on *Symbolism and Belief* Edwyn Bevan suggests that 'symbolism' is a theologically suspect term because to say of a statement that it is 'symbolical', or of a supposed 'event' that it is a 'symbol', impugns its historicity.[16]

For instance, if I speak of the account of the resurrection as 'symbolical' I am likely to be thought to cast doubt on the physical resurrection of Jesus after his death, in the sense in which such a resurrection is attested to by the given account of the discovery of the empty tomb in which he was buried. If I did so doubt the physical resurrection of Jesus, but nevertheless continued to assert that I "believed in the resurrection", I would not mean the same thing by that credal assertion as those who have assented to the same form of words in their traditional sense. For at least part of what the latter assent to is the proposition: 'Jesus' physical body did not decay in the tomb and was not taken out of it in deception, but is in some way involved in his resurrected life.' And this would be in no wise part of what I assented to by the same formula.

Whether, or how far, this different content of belief matters is another question. That it is a difference, and one which many people take to be of vital importance, is indubitable. And it is, at all events, likely to have further consequences, especially if I don't confine myself to the designation of a *particular* narrative of the Scriptures, and the consequent credal proposition, as 'symbolical' in this sense, but apply it generally.

Moreover, extension of this use of the term 'symbolical' (i.e., with its anti-historical implication) reverses, or at least changes, the emphasis between an event and its meaning and significance. Christianity has, by and large, claimed that certain consequences follow upon events having happened. The pursuit of the Christian is to be like Christ, Christ-like. His behaviour towards others is (supposedly) determined by the words of Christ: "Love one another as I have loved you." What Christ did and said is therefore important as the basis of a Christian's own actions. But, as Bevan notes, "If you say you regard the belief that Jesus gave himself voluntarily as a sacrifice upon the cross as a symbol only, what you mean is that whether any real man ever did do what Jesus is alleged to have done is relatively unimportant for religion: what is important is the general obligation of men to sacrifice themselves for other men, the general beauty of such self-immolation." (*Symbolism and Belief*, p. 235.) In such a case, the motive for the Christian's own actions ceases to be what Christ did, and becomes some principle of which Christ's life, whether the recorded events actually happened or not, is but an inspiring illustration. And that changes the relationship between Christ and his followers.

There is no doubt that in a statement such as: 'The first two chapters of the Book of Genesis are a symbolical narrative of events,' the historical nature of those events is usually either impugned or regarded as unimportant. Hence it is not surprising that any similar statement should be thought to convey the same implication. But is this necessarily the case? If we admit that all historical narrative is necessarily selective, it may be possible to call a given narrative 'symbolical' not because the events it selects never happened but because of some other principle of selection which we descry therein.

It would also be possible to say something like this: 'The writer of the Book of Genesis gave us this account of the creation of man and woman as a symbol of the relationship which exists between them.' Unless we are careful, we are likely, I think, to suppose that such a statement also means that the account, as given, is not historical, did not happen as described. But no such implication need be supposed. There are at least some instances where the terms 'history' and 'symbol' are not opposed in this way. Thus D. G. James, interpreting Coleridge, says: "Not only is the symbol not a 'mere symbol'; it is also event. If the symbol is 'consubstantial with the truth of which it is the conductor', it is also embedded in, or rather is a part of, history." (*The Romantic Comedy*, p. 207.)

The designation of certain statements as 'symbolical' or certain events as 'symbols' does not, then, always imply that the events referred to did not happen as described. A given phraseology ('mere symbol', for example) may carry such an implication. But there are other instances where no such implication may be intended. In such cases it may be necessary to establish what the relationship between history and 'symbol' is for the given writer.

3.   Bevan discusses the consequences of that sense of the term 'symbolism' which, in application to dogma, threatens to dissolve Christianity's historical content. But he first points out that to say of a dogma that it is 'symbol' can mean that behind *that* formulation we can see *and hence* also come to express better, the idea or reality for which that dogma as symbol stands, or the truth which it seeks to state. Thus, in condemning Modernism, the Vatican was condemning the assertion that dogmas were symbols of this kind, i.e., "behind which we could see" and which therefore we could come to re-state in the sense of 'improve'. An example, par excellence, of one who held such a position is Marcel Hébert for whom to say that the creed was a symbol or a symbolical statement of faith, meant that a re-statement of its contents more consonant with advanced knowledge could be expressed thus:

I believe in the objective value of the idea of God, of an absolute and perfect ideal, distinct, though not separated, from the world which He draws and directs towards the greater good, One and Three, because He can be called infinite activity, infinite mind, infinite love. And I believe in Him in whom there was realised in an exceptional or unique degree the union of the divine with human nature, Jesus Christ, whose luminous superiority, impressing simple hearts, is for them symbolised by the idea of a Virgin Birth, whose powerful action after His death caused in the mind of the apostles and disciples the visions and appearances narrated in the Gospels, and is symbolised by the myth of a descent into Hell and an ascension to the upper regions of the sky . . . I believe in the survival of that which constitutes our moral personality, in the eternal life which is already present in every soul leading a higher life, and which popular imagination has symbolised in the ideas of the Resurrection of the body and of eternal felicity.[17]

That an essential quality of a 'symbol', or of a 'symbolic expression', is the possibility of an eventual re-formulation is an integral part of some definitions of the terms, as, for instance, Jung's. And therefore it is not surprising that a statement such as "dogmas are symbols" should sometimes be understood in this sense. But, as Bevan points out, to call dogmas 'symbols' is not to imply that they are, necessarily, thus re-statable. The reason he gives (though one could think of others) is that there are two classes of symbols: those behind which we can see, and those behind which we cannot see. He suggests that in the Vatican vocabulary statements of the latter kind are called not 'symbolical' but 'analogical'. But since scholasticism upholds the principle that all our language about God is necessarily analogical (cf. below, section 5), those who hold that analogical statements are a kind of symbolical statement (symbols behind which we cannot see) find in the Vatican's unqualified condemnation of symbolism a condemnation of its own most cherished principle. But the Vatican condemns all symbolism because it fails to realize that the term is sometimes used in the sense which *it* reserves for 'analogy'. Hence the confusion, and the sometimes unwarranted suspicion of the term 'symbolism' as applied to religious statements.

It is clear, then, that this is another point to bear in mind when looking at the implications of a given use of the terms 'symbol' and 'symbolism' in religious discourse. Does the writer suggest thereby that the statements in question are capable of better, more accurate, more satisfactory re-formulation? Or, on the contrary, does he, by asserting their symbolical nature, draw attention rather to *this* formulation as the only one which, under circumstances of our human condition, it is possible for us to make?

4.   The uneasiness which may be felt in saying that 'symbolical language' is the only kind of language we can use when speaking of God does not come simply from the definitions of the sort just discussed. It comes also from identifying 'symbols' and 'symbolical expressions' with what is vague and imprecise:

a related point, of course, but one of different emphasis and consequence. We may know that we cannot speak of God as he is, and we may know that our knowledge of him must necessarily be cut according to the cloth of our humanity. But yet we may not wish to say either that our knowledge of God is 'vague', or that the statements we can make about him or our relations with him are 'vague'. Yet this is just what the terms 'symbol' and 'symbolical' so often suggest: an inescapable 'vagueness'.

Of the various reasons which may be adduced for linking the term 'symbolical' and 'vague' I wish to stress only one. This is that the terms 'symbol' and 'symbolical' are connected to what is imaginative, and that statements which are 'imaginative' are, if not positively misleading, then lacking in precision. The notion that imaginative language lacks clarity stems from the Renaissance attempt to establish the practice and validity of what we might now call modern scientific method, with the consequent emphasis on the necessity of plain statement to record direct observation. Francis Bacon gave voice to this endeavour in his *Advancement of Learning*.[18] It was part of that whole way of thinking about, and apprehending, the world which T. S. Eliot characterized by his phrase "the dissociation of sensibility".[19] One of the underlying tenets of this empirical (and utilitarian) approach to man's knowledge of the world was that what is known clearly can be said clearly, and that clarity will avoid the use of imagery (and hence of symbolical language) except for persuasion and graceful ornament. Such a conviction is, of course, concurrent with the belief that true knowledge, knowledge of which there is no doubt, is the product of the intellect alone; the intellect free from, and unsullied by, emotions (the source of imagination), prejudices, hopes, fears, wishes, time, place, culture, everything that is purely personal, or purely contingent on circumstances. The unclouded intellect alone can free us from the limitations of our human condition. And the product of the intellect, clear reasoning, will issue in statements which are free from imagination. Only that, then, which is 'rational', reasoned, is 'true', and what is rational is opposed to both that which is imaginative, and that which is symbolical.

Here is found both an embryonic epistemology and theory of language. If one accepts it, and therefore maintains: (a) that clarity is necessarily intellective, rational; (b) that symbols and symbolical language are necessarily products of the imagination; and (c) that the statements we make about God must be clear, and that the clearest possible statements are dogmatic formulations; then one will naturally enough take strong exception to any imputation that all religious language – and in particular, the language of dogma – is 'symbolic'.

But, of course, a given writer may not hold such views of language and knowledge, in which case his use of the term 'symbolic', even if linked to 'imaginative' may not carry the implications of vagueness. And this, too, often needs to be determined before we can say what theological implications the term 'symbol' will have for him.

5. There is, however, a further difficulty about statements such as "dogmas are symbols", or "all religious language is symbolic", which also touches upon the distinction between 'imaginative' and 'conceptual' language, and Bevan's two classes of symbols. In what we say about God, we might distinguish between two kinds of statements to begin with: those which speak of God's wrath, or the hand of God, or of seeing God face to face, phrases in which God is spoken of in terms of man's physical or temperamental characteristics; and those which refer to God in terms like 'omnipotent' or 'impassable' or as being "three persons in one nature", phrases in which a directly human reference seems to have been attenuated. The first, we might readily admit, are anthropomorphic: God doesn't really have hands or a face; he is not angry as we are angry. And we may use the term 'symbolic' to describe such phrases: ones where we know clearly that the terms we use are not applicable to God, whether or not we can find substitutes for them.

But we may also come to realize that, because we are human and must inescapably think as human beings in human terms, all our language, however abstract, however conceptualized and non-imaginative, is based on our all too human knowledge and experience of the world around us. Consequently, if we speak of God as omnipotent, for instance, we are still applying to him the concept of power which we derive from human or natural forces around us. We arrive at the conclusion that these terms, too, being equally man-centred, are no more really applicable to God than the others were. Like the first group, they are terms applicable to men and the world of human action which we, because we have and can have no other language, must also use of God. It seems to follow, then, that if we call the first 'symbolic' because they are anthropomorphic, so we should also call the second. The distinction made at the beginning is valueless.

What is being stressed in *this* use of the term 'symbolic', this extension of the term to include not only the obvious anthropomorphisms of the first group, but also the less obvious, but no less man-orientated vocabulary of the second, is precisely this: that *all* our language, whether imaginative or conceptual, whether Biblical or theological and dogmatic, is human language, and that therefore it is a mistake to think that the latter is a closer approximation to a description of God as he really is than the former. God, as 'other', is as 'other' to our concepts as he is to our imaginative representations; as other to our psychology and philosophy, as he is to our temperament and physique. To call language about God 'symbolic' in this sense is to insist that all language inevitably misses the target of proper description by the same fixed distance which removes man from God.

This assertion is troublesome for two reasons. The first that, while it insists, even if rightly, on the parity of all language in respect to God, it nevertheless blurs that distinction within language itself which allows one to say, at least with the semblance of reason, that God is – in some sense – impassable, but which does not allow one to say that God 'in some sense' has feet. The difference may be slight, and too much may be made of it, since there are so many phrases which seem to fall between the two extremes; but the conviction that the difference is of some consequence provides a further reason for the objection to calling all language about God equally 'symbolic'.

This may seem more a literary than a theological difficulty. But it impinges on theology because, to call *all* language about God 'symbolic', stressing by doing so that it is *all* equally anthropomorphic, is to deny that any language about God is analogical. It is to assert that, because God is 'other', all the words we have at our disposal, when applied to God, can be so applied only equivocally. But to say this is to maintain that neither dogma nor even Scripture itself can tell us anything about God himself: though the statements thereof may be couched like descriptions (God is . . . this, or that) at best, they tell us only how we should behave towards him. To affirm, then, that all language about God is symbolical is to deny the possibility of that kind of verbal 'revelation' which – it has been thought – is the basis of Christianity.

6. But such is the oddity of the term 'symbolism' that it is theologically suspect also for the reverse reason. Not, in this case, because it is based on the assertion that God's otherness is so complete that none of our language about him can be analogical. On the contrary, it is also claimed that to call theological language 'symbolic' is to assume a correspondence between the empirical and the non-empirical worlds (and between man and God) such that at least in some cases we can use words of both *in the same sense*. This is to deny the necessity of analogical language since it is to affirm that some language about God, that which is 'symbolic', is univocal. And, if the former meaning of the term seemed to deny the possibility of any 'revelation', this one seems to deny its necessity.

This criticism and that with which Section 5 concluded constitute a kind of 'heads I win, tails you lose' impasse for anyone who says that religious language is symbolical: either too much or too little is said to be assumed by it, and some resolution of this peculiarity is obviously necessary.[20]

7. 'Anthropomorphism' uses terms of absolute being in the same sense as of creatures, and in speaking of God as 'Father' thinks of him as father *in excelsis* raised to superlative degree. This misses the distinction in kind between absolute being and all modes of being. 'Symbolism', as condemned by Catholic theologians, looks on such concepts as imaginative expressions of feeling, while remaining agnostic as to whether there is some real metaphysical relationship which they exemplify. (Dorothy Emmet, *The Nature of Metaphysical Thinking*, p. 181.)

Here another criticism of symbolism is attributed to Catholic theologians. The term 'symbolism' does more than suggest that all language about God is anthropomorphic, with whatever consequences. It also implies that, far from being descriptions of an objective, 'out-there' entity, of whatever kind, 'symbolical' statements are but the expressions of subjective states. And if, as is here supposed, what they express is how we feel, rather than how we think, then to say that religious language is 'symbolic' is to rob it of all claim to certainty and objectivity.

For, such is the assumption, feelings (like the imagination, to which they are linked, and unlike the intellect) are misleading, unreliable guides; are individual and subjective; are volatile and changeable. If not strictly held in check, they are more likely to lead us into perdition – at least of heresy if not damnation – than into the truth.

Nor is this position ameliorated if, as sometimes, religious language, or religious statements of a certain kind, are thought of as expressions of need rather than of feeling. For who is to say that our needs, however basic to our common human nature, must have an objective correlative such that our expressions of *them* become, *ipso facto*, descriptions of *it*?

The same suspicion of implicit agnosticism is attached also to those who call religious language 'symbolic' because it is the record, or description, or expression, of 'experience'; because – such is the assumption here made by such critics – experience, like feelings or needs or imagination (and for the same reason) is too subjective, too individual to give its (however faithful) record the universal certainty required of statements about God, which only clear, rational thinking can attain.

8.   The Catholic theologians, according to Professor Emmet, condemn 'symbolism' not only because it is an expression of feeling, but also because it is agnostic as to whether there is some real metaphysical relationship which such an expression exemplifies. But the charge of agnosticism need not (though it may) rest on the interpretation of symbolic statements as expressions of feeling. A further reason for such a charge can, I think, best be seen by considering some words of Cassirer, who outlines the change which occurred in the view taken of the nature of scientific language when "the naive *copy theory* of knowledge is discredited". When this happens "the fundamental concepts of each science, the instruments with which it propounds its questions and formulates its solutions, are regarded no longer as passive images of something given but as *symbols* created by the intellect itself". (*The Philosophy of Symbolic Forms*, 1, p. 75.)

Possibly by now most people have got used to thinking that the knowledge we have of the world, and the way we express that knowledge, is not a copy, an exact replica, a passive image, and it is surely this which is expressed when all languages, whether those of mathematics or physical sciences, or history, or poetry, or theology are called 'symbolisms'. But what is the consequence? If the 'symbols' with which we work, in which we think, are not "passive images of something *given*", but are "created by the intellect", what guarantee have we that they are 'images' at all? That they are, that is to say, so related to the – or an – out-there world as not to be misleading, as to be in some sense *about* the world? If they are "created by the intellect" how are they better than the fictions which are pure fantasies and which are not related to any world at all? In what sense can they be 'true'?

The usual answer is that in the sciences these 'symbols', hypotheses, theories, laws, help us to order the world of our sense experience in such a way that we can make certain predictions about the behaviour of things in that world; and that hence we can carry out certain operations we may wish to perform, the success of which is both a test of, and a result of, the functional validity of our particular symbolism. In brief, in science "we make 'inner fictions or symbols' . . . so constituted that the necessary logical consequences of the images are always images of the necessary natural consequences of the imaged objects". (Cassirer *ibid*.) That is all that needs to be posited, and all that is shown by the successful predictions which the science enables us to make.

In theology, however, as in poetry, as in history, there is doubt that such predictions can ever be made on the basis of their 'symbolism'. And for theology especially such results, even if they could be had, are somehow beside the point. For neither theology nor, for that matter, poetry, is concerned with this kind of ordering of this kind of experience. Hence, if we speak of theology or poetry as a symbolism in the same sense in which science is spoken of here, there is no guarantee that, if it is a creation of the intellect, even the kind of relation described above holds good in this case. So, if we speak thus, we must either simply assert that some relation which is not misleading does hold good between our 'symbol' and that to which it supposedly refers; or we must demonstrate that it does so, which may mean that we are forced to give some account of how such symbols are created; or we must abandon the attempt altogether and remain content within the symbolism alone, without enquiring into its referential qualifications.

It is this agnosticism which is unpalatable to many

theologians, because it seems to trap the language of theology – which has been supposed to tell us about how things are – in an eternal 'don't know'. And what is the good of language about God if all it tells us is how we think?

The repudiation of 'symbolism' understood in this sense, is, therefore, also a repudiation of a Cassirer-like epistemology, which stems from Kant, and which denies that we can know things as they really are. It is based on the contrary assertion that our knowledge of the world, and of the languages in which we reproduce that knowledge, is, indeed, 're-production', in some sense of that word which will carry the connotation of a known, real, affinity between the thing and its reproduction, however unspecified that affinity may be.

'Symbolism', then, is a theologically suspect term for a variety of reasons: because it is said to impugn Christianity's claim to be true, or to be historical; because it involves the assertion that religious language can *tell* us nothing about *God*, but only about how we feel, or what we experience; because it implies that we can *know* nothing about God, or because it puts our knowledge of, and language about, God on a par with our knowledge of, and our language about, men. But, as I have indicated, some actual uses of the term 'symbol' and 'symbolism' may not carry one, or another, or any, of these connotations. Even if, for instance, by calling theological (or biblical) language 'symbolic', a writer means to indicate that such language is not, and cannot be, a replica of a given world, but that, on the contrary, he affirms thereby his belief that it is created by the intellect, he may not be wishing to suggest that such symbolism, such a creation, is *no* guide to the world – be it transcendental or historical. Such a writer may grant, furthermore, that the principle of verifiability, applicable to the symbolism of science, is not applicable to theology, and still maintain that the symbolism which is theology is, in its own way, self-authenticating. And to show this, he may be offering some theory of language, some theory of the creation of symbols and symbolisms, which he sees as a guarantee of their authenticity, and of the assertion that – creations of the intellect though they be – the symbols give knowledge of that which they symbolize. Such a writer may be sufficiently Kantian to deny to knowledge and to language the status of copy, of replica, but still perhaps sufficiently Platonist to be concerned to show that (and how) the world presented is known in the presentation. He may not be successful in his endeavour; his theory may founder; but the attempt, if it is serious, is itself sufficient to shield him from any easy charge of agnosticism; it deserves a careful consideration, without the prejudice of some preconceived general theory derived from other sources.

Such a writer was Coleridge and it is to his concept of 'symbol' and its implications that particular attention must be paid first of all.

2

THE TERM 'SYMBOL' AND ITS COGNATES IN THE THOUGHT OF COLERIDGE

The Context of Thought

Coleridge sat on the brow of Highgate Hill, in those years, looking down on London and its smoke-tumult, like a sage escaped from the inanity of life's battle; attracting towards him the thoughts of innumerable brave souls still engaged there. . . . His voice, naturally soft and good, had contracted itself into a plaintive snuffle and sing-song; he spoke as if preaching – you would have said preaching earnestly and also hopelessly the weightiest things. I still recollect his "object" and "subject", terms of continual reference in the Kantean province; and how he sang and snuffled them into "om-m-mject" and "sum-m-mject" with a kind of solemn shake or quaver as he rolled along. No talk, in his century or in any other, could be more surprising. (Carlyle: *Life of Sterling*, ch. VIII, pp. 53–4, 54–5.)

Carlyle's often-quoted description of Coleridge at Highgate in the late 1820s – from a chapter which, taken as a whole, is less cruel than these extracts imply: the attempt of one impatient and irascible lover of his own speech to recall the effect of another spinner of spell-binding monologues – is certainly correct in giving the impression of a man pre-occupied with the relation between subject and object. For much, if not all, of Coleridge's intellectual endeavour was directed to the reconciling of two apparent opposites of his own experience: one, that the mind is active and not passive in the act of knowing and perceiving; the other, that what we know are nevertheless *things*, and not only appearances of things. While he was convinced that the outward object as known and perceived is partly the product of the mind (an insight which, in his

31

Philosophical Lectures of 1818 he attributes to Pythagoras[1]) Coleridge was also certain that the man of common sense is right who holds that what he sees "is the table itself . . . not the phantom of a table from which he may argumentatively deduce the reality of a table which he does not see". (*BL*, 1, XII, p. 179.) But how could this be if, in our act of knowing – sensory or intellective – the constitutions of our minds and bodies played an inalienable part? This was the problem he tried to solve, and all that he writes is an attempt to arrive at a true realism which would accommodate both convictions.

This 'all' includes analyses of the nature of man in himself, and in relation to the 'Nature' external to himself, of which he is both a part and an observer, a relation which involves some notion of the nature of God and his activity; the nature of art as a product of man (both a theory of creativity and of the created object) and its relation to Nature; and the relation of such a product of man's creativity, particularly but not exclusively the Bible, to God. Thus Coleridge's preoccupations with the operation of the mind were at once philosophical and psychological, literary and theological. For him, for instance, the imagination was "not only the synthesizing and mediating faculty in the act of aesthetic creation", it was also "the faculty of insight into ultimate philosophical and religious truths".[2] While Coleridge never used the term 'symbolic' to describe his own theory of the mind's operation, nor as an adjective to qualify 'knowledge', it is within this complex of thought, diffuse and diffused as it is, that he attempts to define what he means by 'symbol'. It is, therefore, impossible to arrive at any understanding of what that term meant for him without reference to, or outside the context of, his epistemology, cosmogony and ontology. His was an interlinking universe in which it is difficult to isolate any one element without presupposing what has been said about others. However, since it was his often repeated suggestion that an understanding of the universe and its laws is most easily reached by a careful introspection into the workings of the mind, the attempt to unravel the significance of Coleridge's concept of 'symbol' had best begin here.

1. *The constitution of man's mind*
What is most relevant to this pursuit in Coleridge's description of the constitution of man's mind is the nature and the function

of Reason, Understanding and Imagination, with the consequent definition of Ideas, since

> an IDEA in the *highest* sense of the word, cannot be conveyed but by a
> *symbol*. (*BL*, 1, IX, p. 100.)

The first prerequisite here, as with most terms that Coleridge
uses, is that we should dispossess ourselves of the meanings we
may commonly attach to such words. It should also be noted at
the outset that, though Coleridge uses a 'faculty' vocabulary,
he rejects the notion that the powers of the mind are separate
faculties acting independently. Fundamentally, as he says of
Reason and Religion, they differ only as different applications
of the same power, so that "every intellectual act, however you
may distinguish it by name in respect of the originating faculties, is truly the act of the entire man". (*TT*, 29.7.1830.) The
difference but interdependence which Coleridge envisaged can
be illustrated by what he says, in one instance, of Reason: "The
reason . . . without being either the sense, the understanding or
the imagination, contains all three within itself, even as the
mind contains its thoughts and is present in and through them
all; or as the expression pervades the different features of an
intelligent countenance". (*SM*, p. 461.) Elsewhere, too, he says
that though the Understanding in man differs from even the
noblest form of instinct in other creatures, it does so "not in
itself or its own essential properties, but in consequence of its
co-existence with far higher powers of a diverse kind in one and
the same subject. Instinct in a rational, responsible, and self-
conscious animal is Understanding". (*AR*, p. 261.)

Nevertheless, though the powers of the mind – and, as we
shall see, not only the powers of the mind – must not be thought
of in separation, and cannot be understood when isolated the
one from the other, yet the distinctions between them were
crucial for Coleridge. And indeed the chief object of *The Friend*
was to drive home the distinction between Understanding and
Reason: a difference which he enlarged upon and repeated in
subsequent writing.[3]

2. *The Understanding*
In the present context least need perhaps be said about the
Understanding, which approximates most nearly to what is
commonly meant by 'reasoning'. Like all the Coleridgean

33

powers of the mind, the Understanding is Janus-faced, turned both towards sense-experience, and towards the Reason. As turned towards the external world of Nature, and of our sense-experience of this outer world,

it may be defined as the conception of the Sensuous, or the faculty by which we generalize and arrange the phaenomena of perception: that faculty, the functions of which contain the rules and constitute the possibility of outward Experience. (*F*, 1. p. 156.)

This definition is repeated and expanded in *The Statesman's Manual*, where Coleridge says that the Understanding

concerns itself exclusively with the quantities and qualities and relations of particulars in time and space ... it is the science of phaenomena and their subsumption under distinct kinds and sorts (genus and species). Its functions supply the rules and constitute the possibility of experience, but remain mere logical forms, except as far as materials are given by the senses or sensations. (*SM*, p. 456.)

Again, Understanding is said to be

the creaturely mind of the individual, the acts of which are posterior to the things it records and arranges. (*SM*, p. 430.)

It is, then, the faculty whereby we reflect, classify, abstract and generalize (*AR*, p. 247), but it can work only on information given it by the senses or some other faculty; and its powers of abstraction – wherein man is distinguished from the animals, and in the development of which "the superiority of man over man largely consists" – is only possible because, in man, the Understanding is conjoined with Reason. It is pre-eminently one of the tools of the scientist, who must, as Coleridge notes (*BL*, 1, xii, p. 175), begin with Nature, with the material and phenomenal world, though his business is also to arrive at conclusions freed from the particulars with which he starts, and to formulate ever more-inclusive laws.

The Understanding is discursive, and its method that of logic and step by step reasoning. But since its starting point is phenomena, it yields knowledge only of "superficies without substance" whose characteristic is "clearness without depth". (*SM*, p. 460.) Its conclusions must always remain hypothetical ("timid and uncertain" says Coleridge), for it has "no way of giving permanence to things, but by reducing them to abstractions". (*SM*, p. 431.) For a proper and profound understanding (*sic*) of the world, the Understanding is indispensable but insufficient.

3. *The Reason*

It is otherwise with Reason, which Coleridge sometimes differentiates into two components. As Speculative Reason it penetrates and coalesces with the Understanding, just as the latter informs sense-perception; but as Practical Reason it has also, we shall see, another aspect, which enables Coleridge to say that

Reason is the power of universal and necessary convictions, the source and substance of truths above sense, and having their evidence in themselves. (*AR*, p. 241.)

Herein it is already distinguished from the Understanding, from which it also differs in the objects to which it is directed. These are not the fleeting phenomena of the external world, but "spiritual objects", "the Universal, the Eternal, the Necessary . . ." (*F*, 1, p. 155). And Reason, unlike Understanding, is not discursive but is a direct aspect of truth, an inward beholding, having a similar relation to the intelligible or spiritual, as Sense has to the material or phenomenal. (*AR*, p. 246.)

Closely connected with this is the claim that Reason is "the knowledge of the whole considered as one", "the science of the universal, having the ideas of oneness and allness as its two elements or primary factors". (*SM*, p. 456.) We have seen that the Understanding, enlightened by Reason, attempts to subsume particulars under general laws; but it is "the office, and as it were, the instinct of reason, to bring a unity into all our conceptions and several knowledges. On this all system depends; and without this we could reflect connectedly neither on nature nor on our own minds". (*AR*, p. 210.) And it is Reason which furnishes man "with PRINCIPLES distinguished from the maxims and generalizations of outward experience by their absolute and essential universality and necessity". (*F*, 1, p. 112.)

This insistence on necessity – which is not the necessity of a conclusion drawn correctly from premises – cannot be understood without reference to that second aspect of Reason already alluded to, and on account of which Coleridge can say that Reason "cannot in strict language be called a faculty, much less a personal property of any human mind. He with whom it is present can as little appropriate it, whether totally or by partition, as he can claim ownership in the breathing air". (*SM*, p. 461.) This other essential quality of Reason, or rather its very nature, is expressed as early as *The Friend* where Coleridge writes:

I should have no objection to define Reason with Jacobi . . . as an organ bearing the same relation to spiritual objects, the Universal, the Eternal, and the Necessary, as the eye bears to the material and contingent phænomena. But then it must be added, that it is an organ identical with its appropriate objects. Thus God, the Soul, eternal Truth, etc. are objects of Reason; but they are themselves *reason*. (*F*, 1. pp. 155–6.)

To say that 'God is Truth', or that the soul is the seat of Reason – whatever these propositions may mean – is to use reputable theological language; to say that Reason is God (or truth) has possibly unacceptable overtones, and some attention must here be given to what Coleridge meant by it. What he did not intend is that God should be thought of as co-terminous with Reason in man; nor did he mean that 'God' was the projected ideal of man's highest potential, as his frequent references to Reason as being "from God" as well as being God sufficiently indicate.[4] God and man are distinct. Nevertheless God made man alone among his creatures in his own image and likeness; and he also saved him – and continues to save him – from the disintegration of sinfulness and sin. It is by virtue of Reason, as we have seen, that man is different from the beasts, and it is therefore by virtue of Reason that we are made in God's image. But this 'image' is not a distant reflection, nor a superficial likeness, but an inward contiguity. This is so because Reason, comprising conscience, will, and the possibility of faith and religion (as white light is all the colours of the rainbow) can be seen also as "the indwelling WORD of an holy and omnipotent legislator" (*F*, 1, p. 112): the God without us, present within us. Reason is the light – Christ, God the Son – by which we see light (God the Father, and the things of God as they are). It is "the spirit of the regenerated man"; that in us which is "pre-eminently spiritual, and a spirit, even our spirit, through an effluence of the same grace by which we are privileged to say, Our Father!" (*AR*, p. 242.)

Seen thus, Coleridge's insistence that God, truth, etc., are not only the objects of Reason, but are Reason, has a decidedly Pauline, and Johannine, ring. And it also serves to explain why Coleridge held that Reason is "the knowledge of the whole considered as one". It is the knowledge of things as God knows them. But our tendency to do this – to unify our knowledge, without which we could not reflect as we do, connectedly, on Nature and our own minds – is also an evidence, for Coleridge, of "a One as the ground and cause of the universe, and which, in all succession and through all changes, is the subject neither of time nor change". (*AR*, pp. 210–11.) It is reflection on the functioning of the mind which leads Coleridge to his apprehension of God as Reason, and of God as a unitive cause of the universe.

4. *Ideas*

It will be most convenient to say something of Coleridge's notion of Ideas in the context of this discussion of Reason, and before turning to the other power of man's mind, the Imagination. Ideas are sometimes spoken of as the products of Reason, but they can also be considered as Reason itself in its creative aspect.[5] Like Reason, they appertain, though differently in each, to both God and man. What Ideas are *not* is set forth in the glossary of Appendix E to *The Statesman's Manual*. An Idea is neither a sensation, nor a perception; neither a sensible intuition, nor a conception; neither an abstraction nor a generalization.[6] What an Idea is, is here given in terms of its genesis, and to this we shall come back later. For the present purpose, the following statements are most relevant:

... every idea is living, productive, partaketh of infinity and ... containeth an endless power of semination (*SM*, p. 433),

and

Essence, in its primary signification, means the principle of *individuation*, the inmost principle of the possibility of any thing, as that particular thing. It is equivalent to the *idea* of a thing, when ever we use the word, idea, with philosophic precision. (*BL*, 2. xviii, p. 47.)

Furthermore it is the 'creative IDEA' of the Supreme Being which not only appoints to each thing its *position*, but in that position, and in consequence of that position, gives it its qualities. (*F*, 1, p. 459.)

37

In these scattered statements four elements indispensable to understanding Coleridge's terminology can be discerned:

(1) that an Idea makes a thing what it is, or what it will or would be when or if given existence;
(2) that the qualities and characteristics a particular thing exhibits are determined by this inner essence or Idea, but consequent upon the place that particular thing has in relation to other things, taken individually or as a whole;
(3) that an Idea is not a static, abstractable something, an ideal to which things tend or approach, or which they resemble; but is the dynamic within the thing, "living, productive . . . and capable of semination";
(4) that an Idea is God's creative act, and itself partakes of infinity.

Hence it is that Coleridge maintains – in that issue which he considers "the highest problem of philosophy" – that Ideas are "constitutive, and one with the power and life of nature" (*SM*, p. 484), and not regulative only.[7] And hence, when we grasp, know and acknowledge, the Idea of any thing, we know what that thing is in its innermost essence: the thing as it is, and not only as it appears to be; we know it in its relation to other things, and in its mode of development. To have an Idea of Nature, or of any natural object, is to see it not as *natura naturata* (nature as composed of discrete objects, and in so far as it is available to sensory experience) but as *natura naturans* (nature as embodying a developing potential, something which is, but is also still becoming itself, not as discrete only, but in relation to all other things), a point essential to Coleridge's concept of creativity. To the notion of *our* Ideas as potentially productive and creative we shall return later. What I want to emphasize here is the picture of Nature which is implied in the above: the 'power' within Nature is the power of God, is God, his Idea within each thing; each thing being what it is because of this, and consequently because of its particular place in, and interaction with, the whole of which it is a part. Thus to understand the part is to understand the whole, for no understanding of a thing can be reached without knowing its place within, and relation to, the whole.

5. *Man's relationship to Nature: 'Idea' and 'Law'*
In the description of Coleridge's scheme of things so far, we have seen something of the relation which obtains between God

and man, and between God and Nature. We have also seen that the Understanding in man is the instinct within all animals, but raised to a higher degree by its conjunction with Reason. Something further must now be said of the relationship in which man stands to Nature.

Man is himself, of course, part of nature, but – by virtue of Reason – self-conscious, aware of his own individuality and distinctness from what is around him, as well as of his inter-action with it. This is an awareness which, as has been noted, presents man with the problem of knowledge. That man can systematize his awareness, can make sense of what would otherwise be miasmic and chaotic is (again) due to the nature of his Reason-impregnated Understanding, for "Without this latent presence of the 'I am' all modes of existence in the external world would flit before us as colored shadows . . ." (*SM*, p. 465.) But the possibility of awareness as such, as well as our ability to make sense of it, means, for Coleridge, that there must be a 'rapport', a congruence, an affinity, indeed an interaction, between the powers of perception and knowledge (the senses and the Reason/Understanding) and what is per-ceived and known; between the knowing subject and the known object. Homogeneity, to some degree, is a prerequisite of all awareness and knowledge. In fact, we have seen that, and in what wise, such an affinity or homogeneity exists for Coleridge. For what we know (intellectively) is the Idea of a thing, and an Idea is Reason in action; but our power of thus knowing is also Reason acting within us. Indeed "that which we find in our-selves is (*gradu mutato*) the substance and the life of all our knowledge". (*SM*, p. 465.) Consequently the terms "Idea" and "Law" are interchangeable; or rather (once again) they are but two sides of the same penny, so that "an idea conceived as subsisting in an object becomes a law; and a law contemplated subjectively in a mind is an idea". (*AR*, p. 219n.)

This coincidence of Law and Idea is an often repeated obser-vation. And the concomitant conviction that "the mind of man, in its own primary and constituent forms represents the laws of nature" (*SM*, p. 465), led Coleridge to prefer that philosophical method which he attributed to Plato, and in which

in order to arrive at the truth, we are in the *first* place (for there is no doubt among thinking men that both must be consulted – the ques-tion of priority is the point) . . . in the *first* place, and in order to gain the principles of truth, we are to go into ourselves and in our own spirits to discover the law by which the whole universe is acting, and then modestly to go forth and question this, that, and the other, how far it will give a favorable response to our own individual conception of that truth. (*PL*, 5, p. 188.)

This preference was not, however, an arbitrary prejudice. It was, Coleridge held, confirmed in its results. For, beginning from "a profound meditation on those laws which the pure reason in man reveals to him, with the confident anticipation and faith that to this will be found to correspond certain laws in nature," man will find, when looking abroad into nature, that in contemplating the nature of his own mind, he has been fathoming nature, and that "nature itself is but the greater mirror in which he beholds his own present and his own past being in the law". (*PL*, 11, pp. 333–4.) Additionally, he thereby "learns to reverence while he feels the necessity of that one great Being whose eternal reason is the ground and absolute condition of the ideas in the mind, and no less the ground and the absolute cause of all the correspondent realities in nature – the reality of nature for ever consisting in the law by which each thing is that which it is". (*PL*, 11, p. 334.) It is indeed the coincidence of the constituent forms of the mind with the laws of Nature, thus observed, which "is a mystery which of itself should suffice to make us religious: for it is a problem of which God is the only solution". (*SM*, p. 465.)

6. *The Imagination*

As early as 1802 Coleridge had written to Sotheby saying he believed and felt "that each Thing has a Life of its own, & yet they are all one life".[8] Having obtained some idea of what he meant by this we can now turn to Coleridge's concept of the Imagination, that other power of man's mind, to which, in one of his letters, Coleridge refers as "a dim Analogue of Creation".[9]

First of all, then, the Imagination is

a repetition in the finite mind of the eternal act of creation in the infinite I AM. (*BL*, 1, xiii, p. 202.)

That is to say, just as God creates the objects of the universe, so man, being made in God's image, re-creates that God-created universe for himself, by reason of his truly imaginative –

insightful – perception of it. In Coleridge's categorical scheme this is equivalent to saying that Imagination is Reason, but on the human scale, or from the human angle. Consequently much that can be said of Reason can be said of Imagination; and that Coleridge speaks of both in similar (though not identical) terms shows the continuity (though also the distinctness) of the two powers. Reason, we have seen, is the power which, when conjoined to the Understanding, gives the latter a new dimension; but it is when the Understanding is impregnated by the Imagination that it becomes not discursive but "intuitive, and a living power". It is by virtue of Imagination that knowledge is given depth as well as clarity. (*SM*, p. 461.)

Or the Imagination can be seen as that power by which a poet "described in *ideal* perfection, brings the whole soul of man into activity". (*BL*, 2, xiv, p. 12.) But thence, too, it is a power enabling men to penetrate and comprehend Ideas since these are also "truths . . . the knowledge and acknowledgement of which requires the whole Man, the free Will, no less than the intellect".[10] And thus the Imagination is "the living Power and prime Agent of all human Perception". (*BL*, 1, xiii, p. 202.)

So far, the emphasis is on Imagination as insight, albeit an insight which re-creates the world as it is for our knowing, and to this aspect of imagination Coleridge gives the name "Primary Imagination". But (like Reason) it has another, more purely creative, aspect. For the Imagination (still in repetition of the eternal act of creation in the infinite I AM), when activated by the will, is the power (which Coleridge calls the "Secondary Imagination") whereby man himself can create new entities. These (when they are products of the Imagination) will not, however, be 'copies' of already existing beings. For copies reproduce only the external and superficial likeness, while the Imagination – being insight – is reproductive of the inner, vital, organizing principle of its object – its Idea. The resulting product is, in Coleridge's terminology, not a copy but an "imitation".

This distinction is important for Coleridge, and will be relevant to the concept of 'symbol'. In the essay 'On Poesy or Art' an imitation is characterized as a reproduction in which

two elements must co-exist, and must not only co-exist, but must be perceived as co-existing. These two constituent elements are likeness

and unlikeness, or sameness and difference, and in all genuine creations of art there must be a union of these disparates . . . a reconcilement of both in one. (*BL*, 2, p. 256.)

How, then, is an "imitation" created? To understand this we
must look further at the activity of the Imagination, both as
insight and as creative power. As insight, Imagination can be
directed (like Understanding) to the world as object: the given
material things of the natural world, to man and to men's
actions. But in this, its penetrative function, it "dissolves,
diffuses, dissipates" (*BL*, 1, xiii, p. 202) these received elements, not, as Understanding does, to analyse them, and produce them serially, but in order that it can modify and unify
them into new creations. The Imagination is essentially a
"synthesizing", "coadunating" power, which "blends, and (as
it were) *fuses*" (*BL*, 2, xiv, p. 12) whatever comes or is brought
into its province. Here it is different from Reason, which creates
Ideas "by the necessity of its own excellence"; instead, like
Understanding, the creating Imagination works upon given
material. Nevertheless, like Reason, which "manifests itself in
man by the tendency to comprehension of all as one", so
Imagination "acts chiefly by creating out of many things . . . a
oneness, even as nature, the greatest of poets, acts upon us,
when we open our eyes upon an extended prospect". Thus, too,
it "reveals itself in the balance or reconciliation of opposite or
discordant qualities: of sameness, with difference; of the general, with the concrete; the idea, with the image; the individual,
with the representative . . ." (*BL*, 2, xiv, p. 12); in products,
therefore, which (be they of the arts or the sciences) are
imitations. And in Coleridge an imitation is the product of
Imaginative insight, which dissolves its elements and fuses
them anew. To borrow a chemical analogy: it is, for Coleridge,
a true compound, and not a mixture, amalgam, or suspension.
The functions of the Imagination, and its products, are reciprocal, and cannot be described independently.

Though the Imagination, as insight, is a power possessed by
all, in its specifically creative aspect it is most particularly the
prerogative and essential quality of the man of genius, be he
artist, poet, scientist, mathematician, philosopher, historian:
that is to say, if his avocation includes the re-presentation of his
apprehension of the world, its materials, its events, in new

form. And Coleridge's account of the Imagination as a power of mind, is also a theory of how such works (when they are works of genius) are produced, as well as a statement – however sketchy – of the criterion for distinguishing these from other products and artefacts. The man of genius, the artist, does not copy Nature, does not present us with its superficial likeness. He must first "master its essence, the *natura naturans*",[11] which, as we have seen, is the Idea within Nature, its organizing and vitalizing principle. Having done this, he will be able to apply "the same energies to other circumstances and different materials", which is to 'imitate', as Nature 'imitates' itself in its various products (*PL*, 10, p. 252). And he applies "the same energies" to his own creations, not only because he has discovered what these are in Nature, but because he himself repeats the continuing creative activity of the "infinite I AM".

This account of the creativity of the man of genius indicates the relationship in which his products stand to Nature. Briefly, they are imitations, in Coleridge's particular sense. But it can also be said that, as the Imagination is, as it were, Reason on the human scale, so the products of the Imagination are the products of the "infinite I AM", on the human scale: they are Nature presented for man's Understanding. Not, it should be remembered, the objects of Nature; for there would be little point in presenting for man's understanding something which is so readily perceived itself; not *natura naturata* but the *natura naturans*: the organizing, vital, developing power which makes each thing what it is in relation to all others. This is, as we have seen, graspable by, present to, Reason in man; but the products of the Imagination make it available also to the Understanding. Art makes what is implicit explicit and thus available for reflection as well as for intuition.

It is to this kind of picture of the mind, its powers, the inter-relationship between them and between God the Creator, Nature his creation, and man and his products (simplified though the above account has necessarily been), that Coleridge's concept of 'symbol' must be related, and within which it must be understood. Thus to relate it will be the object of the following section.

'Symbol' and its Cognates in Coleridge

Coleridge's Concept of 'Symbol'

What has been said so far about the context of thought in which Coleridge used the term 'symbol' goes a long way towards explaining what that word meant for him. The creations of genius as these have been described in their relation to God's original creating power, to Ideas, and to the powers of man's mind, are, precisely, 'symbols'. The further, and now direct, consideration of the concept of symbol will therefore also serve to fill in the larger picture which has already been outlined.

To establish the connection between a 'symbol' and the Imaginative creations of genius, it is necessary to look at the definition of an Idea given in *The Statesman's Manual*. Here, in Appendix E, Coleridge says that an Idea is

an educt of the imagination actuated by the pure reason, to which there neither is nor can be an adequate correspondent in the world of the senses. (p. 484.)

In the body of the same work occurs his much quoted reference to 'symbols' which are there given the following genesis and characteristics: they are "the living educts of the imagination" when the Imagination incorporates "the reason in images of sense" and organizes "the flux of the sense by the permanence and self-encircling energies of the reason". Hence symbols are "harmonious in themselves and consubstantial with the truths of which they are the conductors". (*SM*, p. 436.)

The parallelism here between "symbol" and "Idea" is obvious. When moreover it is added that Ideas are also referred to as "living Truths", and that, in the *Biographia*, as already quoted, Coleridge says that

an IDEA in the *highest* sense of that word cannot be expressed but by a *symbol* (*BL*, 1, IX, p. 100)

the conclusion, that a symbol has the same genesis as an Idea, but is its outward, sensible complement, is inescapable. But this is precisely what Coleridge also maintains, as we have seen, of 'art' in the extended sense of that word in which I have used it in the previous section to mean any product of genius. Hence much that has already been said about "Ideas", and about their sensible complements is also true of 'symbols'. This now needs amplification.

44

If we discount as incidental those instances of the term in Coleridge's writings where no indication of the nature of a symbol is suggested, there remains, even so, a wide variety of things to which the term is explicitly applied. A list would include such heterogeneous entities as numbers, geometry, certain paintings and sculptures, music, the political and historical narratives of the Bible, Adam, Don Juan, the events of Christ's life, the sacrament of marriage, various philosophical 'isms', Nature itself. Evidently we must look for the principles in accordance with which one term can be used so widely.

1. *Number and Geometry*

In some cases these principles can be readily seen (if not so readily acknowledged). Thus Coleridge attributes to Pythagoras the supposition that:

what in men the ideas were, as we should say, those in the world were the laws; that the ideas partook according to the power of the man, of a constitutive character, in the same manner as the laws did in external nature. (*PL*, 2, pp. 107–8.)

And Pythagoras conceived that number was

the best symbol, if I may so say, of the representation of the laws of nature considered as homogeneous with the pure reason in man,

for he observed that "in numbers considered philosophically there was a perpetual reference to a unity that was yet infinite, and yet that in each number there was an integral or individual that still contained in its nature something progressive, that went beyond it". (*ibid.*)

That Coleridge may have been mistaken in attributing such perceptions and intentions to Pythagoras is not the point, as it is also beside the point to ask whether, in fact, numbers do exhibit such characteristics, and whether the concept of number is of such a nature. What is important is that, for Coleridge, number and numbers are symbols, not because of some convention, but because they exhibit the homogeneity of Idea and Law, of which they are a presentation; and because they combine in themselves those kinds of opposites which Imagination reconciles, and which are characteristic of an 'imitation'.

With regard to this latter quality of symbols, geometry, as

45

symbol, is singular, since it alone does not "involve an apparent contradiction". Nevertheless geometry also is a true product of the Imagination; and although it is a product of the mind, it is also discovered to be true of Nature, and thus exhibits in a visible structure the interaction between mind and law, man and Nature, knower and known, which is the peculiar quality of symbols. Coleridge puts it thus – this time as a description of the "true Baconic philosophy" – which

consists in this, in a profound meditation on those laws which the pure reason in man reveals to him, with the confident anticipation and faith that to this will be found to correspond certain laws in nature. If there be aught that can be said to be purely in the human mind, it is surely those acts of its own imagination which the mathematician alone avails himself of, for I need not I am sure tell you that a line upon a slate is but a picture of that act of the imagination which the mathematician alone consults. That it is the picture only is evident, for never could we learn the art of the imagination, or form an idea of a line in the mathematical sense, from that picture of it which we draw beforehand. Otherwise how could we draw it without depth or breadth? It becomes, evidently too, an act of the imagination. Out of these simple acts the mind still proceeding , raises that wonderful superstructure of geometry . . . (PL, 11, p. 333),

and it is this superstructure which is found to be also a fathoming of nature, as already quoted above.

2. *Painting, sculpture and other artefacts*

Some of Coleridge's other examples are more usual. The reason why certain paintings and sculptures are symbols can best be understood with reference to his definition of beauty. In the essay 'On the Principles of Genial Criticism concerning the Fine Arts', Coleridge writes:

The BEAUTIFUL, contemplated in its essentials . . . is that in which the *many*, still seen as many, becomes one. (*BL*, 2, p. 232.)

And:

The most general definition of beauty . . . is . . . Multeity in Unity. (*ibid.*)

Or again:

The safest definition, then, of Beauty, as well as the oldest, is that of Pythagoras: THE REDUCTION OF MANY TO ONE. (*ibid.* p. 238.)

All these he considers as equivalent to the definition of beauty as

the subjection of matter to spirit so as to be transformed into a symbol, in and through which the spirit reveals itself. (*ibid.* p. 239.)

Beautiful objects are therefore symbols, and they exhibit "Multeity in Unity" and reveal the spirit in being thus organized. The examples here given of beauty are various, but those which are pursued furthest are that of an ordinary wheel, and of Raphael's *Galatea*. In the arrangement of rays with respect to the circumference in the former, Coleridge finds "many different images are distinctly comprehended at one glance, as forming one whole, and each part in some harmonious relation to each and all". (*ibid.* p. 233.) About the latter (also a composition of "rays and chords within the area of a circular group") he thinks that "in the junctions of the figures, is the balance, the perfect reconciliation, effected between these two conflicting principles of the FREE LIFE, and of the confining FORM!" (*ibid.* p. 235.) More is said about the paintings of Raphael and Michael Angelo in the *Philosophical Lectures*. Asking why we go on looking at such paintings after "having satisfied all our curiosity concerning the mere outline" Coleridge answers that in such works of art "the mighty spirit still coming from within had succeeded in taming the untractable matter and in reducing external form to a symbol of the inward and imaginable beauty;" and because "there is a divine something corresponding to something within, which no image can exhaust". (*PL*, 5, pp. 193–4.)

These extracts indicate why (or when) certain pictures, sculptures, or indeed other artefacts are 'symbols'. It is when in them the form and matter are so combined that they exhibit a unity in the distinctness of many parts; when they are the externalizations of an inward beauty, which is itself a correspondence to something divine.

But the vocabulary used in these analyses of the beautiful cannot but remind the reader that the knowledge of the one in the many is a function of Reason; and that the creation of objects in which "opposites are reconciled" and unity combined with multeity is the function of the Imagination; and that the "something divine" and the "something within" which is externalized, and apprehended in the externalization is "an Idea". And thus we can be led to see the relationship between

47

the use of the term 'symbol' in connection with sculpture, painting, and other such objects, and its previous use of geometrical structures. Beauty (and enjoyment) may not be the purposes for which geometrical structures are constructed (though a mathematician may find such structures a source both of beauty and enjoyment); and intellectual guidance is not (normally) the reason why we value works of art (though a painting or sculpture may serve useful purposes). But both geometry and the objects of art are the sensible counterparts of a Reason-actuated-Imagination; and as such they are both embodiments of Ideas, not as copies, but as imitations in which the Idea embodied is also the empowering, unifying, and present force.

3. *Bible narratives*

It is in considering the Bible as history in contrast to other historical and political accounts of events that Coleridge speaks of symbols in the terms already indicated. Coleridge is well aware that no account, no description, however historical or factual, can be free from selection and interpretation, since, as we have seen, he maintains that the mind is never passive, a mere recorder, but always active in its apprehension of the world and its events. But his contention here is that "the histories of highest note in the present age" are events as interpreted by the Understanding *only*: "the product of an unenlivened generalizing understanding". (*SM*, p. 436.) Hence such "histories and political economies" are no more than abstractions and generalizations: the connections made in them between one event and another are superficial, spurious and arbitrary associations made according to the theories of the prevalent "mechanical philosophies". These were incapable of giving insight into the true organic, internal development and interdependence of the particulars which were their subject matter. It is only the histories and political economies of Scripture which are

living educts of the imagination; of that reconciling and mediatory power, which incorporating the reason in images of the sense, and organizing (as it were) the flux of the senses by the permanence and self-encircling energies of the reason, gives birth to a system of symbols, harmonious in themselves, and consubstantial with the truths of which they are the conductors. (*SM*, p. 436.)

Like geometry, like art, the Scriptural narratives are presentations of Ideas, and as such are symbols. As symbols and like
other symbols they exhibit a "reconciliation of opposites", of,
for instance, the "individual and the representative" for in the
Scriptures "both facts and persons must of necessity have a
two-fold significance, a past and future, a temporary and a
perpetual, a particular and a universal application. They must
be at once portraits and ideals." (*SM*, p. 437.)

What Coleridge means by this, and the reason why, for him,
there is no opposition between "history" and "symbol" – an
important point to note – is to be seen in his treatment of the
story of the fall. This is to be found in *Aids to Reflection* – typically
in a long footnote appended to a quotation from Jeremy Taylor.
To understand, first, why Coleridge should see Adam as a
representative of mankind it is necessary to grasp his concept of
sin, which is expounded in this footnote. All sin consists in this,
that we allow ourselves to be guided by the Understanding
"without, or in contravention to the reason – (that is, the
spiritual mind of St. Paul, and *the light that lighteth every man* of St.
John)". (*AR*, p. 268n.) Without the guidance of Reason, the
Understanding, which is "the faculty of means to approximate
and medial ends", and not "the determinant of the ultimate
end", though remaining an intelligential, becomes "the sophis-
tic principle, the wily tempter to evil and counterfeit good".
Because, in itself, the Understanding is concerned only with
proximate ends, when severed from Reason it is "ever in league
with, and always first applying to, the desire, as the inferior
nature in man . . . and through the desire, prevailing on the will
. . . against the command of the universal reason and against
the light of reason in the will itself". (*AR*, p. 268n.)

As this note also explains, Coleridge sees each human being
as a compound of feminine and masculine, this basic fact of
human nature being externalised in the separate sexes. The
appetitive inclinations in all human beings, the desire, he sees
as "the woman in our humanity" whilst the will he calls its
"manhood, virtus". When we also remember (what Coleridge
again stresses here) that the Understanding, which leagues
with desire, is "analogous to" and an extension of "the instinct
of the more intelligent animals", we can see why Coleridge can
say that in the Genesis narrative of the fall, the author "gives a
just and faithful explanation of the birth and parentage and

49

successive moments of phenomenal sin . . . that is of sin as it reveals itself in time, and is an immediate object of consciousness". (*AR*, p. 269n.) For Coleridge's analysis of sin is that it is the will (the manhood in man) succumbing to desire (the woman in man) itself actuated by the Understanding (the intellective principle man has in common with the higher animals) acting without the light of Reason (conscience, and the light of God in man) and hence transgressing the commands of Reason (conscience, and the laws of God). And the Mosaic story has the same elements: Man (Adam) tempted by Woman (Eve) at the instigation of a Higher Animal (the most cunning of the beasts of the field) to transgress the command of God. But furthermore, if all sin is like this then the first man to sin sinned thus, and we all sin as he did, and hence also "The first human sinner is the adequate representative of all his successors. And with no less truth may it be said, that it is the same Adam that falls in every man, and from the same reluctance to abandon the too dear and undivorceable Eve: and the same Eve is tempted by the same serpentine and perverted understanding." (*ibid.*)

However, it is still possible to ask: yes, but even though the story thus represents what always happens, and therefore too what originally happened when the first man sinned, are the external events, as recounted, 'historical'? Was there *a* man who was tempted by *a* woman at the instigation of *a* creature? Coleridge sees that the story may be allegorical, but he himself asks "Why not at once symbol and history?" (*ibid.* p. 270n.) and he then goes on to explain that, indeed, to be symbol, it must also be history, for the point about symbol is that it is "a sign included in the idea which it represents; that is, an actual part chosen to represent the whole . . .". The implication is, that if it did not happen it is no actual part of the history of the human race of which it is a symbolical rendering. Whatever the logic of this argument, the note does show that Coleridge did not think that symbol and history were incompatible, but rather the contrary; and it also is one of the few instances where his theoretical definition is applied to a specific example, and its meaning, therefore, made more explicit.

Enough has now been said to indicate why, in Coleridge's view, such a seemingly heterogeneous collection of entities as geometry, art, and the Bible considered as history, can be subsumed under the one term 'symbol'. It is because in all there is "a translucence of the special in the individual, or of the general in the special, or of the universal in the general" (*SM*, p. 437); and above all, "the translucence of the eternal through and in the temporal" (*SM*, p. 437). Though they differ in the material, or subject matter, in which this "translucence" occurs, in each the material or subject matter is so organized and presented that in each, as in the Bible, "the same mystery . . . reveals itself" "freed from the phaenomena of time and space". This "hidden mystery in every the minutest form of existence" is, as we have seen, "the actual immanence or in-being of all in each" (*SM*, p. 450). In each, such a translucence is possible because every symbol "always partakes of the reality which it renders intelligible", and every symbol is "a living part in the unity of which it is a representative",[12] because each is empowered by the same creative force and springs from the same source of energy, as the whole, which it can therefore 'enunciate'.

4. *The interaction of God and man*

So far, 'symbols' – geometry, art, the Bible – have been discussed as if they were all the products of man's mind, though working on a given material. And so, of course, they are. But what has previously been said about Reason in man as coincident with Supreme Reason and of the Imagination as a repetition of the creative activity of God, should indicate that no symbol is a product of man alone, unenlightened and unempowered by the God who, for Coleridge, was the supreme creator and evolver; the indwelling presence and power disclosed to us within symbols, and, as distinct, through them. But, as might be expected, the coincidence of the activity of God and the activity of man – this aspect of 'symbol' – is best seen in what Coleridge says of the events of the life of Christ. In notes on Donne he writes:

the crucifixion, resurrection and ascension of Christ himself in the flesh, were the epiphanies, the sacramental acts, and *phænomena* of the *Deus patiens*, the visible words of the invisible Word that was in the beginning, symbols in time and historic fact of the redemptive functions, passions and procedures of the Lamb crucified from the foundation of the world; the incarnation, cross, and passion, – in short, the whole life of Christ in the flesh, dwelling a man among men, being essential and substantive parts of the process, the total of which they represented; and on this account proper symbols of the acts and passions of the Christ dwelling in man, as the Spirit of truth. (Shedd, 5, pp. 83–4.)

If we look at this closely we shall see that here are united four characteristics of 'symbols', of those sensible counterparts of Ideas which are the educts of the joint activity of Reason and Imagination, both of which find their origin in God. For the events, acts, words, of Christ's life are symbols because

(1) they are the acts of "a man among men" but also (since Christ is "the Word that was in the beginning") the acts of God;
(2) in Christ, and therefore in his actions, the invisible God is rendered visible; the infinite is present in the finite; the eternal translucent in the temporal;
(3) moreover, and consequently, the events of his life are the visible and historical part of the whole creative and redemptive plan, which is a continuing process. Here the eternal is translucent in the temporal and the macrocosm realized in the microcosm: the whole of redemption and creation is in this part effected, and presented for man's cognizance;
(4) as the acts of Christ, they are continuous with the activity of Christ within each man, by whose power the outward events can be recognised for what they are.

The interaction between man and God in a symbol; the way in which a symbol is part of that which it enunciates; the way in which the part as well as the whole both tend towards and at the same time contain, exhibit, and are empowered by, that towards which they tend, Coleridge sought to express as early as about 1805. He then wrote:

The best, the truly lovely in each & all is God. Therefore the truly Beloved is the symbol of God to whomever it is truly beloved by! – but it may become perfect & maintained lovely by the function of the two/The Lover worships in his Beloved that final consummation ⟨of itself which is . . . ?⟩produced in his own soul by the action of the soul of the Beloved upon it . . . ⟨which is in part?⟩ the consequence of the reaction of his (so ammeliorated & regenerated) Soul upon the Soul of his Beloved/till each contemplates the Soul of the other as involving his own, both in its giving and its receivings, and thus still keeping alive its *outness*, its *self-oblivion* united with *Self-warmth*, & still approximates to God! Where shall I find an image for this sublime

Symbol ⟨which ever?⟩ involving the presence of Deity, yet tends towards it ever! (*N*, 2, no. 2540.)[13]

Two decades later, in the *Aids to Reflection*, Coleridge returns to what is a similar thought:

It might be a mean of preventing many unhappy marriages, if the youth of both sexes had it early impressed on their minds, that marriage contracted between Christians is a true and perfect symbol or mystery; that is, the actualizing faith being supposed to exist in the receivers, it is an outward sign, co-essential with that which it signifies, or a living part of that, the whole of which it represents. Marriage, therefore, in the Christian sense (Ephesians v. 22–3) as symbolical of the union of the soul with Christ the Mediator, and with God through Christ, is perfectly a sacramental ordinance. (*AR*, p. 138n.)

This phraseology, which might seem tired and empty to those used to certain formulations of the catechism, acquires, in the context of Coleridge's thought, a new richness and resonance of meaning. A symbol, so theologically suspect in some contexts, is here seen to be one with the whole Christian affirmation of incarnation: it is that wherein God is made present to men in the circumstances of their own lives. Indeed, Coleridge's insistence that in a symbol the creative work of God and the creative work of man are coexistent, and in a particular way interdependent – that in a symbol the historical and the representational (history and myth) coincide, may suggest an answer to the Modernist dilemma. For Modernism, in attempting to free scriptural and theological truths from too literal an interpretation, was always in danger of evacuating them of any historical or God-given and God-revealing content. The Coleridgean notion of symbol suggests not only that, but also how, the necessary balance may be achieved.

5. *Nature*

A further instance of Coleridge's use of the term 'symbol', in which, on reflection, the same qualities become apparent, must be considered: his application of it to Nature. In a *Notebook* entry for Saturday Night, April 14th, 1805, Coleridge wrote:

In looking at objects of Nature while I am thinking, as at yonder moon dim-glimmering thro' the dewy window pane, I seem rather to be seeking, as it were *asking*, a symbolical language for something within me that already and forever exists, than observing anything new. Even when that latter is the case, yet still I have always an obscure feeling as if that new phænomenon were the dim Awaking of a forgotten or hidden Truth of my inner Nature / It is still interesting as a Word, a Symbol! It is Λογος, the Creator! (and the Evolver!) (*N*, 2, no. 2546.)

The thoughtful contemplation of Nature generates the search for a counterpart, a symbolical language in Nature, to something within oneself which "already and forever exists". But it also awakens that forgotten and hidden truth, while what is contemplated (the new phenomenon) is at the same time seen as "Word" as "Symbol", as "Logos", Coleridge's favourite synonym for Christ. So the identity of the inwardness of nature, the hidden Truth within man, and the creative power of Christ is apprehended, the two former reciprocal, and symbols of the latter.

Again, Coleridge re-expresses this idea later, this time in *The Statesman's Manual*, thus:

I seem to myself to behold in the quiet objects, on which I am gazing, more than an arbitrary illustration, more than a mere *simile*, the work of my own fancy. I feel an awe, as if there were before my eyes the same power as that of the reason – the same power in a lower dignity, and therefore a symbol established in the truth of things. I feel it alike, whether I contemplate a single tree or flower, or meditate on vegetation throughout the world, as one of the great organs of the life of nature. (*SM*, p. 462.)

When we remember that Reason, as Coleridge understood it, was both the "something within" man, and was Christ, the Logos, this extract throws further light on the relationships indicated in the previous one. In the objects gazed at, Coleridge insists, is found not merely an "arbitrary illustration" of the "something within". The awe engendered by the contemplation of Nature belies the possibility that there is here merely a superficial parallelism such as that of a simile; and it belies the possibility that the coincidence apprehended is simply the construction of fancy which is an "aggregating power"[14] only (and not like Imagination "coadunating"), and which is (as such) a construction of man's Understanding. The awe felt is (for Coleridge) an indication that within Nature the same power is at work as within himself. It is "reason" in a "lower dignity". Hence what he contemplates is a symbol; namely: an inward truth one with its visible complement, and perceived and perceivable because one with the power by which it is perceived. Furthermore, this evidence that what is seen is such a symbol is apprehended alike in the contemplation of each part or of the whole as one of the organs of the life of Nature.

One final example will serve to supplement the foregoing. In the essay 'On Poesy or Art', Coleridge is, as we have seen, concerned with the nature of artistic activity, and hence with the nature of the art product. And here he writes: "The artist must imitate that which is within the thing, that which is active through form and figure, and discourses to us by symbols – the *Natur-geist* or spirit of nature" (*BL*, 2, p. 259); in other words, what is 'symbol' here is the *natura naturata*, and it is symbol of the *natura naturans*. If, then, we look at the three extracts together, we will discover a kind of hierarchy of symbols, or rather a kind of nest of symbols which fit one in another. If we start from the *natura naturata*, the visible forms, the things, which embody the *natura naturans*, which in turn informs them, and makes them what they are, and is, indeed, the presence of God within them as his creative Idea, the *natura naturata* is seen as the symbol, the visible counterpart, of the *natura naturans*. But if this latter is also seen as "continuous with the same power as that of reason" but "in a lower dignity", then the *natura naturans* can be apprehended as symbol of Reason in man. It must be noted, however, that the *natura naturans* can be thus apprehended as symbol only because it is seen in its own visible symbol as *natura naturata*. And Reason in man is the symbol of God, as continuous (in a lower dignity) with his activity; but, again, it is symbol also because its activity is perceptible in its outward forms: when Ideas are presented to the senses in the products of the Imagination, themselves therefore symbols, as the *natura naturata* is of the *natura naturans*.

It is, indeed, difficult to find an image for, or even to give a comprehensive description of, this kind of complex, interlocking, and essentially dynamic structure, each part of which is a symbol of another in a "higher dignity" with which it is nevertheless continuous, and in which each part, as well as the whole, is ultimately the symbol of the structure's apex, cohesive energy and independent cause – God. The images which Coleridge repeatedly returned to were those of light – as it affects and is affected by the seeing eye, and as it acts upon glass, which can be reflector, refractor or transparent surface.[15] What remains to be discovered is how a concept which is most aptly, though not even then comprehensively, illustrated by so complex an image can be related to the nature and function of language.

6. *Language*

In all that Coleridge says about language and words as such, and about such language constructs as poems, plays and prose works – and obviously this is much – he does not often refer to them explicitly as 'symbols'. Indeed I know no instance in which a work of literature is spoken of as a symbol. Nevertheless there are two ways in which the terms are linked and the concepts coincide.

In the first place, all that has been said of the products of the Imagination is, *ipso facto*, applicable to those forms of language which are imaginative in this sense, whether they are plays, poems, or prose works of fact or fiction. But equally obviously, not all such works are 'symbols' just by virtue of being language constructs. Those which are will exhibit the appropriate characteristics of symbols; these will, at least in theory, distinguish them from language constructs which are not products of the Imagination. The point need not be laboured; nor is it my concern to discuss the question whether Coleridge's distinction between Imagination and Fancy is valuable in practice.

But there is a second link between language, words, and symbols. We have seen that Coleridge referred to Christ as "Logos". Behind this usage lies the thought of the beginning of John's Gospel: that the Word was God and was with God; and that through the Word all things were made. Coleridge's view is supplemented by other passages in the New Testament, such as the words of Paul in Colossians, that in, and through, and for Christ, the Son of God, all things were created, and that in him all things hold together. (See Colossians i. 15ff.) The Word, then, is creative. And it is creative in two senses: as origin, and as such distinct from the creation; but also as that within each thing, and all things, whereby each and all are what they are. The Word is also life, as John explicitly says. And that life, for John, as for Coleridge, is also light: "In him (Christ)", says John, "was life, and the life was the light of men"; whereas for

Coleridge, as we have seen, Christ, the Word, is also the Reason in man: that which enables us to see those things which are imperceptible to the senses and incomprehensible by the Understanding. The Word is the light *by* which we see, and it is also the power of seeing, as well as that which we see.

However, it is not only Christ who is "the Word", otherwise what has been said so far would have no particular relevance to language. The Bible, too, is referred to as "the Word of God". Now this is a commonplace, and again need not take us much further. But what must be noted, in view of what has been said about the connection of Word, Life, and Light, is the way in which Coleridge speaks of the Bible as "The Word of God". It is after he has explained why and how the Bible differs from other histories and political economies, how and why it is 'symbol', and what a 'symbol' does, that Coleridge adds:

Hence, by a derivative, indeed, but not a divided, influence, and though in a secondary yet in more than a metaphorical sense, the Sacred Book is worthily entitled *the Word of God*. (*SM*, p. 437.)

What is important in this is that the Bible, which is a language construct, and a symbol, is not "the Word of God" metaphorically only; it is "the Word of God" because it is one with it. That is to say, what can be said of the activity of Christ, the Word, can, in a derivative, but not simply metaphorical, sense be said of the Bible. The Bible, then, is not simply a *record*, even though of things as they are and not only as they appear to be. It is also a creative agent, whereby (and not only wherein) we can see them as such.

But this is because the Bible is also 'symbol'. Hence, also by a derivative, though not divided, influence, and not only metaphorically, all language constructs which are symbols (as all symbols) have a like creative power. They are constructs which enable us to 'see'. And what we are enabled to 'see' is not only the purely human notions and conceptions (ideas in that sense) which any theory of language will grant, and which is all that the theory of language which considers words as one to one counters of thoughts will allow. No: words, language constructs, when they are symbols, are counterparts of Ideas in the Coleridgean sense; of thinking, rather than thoughts; of an ongoing, creative process which, though human, is also of God. Such language constructs, then, present to us, and enable us to

57

'see', to experience, and to think about, the world as it is transcendentally, in the Divine (and therefore real) dimension. Language may accurately and clearly state, and hence convey (provided the hearer or reader is capable of understanding) thoughts, feelings, individual objects of nature – the *natura naturata*. But in that language which is symbolic such statements and descriptions will be re-creative also of the *natura naturans*, the power whereby things are as they are, provided that the reader or listener allows the light of Reason to function within him. In and through symbols the light of Christ within man (his Indwelling Spirit) thus brings him into contact with the power of Christ without him. But it is only symbols which have the potentiality of being seen in this way, of being thus creative and illuminating, and in thus bringing us into contact with the Divine, which is within and without, and in whom we are. To repeat: language, as symbol, is not descriptive only, it is also creative; creative by its own power as symbol, which is the power within us which enables us to see it as symbol: but creative only when we allow that power to act. But when this happens we will also see that not only Christ, and not only the Bible, are the Word of God. For then, when we are taught by Reason, "will that other great Bible of God, the Book of Nature, become transparent to us, when we regard the forms of matter as words, as symbols valuable only as being the expression, an unrolled but yet a glorious fragment, of the wisdom of the Supreme Being". (*PL*, 12, p. 367.)

These considerations show that symbols, even when they are language constructs, are never just figures of speech or literary devices. Coleridge explicitly says that by a symbol he means

not a metaphor or allegory or any other figure of speech or form of fancy (*SM*, p. 465),

and this should be taken seriously. The difference between symbols on the one hand, and metaphors and allegories on the other, is not between two different kinds of figurative expressions, but between two different kinds of things which differ *toto genere*. This fundamental cleavage is, I think, often forgotten especially in literary discussions where a symbol is taken to be a different kind of literary device, but a literary device all the same. This is at least partly due to the fact that Coleridge insists on the distinction between allegory and symbol so frequently that the tendency to consider the two as two species of the same genus is reinforced. Moreover, Coleridge's examples do not always help to clarify the distinction he is making. His insistence that a symbol is part of that which it represents can only too easily lead the unwary, who fail to consider this within the whole context of his thought, into the belief that Coleridge confused symbol with synecdoche. That this is not the case should now be clear.

The particular distinctions which Coleridge makes between metaphors and allegories on the one hand (metaphors for him being essentially allegorical), and symbols on the other, can be briefly sketched. Metaphors and allegories are both "forms of fancy" (and not Imagination); they are translations

of abstract notions into picture language, which is itself nothing but an abstraction from objects of the senses (*SM*, p. 436);

they are "grounded on an apparent likeness of things essentially different" (*AR*, p. 197); are always "spoken consciously" and arrived at by "outward observation or historically".[16] In other words, it can in general be said that metaphors and allegories are products of the Understanding, and as such can only deal with, and appertain to, that which appears and not that which is.

Symbols, on the other hand are, for Coleridge, the visible tips of an ontological iceberg. They presuppose, and also indicate, the whole Coleridgean scheme of things, outside which they simply cease to be (and to mean) what he conceived them to be (and to mean). If there is no eternal, symbols cannot be translucent of it; if the relationship between God, man, Nature, and art is not such as Coleridge has described, then symbols cannot be "part of that which they represent" in the way he envisaged. If, then, these things are not so, there are simply no 'symbols' in the Coleridgean sense, but only various kinds of metaphors, allegories, and other figures of speech. To say that 'this is a symbol' in the Coleridgean sense, is also to make a statement about the structure of each component of the universe, and about the inter-relationship between all created things and their creator, whereas to say 'this is a metaphor' or 'this is an allegory' implies no such general metaphysics. For to construct, or recognize, a metaphor or an allegory, all we need accept is that the world is a collection of disparate things, as it appears to be, some of which have a fortuitous resemblance to one another, which we recognize and in our speech emphasize. Thus it is (to repeat) that they express different subjects with a resemblance. But symbols, as we have seen, always "express the same subject" (the Ideas of Reason) but "with a difference" (in and through different media), and thus presuppose that there is an inner 'unity' which can be manifested in various forms. And, to fulfil the other requirements of a symbol, this unity must be of a particular kind.

Finally, I would like to add a comment about one other – apparently discordant – reference to the world as 'symbolical' in Coleridge's writing. It occurs in his poem 'The Destiny of Nations', first published in its entirety in 1817; but partly written as early as 1796, with some passages forming part of Southey's *Joan of Arc*. The relevant lines, as most often quoted, run as follows:

For all that meets the bodily sense I deem
Symbolical, one mighty alphabet
For infant minds; and we in this low world
Placed with our backs to bright Reality,
That we may learn with young unwounded ken
The substance from the shadow.

Now this, as Mary Rahme points out,[17] is reminiscent of Plato's cave analogy, in which what we see are the shadows of a Reality which we are *not* looking at directly. The comparison suggests that, in the lines quoted, the relation between a symbol and the Reality which is symbolized is that between shadow and thing, and that to apprehend the thing we must look away from the shadow at the thing itself. What, then, of Coleridge's description of a 'symbol' as "translucent", which, quite apart from the suggestion of light, also indicates that it is by looking *at* (and not away from) the symbol that we see the Reality? And, even if we consider a shadow as "a part of that which it represents" can it be so in a way in which Coleridge's whole metaphysic seems to suggest? There are, then, apparent discrepancies between the lines quoted (when the parallelism with Plato is emphasized) and what Coleridge says elsewhere, and it seems to me therefore inaccurate to say without further comment (as Mary Rahme does) that they sum up Coleridge's ideas on "the symbolic nature of the physical universe".

I do not think, however, that Coleridge was being simply inconsistent. In the first place it is impossible to assume that, though he obviously did have Plato's cave in mind, the implications of the image were, for him, what they were for Plato. As we have seen in the cases of Pythagoras and Bacon, Coleridge was quite capable of seeing the work of others in his own light, and interpreting it accordingly. The allusion here cannot, therefore, be taken at its face value, especially when we remember that Coleridge's Ideas were not the Platonic Ideals which the cave analogy seeks to illustrate.

This must be borne in mind since the elements of Coleridge's thought are so inter-related that each is always relevant, and hence it is that the actual context of this particular passage, as well as its genesis in earlier versions, is more important than it would be in the case of other poets.

The "preluding strain" of this poem is intended to be addressed to God, "the I AM, the Word, the Life, the Living God", and for such a symphony, the best of instruments is required, which, for Coleridge, is the Harp, seized "from Freedom's trophied dome", whose music will "force back / Man's free and stirring spirit that lies entranced". The poem then continues:

For what is Freedom, but the unfettered use
Of all the powers which God for use had given?
But chiefly this, him First, him Last to view
Through meaner powers and secondary things
Effulgent, as through clouds that veil his blaze.
For all that meets the bodily sense I deem
Symbolical, one mighty alphabet
For infant minds; and we in this low world
Placed with our backs to bright Reality
That we may learn with young unwounded ken
The substance from its shadow. Infinite Love,
Whose latence is the plenitude of All,
Thou with retracted beams, and self-eclipse
Veiling, revealest thine eternal sun.
('The Destiny of Nations', ll. 13–26.)

When the whole of this passage is read, the central image, in which there appears to be the suggestion that "all that meets the bodily sense" is the shadow of a "bright Reality", is qualified by the two other images which flank it. In these, Reality – God, spoken of in various terms – is seen to be "effulgent" *in* the "secondary things" as in "clouds". These "clouds", moreover, are not seen as an interposition between the Reality and us, but are spoken of as the "self-eclipse" of that Reality, effected in order that the Reality may become visible; the point being that we cannot see or look at the sun *at all* unless its beams are thus retracted. In these two flanking images, then, that which we perceive by our senses is a direct apprehension of the Reality, albeit modified, and not its "shadow" *from* which (as in the cave analogy) we must turn away our gaze in order to see the Reality itself. In an earlier version, indeed, the shadow image is absent, the relevant lines being:

For what is Freedom but the unfettered use
Of all the powers which God for use had given?
But chiefly this, him first to view, him last,
Through shapes and sounds and all the world of sense,
The change of empires, and the deeds of Man
Translucent, as thro' clouds that veil the Light. (1796.)

As Gerard has pointed out, the word "translucent" is important here since it later becomes "central to Coleridge's full-blown definition of the symbol".[18] That definition, in *The Statesman's Manual*, appeared in 1816. Why, then, did Coleridge in the 1817 version of 'The Destiny of Nations' not keep to it, but instead expand the lines in the way he did? I would suggest that this is not because he had ceased to think of symbols, of things in this world, as "translucent" of God, replacing this by an entirely different concept of symbol as "shadow". Were this so, he would surely not have kept (and extended) the light images as he did. It is, I think, because the central image of this passage as it eventually appears, adds to the original concept of symbol, and without inconsistency. This can be made clear if we think of that element of Plato's cave analogy which is missing in Coleridge's allusion to it. According to Plato, it is only those who have – painfully – averted their gaze from the shadow world to look at the Reality itself, who will eventually be able to discern the true meaning of the shadows on the cave wall. But in Coleridge's lines there is no hint that such a turning away is necessary. The suggestion is, rather, that it is by continuing to sit "with our backs to bright Reality", continuing, therefore, to look at the shadows before us, that, nevertheless, we learn to distinguish "the substance from the shadow".[19] What, then, can such a "substance" be? What can be better seen by looking *at* shadows than can be seen by turning away from them, even if (eventually) to return? I suggest that this is that aspect of "Reality" which is its pattern, its movement, its developing process. We have seen that in this passage the "Reality" is God, who is seen both as the "latence" and "plenitude of *all*"; and is revealed in "powers" as well as "things". What is still missing, if we compare this with Coleridge's concept of God in relation to the universe as previously sketched, is the notion of the universe as a developing pattern, whose movement, as well as that movement's ultimate resolution, is God. It is this lack which is made good in Coleridge's (as distinct from Plato's) image here. For in fact it *is* easier for us to discern a pattern of movement, to see things in close interrelation, in a two-dimensional shadow projection, than it is if we look at a multitude of detailed things in a coloured and three-dimensional perspective. In other words, the "shadow" in Coleridge's image may be predominantly a modification, a simplification, of Reality, *in* which we discern Reality in this particular way, namely as pattern. It is not "shadow" in the sense of being a pale reflection, a ghostlike anticipation, an 'adumbration' of something 'more real', 'more substantial'. It is attached to Reality not simply at one (invisible) point, as the shadow of a tree is linked to it only at its base, and part of it in that sense. The Reality, as pattern, transfuses the shadow and is made visible in it.

Interpreted in this way – and I think careful attention to the words endorses this view – there is no inconsistency between the image of symbol as "shadow" and its definition as "translucent". The shadow-play, like the clouds, is an effect which embodies and thus makes visible to us the inner nature of Reality – God – not as it appears, but as it is. And a symbol is a tangible, visible creation (an appearance in that sense) of this sort, in which, because it is perceptible, we can see Reality not only as it appears but as it is. Moreover, as an embodiment of the inner Reality of all and each, the outwardness of an inwardness, a symbol renders that Reality (in itself susceptible only to direct apprehension by Reason) comprehensible also by the Understanding, and open, therefore, to discursive thought.

'Symbol' and its Cognates in Coleridge

Some Final Reflections

In the foregoing sections I have attempted to give an exposition of what Coleridge meant by 'symbol', and have tried to show how, in Coleridge's thought, this is inextricably related to a particular concept of a triune God, and his relationship to man and to Nature. With the question of the originality of such a concept of 'symbol', especially in comparison with thinkers like Schelling and Schlegel upon whom Coleridge so heavily drew, or even more particularly with Goethe, I am not equipped to deal. The verbal similarities, and sometimes wholesale plagiarisms, of relevant passages have been already well documented by Patricia Ward[20] and Norman Fruman;[21] on the other hand, MacFarland[22] has suggested that such verbal similarities do not necessarily constitute a lack of originality, since in Coleridge's work (which he compares to a mosaic) they are parts of a total picture very different from that drawn by those from whom these passages are lifted. This, I would suggest, is particularly applicable to Coleridge's use of the term 'symbol'. Even if some – or many – of Coleridge's words on the subject are culled from others, it is only if these others have a similarly articulated *Weltanschauung* that the term will, in his work, bear the same meaning as in theirs.

The question at issue, then, is how far Coleridge's *Weltanschauung* is sufficiently well articulated to form a whole in which even the second-hand material performs new functions. I have only been concerned with this question from a particular point of view: that of the concept of 'symbol' itself, and I have tried to show that, looked at from this angle there does appear to be a certain coherence in Coleridge's theology, metaphysics, and aesthetics in which the term 'symbol' has a particular and important meaning. But it would be idle to pretend that this articulation is either easy to discern or even complete. Even in the limited question of Coleridge's use of the term 'symbol', loose ends and unsolved problems become apparent.

In the first place, for instance, in spite of the general consistency with which Coleridge uses the term, which itself is not obvious, there are occasions when Coleridge uses the word as it were casually, and without any regard to what he vehemently says elsewhere. But, what is more important, he does not pay attention to the theological problems which his use of the term

raises. His use of the term 'symbol' in respect of biblical narratives may not, it is true, impugn their historicity; and when he
applies it to Christ he does not deny his Divinity, nor the
importance of his historical existence, nor his essential uniqueness. But the question which Coleridge's use of the term raises,
and with which he does not deal, is of the status of the Bible as a
source of revelation *vis-à-vis* other language constructs (plays,
poems – perhaps especially, for Coleridge, the works of Shakespeare) which from his general account must also be considered
'symbols' in his sense of the word, though he nowhere calls
them such. It would appear that, as sources of our knowledge of
God and his dealings with men, and relationship to all created
beings, the Bible, Nature, and those literary (or other art)
works which are products of the Imagination (both as insight
and creative power) rather than Fancy, are all equally valuable, all equally sources of 'revelation'. It is not that, like the
deists, Coleridge considers that man can attain to a knowledge
of God by his own unaided powers, and that therefore no
special revelation is necessary. For, as we have seen, he insists
that the recognition of symbol as symbol, as well as the creation
of symbols, and the consequent knowledge of God and the
Universe as his creation which these provide, depend upon the
power, the spirit, of Christ working within man (only by his
light do we see light). It is, rather, that other works of men are
raised to the same status as sources of revelation as the Bible
and this, equally, brings its uniqueness to question. While it
cannot be denied that Coleridge held the Bible in very high
regard, and that he did, in some way, think of it as a special kind
of work, the question of its parity with other works, raised by
Coleridge's concept of 'symbol', is never explicitly tackled.

A similar difficulty becomes apparent in Coleridge's use of
the term in one of his early notebooks. Here, in 1804, he could
write that Newtonianism, Berkeleyism and whatever finer
'isms' these might eventually be translated into, all "remain
symbols of Truth, actual tho' dim perceptions of it". (*N*, 2, no.
2541.) By this he meant, as the note goes on to suggest, that all
such 'isms' are perceptions of an 'object' absolutely, though
differently, seen. It is interesting to note here – in anticipation
of what will later be said of Carlyle – that, even though translated into finer 'isms' the earlier apprehensions of the 'object'
remain symbols; and – in anticipation of what is to be said of

Newman – that 'symbols' once again seem to be representations of the 'object' seen 'as a whole'. Yet a difficulty arises because Coleridge here seems to imply that there exist, with respect to the object as thus 'seen', some symbols which are better than others. But not only is there nothing in what Coleridge says elsewhere which might help one to judge the fine-ness of a given symbol, and thus place it on a scale of values; there is, on the whole, the contrary impression that symbols cannot be thus balanced one against another, since something either is a product of the Imagination, or not; it either is the visible counterpart of an Idea, or not.

Here, then, there is a further instance in which Coleridge's theory of 'symbol' seems to lack a proper articulation: it is the sort of question the answer to which remains uncertain even when what Coleridge meant by 'symbol' has been teased out. It is, of course, related to the still debated literary question, whether or not Coleridge's distinction between Imagination and Fancy is of any practical value in judging the merit of a poem. The theological implication of this unresolved question is this: that such a view of all philosophical 'isms' – the designation of all as symbols of Truth – raises the question of the status of Christianity as another such 'symbol'. Is it one among many, and still to be translated into further 'symbols'? Or is it in some way unique? And if unique, is it only so with the uniqueness which appertains to all symbols (all are different, if dim, perceptions of Truth), and which, again, if paradoxically, denies to any that primacy which Christianity traditionally claims to possess? To put it another way: if all 'isms' are symbols, and all equally perceptions of Truth (however dim) what is the advantage of Christianity? But if some symbols are clearer perceptions of Truth than others, how are we to judge between them? Even though Coleridge may, here also, maintain that it is only the spirit of Christ working in men which enables them to perceive and construct symbols, this does not provide an answer to the question. And it is because there so often is a lack of such necessary answers to problems raised by Coleridge's theory of 'symbol', that it can be felt to be unsatisfactory, no more than fragmentary, and perhaps, like the whole system which he attempted to build, more in promise than in fulfilment, and consequently easily by-passed.

Nevertheless, unsatisfactory or incomplete as it may be,

Some Final Reflections

Coleridge's concept of 'symbol' is, I would suggest, interesting, perhaps capable of development, and certainly unexpectedly consistent. For, if sometimes uncertainly, Coleridge does attempt to provide some rationale for distinguishing symbolic from non-symbolic presentations of truths, and his theory seeks to preserve the centrality of the action and presence of Christ in symbolic constructions, and the irreplaceability of genuine symbols. All these are important factors in any theory of symbol which might be acceptable to orthodox theology, if applied to such constructs as the Bible. The particularity can perhaps best be seen by contrast with other uses contemporary with his own, an analysis of which will also further point the significant ambiguities which a casual use of the term 'symbol' all too easily obscures.

3

SOME CONTEMPORARIES OF COLERIDGE – CHIEFLY CARLYLE

Hazlitt, De Quincey and Others

". . . it is significant", writes W. J. Bate, "that in the later writing Coleridge should turn increasingly to the word 'symbol' which he did so much to popularise." (*Coleridge*, p. 165.)

It is not contentious, I think, to suggest that if one wanted proof of the extent to which Coleridge's use of the term 'symbol' was both understood and popularized in the nineteenth century, one should turn to the works of Matthew Arnold, who was, after all, not only influenced by Coleridge, but like him was a poet concerned with both literature and religion. But, unfortunately, while there is little doubt that some of Matthew Arnold's insights into the function of literature seem to echo Coleridge, his use of the term 'symbol', as I have noted in the introduction to this book, is practically non-existent. In his inaugural lecture as Professor of Poetry at Oxford, Arnold says that a work of literature "demands the most energetic and harmonious activity of all the powers of the human mind", and speaks of "genius, the activity of the whole mind",[1] a terminology not dissimilar from that of Coleridge in like context. But the term 'symbol' is used of words which have a "definite and fully grasped meaning" in contrast to Pauline terms such as "grace", "new birth", "justification", which, Arnold says, Paul used in "a fluid and passing way, as men use the terms in common discourse, or in eloquence and poetry, to describe approximately, but only approximately, what they have present before their mind, but do not profess that their mind does or can grasp exactly or adequately". ('Literature and Dogma', *Complete Prose Works*, 6, p. 170.) No trace of the Coleridgean use here, rather quite the reverse. And a topsy-turveydom important within discussions of literature and theology.

There is similar neglect – rather than the popularity which Bate suggests – of the Coleridgean (and indeed any other) use of the term 'symbol' by most of Coleridge's nearer contemporaries. This neglect is presaged in Hazlitt's review of *The Statesman's Manual* in *The Examiner* of September 8th and December 29th, 1816, a biting criticism which dismisses the whole sermon as atheistic nonsense (a view widely shared). To illustrate his point Hazlitt quotes at length the passage which includes Coleridge's definition of symbols, where the latter is speaking of them as "consubstantial with the truths of which they are the conductors", and he comments as follows:

So that after all the Bible is not the immediate word of God, except according to the German philosophy, and in *something between a literal and a metaphorical sense*. Of all the cants that ever were canting in this canting world, this is the worst! The author goes on to add that 'it is among the miseries of the present age that it recognises no medium between *literal* and *metaphorical*', and laments that the 'mechanical understanding, in the blindness of its self-complacency, confounds Symbols with Allegories'. This is certainly a sad mistake which he labours learnedly to set right, 'in a diagonal sidelong movement between truth and falsehood'.[2]

And that is Hazlitt's only allusion to Coleridge's definition. In other contexts, Hazlitt's own infrequent use of the term is entirely casual.

Hazlitt, of course, may not be thought a fair representative since, though he was very taken with Coleridge at first meeting, he is not among those who admitted themselves influenced by him – quite the contrary, if we are to judge by the temper of this and other of his reviews. But J. S. Mill, for instance, did admit to such influence,[3] and thought that what Coleridge was trying to say was both coherent and important; more profound, indeed, than men of his time were, as yet, able to judge. Nevertheless, his concept of poetry is far removed from Coleridge's, as one of his very rare uses of the term 'symbol', in a passage praising Tennyson, epitomizes:

Of all the capacities of a poet, that which seems to have arisen earliest in Mr Tennyson, and in which he most excels, is that of scene painting, in the higher sense of the term: not the mere power of producing that rather vapid species of composition usually termed descriptive poetry – for there is not in these volumes one passage of pure description: but the power of *creating* scenery, in keeping with some state of human feeling; so fitted to it as to be the embodied symbol of it, and to summon up the state of feeling itself, with a force not to be surpassed by anything but reality.[4]

Poetry – and symbol – then, are embodiments: but not, as in Coleridge, of a poet's perception of the inwardness of things, but of his feelings on perceiving them. Here – as indeed in Hazlitt – we have the concept of a symbol as something which is principally emotive, and hence possibly peculiar to the individual, and thus subjective.

It may be objected that the whole tenor of Mill's thought was so moulded that – in spite of his appreciation of Coleridge – he could not be expected to assimilate all Coleridge's insights. However, we can look for evidence of Coleridge's influence with respect to the term 'symbol' at De Quincey, who was certainly closer to Coleridge in more ways than that of opium-addiction. De Quincey was acquainted with the German philosophy which forms the background to Coleridge's thought, and he was indeed the first to point out the extent of Coleridge's plagiarism from Schelling. Moreover, as we are led to believe by A. E. Powell in *The Theory of Romantic Poetry*, De Quincey was "thrilled by the symbol"; and we might expect, therefore, at least some attention to Coleridge's pronouncements on the subject. But, though De Quincey, like Coleridge, writes of the effects of the Brocken Spectre (an image which, Prickett suggests, is important for Coleridge's theory of symbol);[5] though he is concerned with the relationship between Biblical narrative and scientific fact;[6] and though, like Coleridge, he does not think of the Arts as attempts to reproduce the superficies of Nature, he nowhere (as far as I am aware) refers to Coleridge's definition of 'symbol', or even attempts to discuss the meaning of the term. And his own unemphatic and infrequent use of the word, though superficially similar to Coleridge's, is seen, on reflection, to be different.

The apparent similarity may be detected in, for instance, De Quincey's linking of "the effect from the symbolic" with "the great catholic principle of *Idem in alio*", and his remark

here (in the context of the description of the Brocken Spectre)
that

the symbol restores the theme, but under new combinations of form or
colouring; gives back, but changes; restores, but idealizes. (*CW*, 1,
p. 51.)

The principle of *idem in alio*, we learn, is "the very first principle
of every Fine Art", which is

to reproduce in the mind some great effect, through the agency of *idem
in alio*. The *idem*, the same impression, is to be restored, but *in alio* in a
different material, – by means of a different instrument. (*CW*, 10,
p. 368.)

This may suggest that art, as symbol, is concerned with
making outward, in a different material, some inward principle
of the thing perceived, and may thus be held reminiscent of
Coleridge. But it also indicates that what is thus reproduced in
the art object is not, after all, the 'isness' of the thing observed,
but its effect: not what the artist sees the thing to be, and what
it really is, but the effect the natural object creates in him. Here,
too, there is no such fusion of subjective and objective in the
symbol as Coleridge posited.

Similarly, with De Quincey's use of the term 'symbol' in his
essay on 'Modern Superstition' (*CW*, 8, pp. 404–51). There are
what seem like echoes of Coleridge; but if echoes, they are
distorted. In the essay in question, De Quincey defines superstition as "the sense of sympathy with the invisible" and calls it
"the great test of man's grandeur, as an earthly combining with
a celestial" (*ibid*. p. 404). This sense he thinks manifests itself
variously at all times of human history, not least his own, and
he classifies its various forms. One class he sees enshrined in the
Metamorphoses of Ovid, where he thinks is displayed

a movement of superstition under the domination of human affections: a mode of spiritual awe, not remarkably profound, which seeks
to reconcile itself with human tenderness or admiration, and which
represents supernatural power as expressing itself by a sympathy
with human distress or passion concurrently with human sympathies,
and as supporting that blended sympathy by a symbol incarnated
with the fixed agencies of nature. (*ibid*. p. 405.)

Here, the reference to a "supernatural" reconciling itself with
the human in "a symbol incarnated with the fixed agencies of

nature" may remind us of Coleridge; but only, I would suggest, till we realize that the reconciliation is between the sympathies of a supernatural and a human, and that the 'symbol' which incarnates these sympathies is not seen as having any essential relation to either. For the story which De Quincey quotes to illustrate his meaning is that of a pair of youthful lovers who

perish by a double suicide originating in a fatal mistake. . . . The tree under which their meeting has been concerted, and which witnesses their tragedy, is supposed ever afterwards to express the divine sympathy with this catastrophe in the gloomy colour of its fruit. . . . And the fruit becomes thenceforward a monument of a double sympathy – sympathy from man, sympathy from a dark power standing behind the agencies of nature and speaking through them. (*ibid*. p. 405.)

Though De Quincey continues this by saying, in terms reminiscent of both Coleridge and Goethe, that "the object of this sympathy is understood to be not the individual catastrophe, but the universal case of unfortunate love . . .", (*ibid.* pp. 405–6), and though, just possibly, the fruit which is here the symbol may be thought of as translucent of the dark power behind it, and of the universal state exemplified by this individual tale, it can certainly not be seen as an essential part of those sympathies whose reconciliation it represents. De Quincey has no metaphysics which would suggest this as – even verbally – an appropriate description. Yet such a metaphysics, and therefore such a partaking of a symbol in that which it represents, is essential to Coleridge's concept (whether or no it is a proper description of any existing things). Thus De Quincey's use is not Coleridge's, and the rest of this essay serves to underline the fact, for it can be seen further that the former's concept of a 'symbol' approximates much more closely to the notion of pre-figuration and omen than Coleridge's definition would allow. And therefore A. E. Powell's book (as others like it) is misleading in that it speaks of 'symbol' in connection with both Coleridge and De Quincey as if the terms were synonymous for both, which, I suggest, they are not.

There is a similar neglect of the Coleridgean term 'symbol' in writers more directly concerned with theology than those so far mentioned. Of these F. D. Maurice may be taken as an example. Maurice thought highly of Coleridge and defended him against critics on a number of occasions. C. R. Sanders[7] also indicates the similarity of their thought on many points, as well as Maurice's respect for Coleridge, in spite of his independence of him on a number of questions. The respect is evident in Maurice's dedicatory letter to the second edition of his *The Kingdom of Christ*;[8] and he also shows himself particularly appreciative of Coleridge's view of Reason, as well as of both *Aids to Reflection* and (though less so) the *Lay Sermons* (of which *The Statesman's Manual* is one). One of the points on which Maurice was suspicious of Coleridge's philosophy was on what seemed to Maurice his disregard of facts. Edward Strachey reports Maurice as one day saying in this connection that "if we ignore facts we change the substances for suppositions – that which really does stand under an appearance for something which we put under it by our imagination" (J. F. Maurice, *Life of F. D. Maurice*, 1, p. 203); and Sanders comments that "Facts were to Maurice the concrete manifestations or embodiments in outward forms of truth or invisible law." (*Coleridge and the Broad Church Movement*, p. 207.) It would seem that Maurice's particular appreciation of Coleridge, as well as his wariness of him on this point of the interpretation of facts would make Maurice, whether in praise or criticism, especially sensitive to what Coleridge had to say about symbols in the context of a discussion of the Bible, as in *The Statesman's Manual*, and *Aids to Reflection*. But no explicit attention to this point is evident, either in Maurice's controversy with H. L. Mansel,[9] or in what he wrote about the Bible and science.[10] Nor does C. R. Sanders, who meticulously documents Maurice's defences of Coleridge, and the coincidences and variances of their thought, ever allude to the concept of 'symbol'. An inexplicable omission if the term had played any significant part in Maurice's work, or if he had singled it out for comment with respect to Coleridge.

I am not, of course, suggesting that the term 'symbol' is entirely absent from Maurice's work. It does occur, as indeed it does in most theological and literary writers here and there, both before and after Coleridge's time. And some of Maurice's uses are, in fact, potentially interesting. There is, for instance, his allusion to "the ordinances of the Christian Church" as "the symbols of Christ's Kingdom, the witnesses for the finished work of Christ, and the bonds of fellowship between Christ and all the redeemed in heaven and earth",[11] where a faint Coleridgean influence might be traced, though there is nothing particularly novel in speaking of sacraments in such general terms. And there is also a reference to "divine symbols" as "media of communication with the Absolute and Eternal, not devised by men but appointed by God, not meant for sages but for all creation".[12]

In the passage in which this reference occurs, Maurice is voicing his dissent from Carlyle who, he indicates, thought of symbols as formularies invented by a few privileged seers, to convey to others less favoured than themselves what these latter could not apprehend directly. Maurice objects, that is to say, to Carlyle's concept of symbols as merely human inventions and as such no more than changeable 'isms' and "repetitions of half truths and falsehoods". To such a view of symbols Maurice's own statement is indeed a contrast, but if one is thinking of the way in which *Coleridge* (and not Carlyle) 'popularized' the term, what is striking is that, in criticizing Carlyle, even Maurice makes no mention of Coleridge, has no reference to *his* concept of symbol. Surely, if Coleridge's ideas had been influential and considered important, Maurice could not have omitted to refer to them in this context, either in dissent or with approval. But here, as elsewhere, he is silent. Nor, it must be added, does Maurice anywhere develop such stray allusions, or pay the term 'symbol' any particular attention in his *Kingdom of Christ*, though its subject matter is relevant to its use.[13] In all these respects Maurice is typical of his generation.

But in all that has been said so far there are two important omissions from those of Coleridge's younger contemporaries whose use of the term 'symbol' is relevant to a discussion of this concept as it appears in nineteenth century theology and literary theory. One of these is Carlyle. And indeed, on the face of it, the 'popularity' of the subsequent use of the term 'symbol' (or the meaning with which it was associated in subsequent theology) could be more readily attributed to his influence than to that of Coleridge, since his use of the term is far more prominent, and his influence at least as potent. As in the case of Maurice, even those influenced by Coleridge appear to have linked the term more with Carlyle than with Coleridge. Precisely for these reasons, however, what Carlyle had to say about 'symbols', and how this relates to the Coleridgean concept as outlined above must be dealt with in a separate section.

The other important theologian omitted so far is, of course, Newman. His use of the term 'symbol' will be discussed in the following chapter.

Carlyle

Carlyle's ambivalent attitude to Coleridge – both as a person and as a thinker – has been well documented in C. R. Sanders' book *Coleridge and the Broad Church Movement*. Sanders, like C. F. Harrold in *Carlyle and German Thought*, affirms that Coleridge made an impact on Carlyle but points to the futility of speculating on the precise influence he had on his younger contemporary. What is certain, as both Sanders and Harrold, as well as Basil Willey,[14] point out, is that their thought appears to have been coincident in a number of matters. Since, as I have tried to show, the term 'symbol' is, for Coleridge at least, essentially a part of his whole *Weltanschauung*, outside which it loses its particular meaning, some of these similarities, as well as the differences, between Coleridge's thought and Carlyle's need to be indicated here, if their concepts of the term 'symbol' are to be seen in comparison and contrast.

One of the points of coincidence is their common repudiation of, and revolt against, what each saw as the mechanistic philosophy and psychology of the preceding century. Carlyle, in his article 'Signs of the Times', first published in the *Edinburgh Review* of 1829, sees the tendency to consider all things in terms of a mechanism as still the most baleful characteristic of his own age.[15] At this early stage of his writing, he remains hopeful that society will realize the follies to which such a concept of man and his world must inevitably lead. In developing his own alternative view of the world in terms more vital and organic than his English predecessors allowed, Carlyle, like Coleridge, was gripped and influenced by the German thought of the time – by Kant, Schelling, Fichte, Jacobi – and much of his early writing is devoted to the attempt to popularize this, at least as it existed in contemporary German literature, most particularly in the works of Goethe.

The way in which Carlyle, in his early writings, thought of the nature and significance of poetry, and of the function of a poet, is also similar to much in Coleridge. These, for instance, are the words in which Carlyle praises Shakespeare: his dramas are "not veri-similar only, but true; nay truer than reality itself, since the essence of unmixed reality is bodied forth in them in expressive symbols . . ." ('The State of German Literature', *CME*, 1, p. 51.) A few years later (1832) speaking of Shakespeare again, and comparing him with Goethe, Carlyle wrote that Shakespeare

does not look *at* a thing, but into it, through it; so that he constructively comprehends it, can take it asunder, and put it together again; the thing melts, as it were, into light under his eyes, and anew *creates* itself before him. That is to say, he is a Thinker in the highest sense of all: he is a Poet. For Goethe, as for Shakespeare, the world lies all translucent, all *fusible* we might call it, encircled with WONDER; the Natural in reality the Supernatural, for to the seer's eyes both become one. What are the *Hamlets* and *Tempests*, the *Fausts* and *Mignons*, but glimpses accorded us into this translucent, wonder-encircled world; revelations of the mystery of mysteries, Man's Life as it actually is? ('Goethe's Works', *CME*, 2, p. 437.)

The true Poet, then, is one "whose eye has been gifted to discern the godlike Mystery of God's Universe" (*CME*, 2, p. 377); and this 'insight' (also a word used by Carlyle) into an inner reality is "bodied forth" in the poet's work. Moreover, a poet like Goethe has the "force to educe reconcilement out of such contradiction as man is now born into"; he, pre-eminently, is able to "reduce chaotic elements into new higher order". (*CME*, 2, p. 435). Here, whether by direct influence or because of a common background, Carlyle's thought, and even his terminology (translucent, reconcilement, fusibility), is reminiscent of Coleridge's, as can be seen most strikingly, perhaps, in an earlier essay on Goethe (1828) in which Carlyle contrasts the "poetry which supplies spouting clubs, and circulates in circulating libraries" with "that Poetry which Masters write, which aims not at 'furnishing a languid mind with fantastic shows and indolent emotions', but *at incorporating the everlasting Reason of man in forms visible to his Sense*, and suitable to it". (*CME*, 1, p. 255, italics mine.)

Such a view of poetry presupposes, as it also reveals, some wider theory of the nature of the universe, and of man; and Carlyle's *Weltanschauung* also appears similar to Coleridge's.

Both, as has been noted, thought of the universe in dynamic and organic terms; and (as the above extracts already indicate) Carlyle, like Coleridge, saw the visible forms of Nature as

Carlyle

expressing in some way an inner reality, which, moreover, he, too, identified as the Divine and godlike. Man, says Carlyle, in an often recurring turn of phrase, "sees the Infinite shadowed forth in something finite; and indeed can and must so see it in *any* finite thing, once tempt him well to *fix* his eyes thereon". ('Goethe's Works', *CME*, 2, p. 389.)

Like Coleridge, too, Carlyle, in his concept of man, is attracted by the Kantian distinction between the Reason and the Understanding, and, somewhat like Coleridge, he extols the powers of the former and underlines the limits of the latter. But – again like Coleridge – though forced to use a faculty vocabulary, he repudiates any absolute distinction between the various powers of man's nature. We ought to know, he says, that "these divisions are at bottom but *names*; that man's spiritual nature, the vital Force which dwells in him, is essentially one and indivisible; that what we call imagination, fancy, understanding, and so forth, are but different figures of the same Power of Insight, all indissolubly connected with each other . . .". ('The Hero as Poet', *HH*, p. 106.) And not only the concept of man, but even the ways in which Carlyle and Coleridge looked at man's history appear similar. As Sanders comments: "The idea of history being a not altogether comprehensible but very marvellous revelation of the 'One Unnameable'; the idea of the unity which lies beneath history and which transcends all considerations of space and time; the idea of the historian's function being the philosophic one of penetrating beneath what is seemingly dead or temporal and discovering what is living and eternal" (Sanders, *Coleridge and the Broad Church Movement*, pp. 167–8), all these ideas are in Coleridge as well as Carlyle.

Such, then, are the general resemblances in Carlyle's and Coleridge's views of the universe and man's place in it. And these points of apparent coincidence in thought can mislead one into thinking and assuming that the meaning of the terms they use – such as 'symbol' – which form part of the expression of their views, is identical.

Mislead: after all, the differences are as important as the similarities, if not more so. Thus, though Carlyle at first held what might be called a 'high' view of the function of a poet, and the nature of poetry, he could also write as early as 1831 (even if perhaps tentatively, in the pseudonymous guise of

Sauertig) that "Fiction, while the feigner of it knows that he is feigning, partakes, more than we suspect, of the nature of *lying*". ('Biography', *CME*, 3, p. 49.) Though Nature is said to "body forth the Finite from the Infinite", Art "only apes her from afar", a verb singularly inapposite to Coleridge's theory of "imitation".[16] And if, even in 1840, Carlyle could still write

Literature, so far as it is Literature, is an 'apocalypse of Nature', a revealing of the 'open secret'. It may well enough be named, in Fichte's style, a 'continuous revelation' of the Godlike in the Terrestrial and Common. The Godlike does ever, in very truth, endure there; is brought out, now in this dialect, now in that, with various degrees of clearness; all true gifted Singers and Speakers are, unconsciously, doing so ('The Hero as Man of Letters', *HH*, p. 163),

eventually, it was only history and the historian who were, for Carlyle, of any account.

Again, Carlyle's rejection of metaphysics, as of literature, is early evident. In his essay 'Characteristics' (1831), he sees philosophy as an evil, even if a necessary one, for "Man is sent hither not to question but to work"; and though "the attempt to shape for ourselves some theorem of the Universe" must often be repeated, there is not the faintest chance that the perennial disease of metaphysics should ascertain "the goings and comings" of that "illimitable ocean of the All" in which "Mankind and our whole existence are but a floating speck" though also an "indissoluble portion . . . partaking of its infinite tendencies". (*CME*, 3, pp. 25–6.) As Harrold says, if both Coleridge and Carlyle "endeavored to promote the 'self-recognition of that spiritual life of the world which fulfils itself in many ways but most completely in religion' they were far from agreeing on the most effective means. 'Action', the key-word in Carlyle's doctrine, contrasts diametrically with Coleridge's faith in the mind's eventual victory over the intractable and bewilderingly involved nature of its own processes". (*Carlyle and German Thought*, pp. 53–4.)

The secondary place which Carlyle gives to thought in relation to action in his scheme of things (in this so different from Coleridge) shows itself also in the lack of particular attention that Carlyle gives to the "powers of man's mind". Though he does, early on, accept a distinction between Reason and Understanding, he eventually shows nothing less than scorn for what he came to consider as Coleridge's mumbo-jumbo on this, Coleridge's favourite, point.[17] And in fact, at least in one very important respect, the Reason never was, for Carlyle, what it was for Coleridge. For both, it might be 'insight'; for both, a gift given to men whereby they can look into the divine heart of things; but only for Coleridge was Reason both the power of seeing, and the most essential inwardness of all that is seen; only for Coleridge was it the creative presence of God within man, possessed equally by all, but the property of none.

It is true that Carlyle writes of "The unspeakable Divine Significance . . . that lies in the being of every man, of every thing, – the Presence of the God who made every man and thing" ('The Hero as Man of Letters', *HH*, p. 156), recognising, that is to say, the God within all men. And it is also true that Coleridge, whilst insisting that all equally possess, or are possessed of, Reason, also maintains that some, though this is by the better exercise of their Understanding, can grasp and present this truth to others more clearly. But Carlyle never identifies man's Reason, or his creative power, with the God within man in the way that Coleridge does and the effect of this difference is most evident in Carlyle's theory of the Hero. For, though the Man of Letters – as Hero – is sent so that "he may discern for himself and make manifest to us" the Divine Idea of the world (the Reality which "lies at the bottom of all Appearance"), what Carlyle presents for our worship is not so much this Idea, but the hero himself. It is not, as in Coleridge, God, the second person of the Trinity, Christ the Logos, who is the source of light and life, but the great man, of whom Carlyle speaks in terms very like those Coleridge uses of Christ, the Word: it is the great man who is "the living light-fountain which it is good and pleasant to be near. The light which enlightens, which has enlightened the darkness of the world; and this not as a kindled lamp only, but rather as a natural luminary shining by the gift of Heaven; a flowing light-fountain, as I say, of native original insight, of manhood and heroic nobleness". ('The Hero as Divinity', *HH*, p. 2.) The gift by which such a one shines is from an unspecified "Heaven", and is after all his own, of "native original insight", and not one with the giver. Carlyle is hero-centric, whereas Coleridge's thought centres on Christ. If both start from the conviction voiced by G. M. Hopkins that "the world is charged with the grandeur of God", and that this is most particularly true in the case of man, when Carlyle dwells on this conviction, God all but disappears, and only Great Men remain.

Such a disappearance of the transcendent God in the exaltation of the godlike in man and nature, is, of course, a version of pantheism which Carlyle, as much as Coleridge, repudiated. Coleridge, however, as MacFarland argues,[18] endeavoured to find an answer to the dilemma of a God whom he recognised as both immanent and transcendent in his particular kind of Trinitarianism, and his particular description of the relation between God and the world. Carlyle, having no philosophy of mind linked to a doctrine of the Trinity, balanced his pantheistic tendencies by a quite different insistence on God's transcendence, one which – in spite of the similarities which have been noted – made his concept of the relation between God and the world essentially unlike Coleridge's. The similarities are linked to the German Idealist influence common to both; the differences have their roots in Carlyle's early religious background against which he fought, but which he was never quite able to reject: Calvinism, as understood by his parents, particularly his father, and as practised in his native home of Ecclefechan.

Calvinism is, of course, many-sided, and it is impossible to do it justice here. But for the present purpose what needs to be stressed are the following elements to be found within it: the emphasis on the essential corruption of the world and the sinfulness of man, which the life, death, resurrection and continuing work of Christ do not affect intrinsically, for Christ's grace is only applied to those whose salvation is already predestined; the emphasis on faith and not works as the hallmarks of salvation (to which Carlyle's vigorous call for action may well be a reaction); and the extrinsic, and purely spiritual, relationship which Christians, individually or as members of a Church organization, bear to the risen Christ. The power of the Holy Spirit sent by Christ after his ascension, for the Calvinist, "does not effect an ontological relation to the glorified Lord, who would thereby be present and active in his Church" (*Sacramentum Mundi*, 1, p. 249), but remains a link of power only. Consequently, Christ is not considered as present in his Church, or in the sacraments, but rather only as working through them. Finally, though to say so is to diminish that side of Calvinist piety expressed in the Heidelberg Catechism, in which the

Christian considers himself as belonging body and soul, both in life and death, not to himself but to his true saviour Jesus Christ, the predominant note of much Calvinist teaching comes from the Old Testament, centred neither on the person of Christ, nor on any concept of the Trinity; on law, rather than on the gospel, on God's omnipotence and power, rather than on his dwelling among men: a God distant, in a Heaven to which some may look forward, rather than present in history and time. One of the effects of such Calvinist doctrine is that the visible, tangible, historical, world with its pleasures and sufferings is considered as of little consequence. Again, Carlyle's eventual emphasis on the importance of even the minutest historical fact, may be a reaction to this. But in Carlyle we find another aspect of this doctrine which he made his own, and which I wish to consider. Harrold puts it thus:

According to the creed of Ecclefechan, the visible world was but a shadow of realities which transcended any earthly grandeur. In comparison with the eternal world, common earthly life was hardly more than a dream. For the stern 'Burgher', both the glamour of life and its enigmatic pain were but transient things; and since the suffering was no more abiding then the joy, life had at best a strange unreality. (*Carlyle and German Thought*, p. 76.)

For Carlyle, this was echoed in lines from Shakespeare which he discovered as a boy and made his own in an almost literal sense:

We are such stuff
As dreams are made on, and our little life
Is rounded with a sleep. (*The Tempest*, IV, i, 156ff.)

But if so, and if, nevertheless, this world is also a revelation of the transcendent God of Carlyle's father, it could be so only as an "Appearance" contrasted with "Reality". And Carlyle's attraction to Fichte and Novalis may be explained partly because he saw their views of the universe as harmonizing these two themes of his own thought: that the word is a manifestation of the power of a transcendent being, but is also a dream and an illusion. What he says of them, is true of himself, for whom "the material Creation is but an Appearance, a typical shadow in which the Deity manifests himself to man. Not only has the unseen world a reality, but the only reality: the rest being not metaphorically, but literally and in scientific strictness, 'a show'; in the words of the Poets, *'Schall und Rauch umnebelnd Himmels Gluth*, Sound and Smoke over-clouding the Splendour of Heaven'". ('Novalis', *CME*, 2, pp. 27–8.)[19]

Thus while on the one hand Carlyle, in his adulation of the hero, comes close to a total identification of man and God such that man is the God to be worshipped; on the other hand he sees the world as the illusion it never was for Coleridge. Harrold remarks that Carlyle "always wavered between a love of nature as suffused with deity and a rejection of her as a cloud on the otherwise dazzling face of Truth" (*Carlyle and German Thought*, p. 81), and that "it was natural for Carlyle to be more inclined . . . to think only of the God behind the vesture". (*ibid.*) For Coleridge, we have seen, the cloud was not a concealment but a means of revelation; there was never any question of rejecting nature as an obstacle to seeing that which was divinely real, or as a cloak which hid God from view. And the different ways in which Coleridge and Carlyle saw the relation between God and the world suggested in these different emphases can be most clearly seen in, as it most profoundly affects, Carlyle's concept of symbol.

Carlyle's most explicit statements concerning symbols occur in Book 3, Chapter III of *Sartor Resartus*, written in the early 1830s, and after some difficulties, published serially in *Fraser's Magazine* of 1833–4. Here, under the fiction of attempting to edit the biography of one Professor Teufelsdröckh, Carlyle inveighs against the deficiencies of society, church and doctrine, choosing the metaphor of clothes, which become outworn, as his predominant image. The central observation of what Levine[20] calls the 'circular' movement of the paragraphs in question is the following:

In the Symbol proper, what we can call a Symbol, there is ever more or less distinctly and directly some embodiment and revelation of the Infinite; the Infinite is made to blend itself with the Finite, to stand visible, and as it were, attainable there. (p. 175.)

It can easily be seen that this is not unlike the concept of the symbol as found in Coleridge, and this general resemblance seems to be accentuated in the attendant thoughts. For instance, the paragraph in which this definition occurs is concerned, at the outset, with man-created things, and it is to these that it initially refers. And the things which man makes ("many a painted Device or simple Seal emblem", to be exact) are 'symbols' when Fantasy (earlier described as "the organ of the Godlike" whereby man "extends down to the infinite depths of the invisible"), "plays into the small domain of Sense, and becomes incorporated therewith".

In such language it is not difficult to find the parallels with a concept of symbols such as Coleridge's, where they are the effects of insight (primary Imagination) produced when man, repeating the creative activity of God in the exercise of the (secondary) Imagination, incorporates the Reason in images of Sense. And there is, too, in this central paragraph, the affirmation that "the Universe is but the vast Symbol of God", and that man himself is such a symbol, also Coleridgean sentiments; whilst further on, Carlyle speaks of true Art as that in which Eternity looks through time, and the Godlike is rendered visible; with which, again, Coleridge might well have agreed.

But the development of these statements (like Coleridge's though they may seem) and the whole context of thought in which they operate, belie any real coincidence of Carlyle's concept of 'symbol' with that of Coleridge: the resemblance is of words only.

First, the development. It will be noticed that Carlyle's definition applies to "symbols proper", suggesting that there are certain artefacts which are not symbols at all. But in fact the paragraph builds up, through the assertions that man "everywhere finds himself encompassed with Symbols, recognised as such or not recognised"; and that, since not only the Universe, but man himself is a symbol of God, *all* that he does is symbolical; to the final statement that "not a Hut he builds but is the visible embodiment of a Thought, but bears visible record of invisible things; but is, in the transcendental sense, symbolical as well as real". (*SR*, 3, III, p. 175.)

This conclusion is obviously contrary to the initial implication that some things are not symbols (or at least not "proper" symbols). But if so, if everything that man does is symbolical, and everything he makes is a symbol (in the initial sense given) then, since there is nothing at all specific in the kind of activity which results in symbols, the earlier reference to Fantasy, in any sense which approximates to that of the Coleridgean Imagination, is not at all to the point. And Carlyle is not after all giving us any indication of how or why it is that the

"Infinite" is embodied and revealed, blended or made visible in, the Finite, whereas such an explanation is precisely what, for Coleridge, distinguishes the symbol from other artefacts or constructs. The ostensible resemblance to Coleridge may remain, but its essential particularity is removed. Or, if we wish to insist on the particularity which is suggested in the first half of the paragraph, then we must conclude that, by the end of it, Carlyle has slipped into a different use of the term 'symbol', where it loses its reference to any Godlike "Infinite" and means, more widely, but also less significantly, any visible, audible, or in any other way sensuous, counterpart of any thought whatsoever. This may be a "visible record of the invisible", but hardly deserves the portentous addition that it is "in a transcendental sense, symbolical as well as real".

The case is not altered by the fact that Carlyle says, further on in the same chapter, that "Symbols . . . have both an extrinsic and intrinsic value; oftenest the former only" (*SR*, 3, III, p. 177), a distinction which, in any case, could not be sustained within the Coleridgean definition. Nor is it possible to maintain that it is Carlyle's "intrinsic" symbols which coincide with Coleridge's definition. True, Carlyle counts as of extrinsic value those symbols which have "no necessary divineness" but only an acquired and accidental one; and, again, he considers that those only have an intrinsic value in which the Godlike manifests itself to sense, and Eternity "Looks more or less visibly through the Time-figure", among which he counts all true works of Art for "in them (if thou know a work of Art from a Daub or Artifice) wilt thou discern Eternity looking through Time; the Godlike rendered visible". (*ibid*. p. 178.)

Nevertheless, once again this apparent distinction between the intrinsic and the extrinsic value of symbols is nullified. For, firstly, even through extrinsic symbols "there glimmers something of the Divine Idea", which can only mean that in them, too, the Godlike is rendered visible, even if more faintly. Secondly, Carlyle admits that extrinsic value may be added to works which already possess an intrinsic one, which indicates, as does the word "value", that his distinction is not an ontological one. Thirdly, under what first appears as a particular class of human products (true works of Art, as opposed to Daubs) Carlyle within a few sentences includes "the lives of heroic god-inspired Men" and "the Death of the Just" – a considerable change of meaning. There is nothing, of course, which prevents the extension of the term "a work of Art" to what is (as here) considered the work of God; and we may indeed see in the lives of men a manifestation of the Godlike, and thus consider them 'symbols' in that there "the Godlike is rendered visible". But such an extension in no way determines in which works of *art* we should consider that "the Godlike is rendered visible": it does not help us to distinguish Art from Daub, or to know when a symbol (supposing us to recognise it) has intrinsic value. Again, it does not give any further real precision to the initial statement that all those things in which the Godlike is rendered visible is a symbol – of some sort. There is, in effect, no theory comparable to Coleridge's only statement, and a statement which is primarily not about art, but about the relations between God and *his* creation.

So we must return to a closer examination of the supposed resemblance between Carlyle's definition and Coleridge's concept. The likeness, I think, lies in Carlyle's terms "revelation", "embodiment", "blend", which suggest that the relationship between the finite symbol and the infinite symbolized therein is, for him, the same as that implied by Coleridge's "translucence" and "partaking". It seems they both insist on an indissoluble fusion between the sensible symbol and the otherwise inexpressible Idea. But a scrutiny of the context in which Carlyle's definition occurs shows that these apparently similar terms do not imply an identical relationship between symbol and referent, so that Carlyle's symbol is not, after all, like Coleridge's.

I have already indicated that Carlyle thinks of the material universe as a "cloud" which conceals the Deity, while in Coleridge the same cloud image occurs as a necessary instrument of revelation. This emphasis is again made plain in Carlyle's other statements concerning symbols in *Sartor Resartus*. Thus Teufelsdröckh, whose biography and philosophy Carlyle is here supposedly editing, prefaces his "speculations on Symbols" by a eulogy on "the benignant efficacies of Concealment" – one of Carlyle's frequent and voluble paeans on the virtues of "SILENCE AND SECRECY". The actual subject of symbols is introduced thus:

Of kin to the incalculable influences of Concealment and connected

with still greater things, is the wondrous agency of *Symbols*. In a
Symbol there is concealment and yet revelation: here therefore by
Silence and by Speech acting together comes a double significance.
(*SR*, 3, III, p. 175.)

Here the idea of concealment is obviously primary – an
emphasis absent from Coleridge. It becomes further obvious in
Carlyle's developed views on Heroes: they are the only ones
who can read the "open secret" (a phrase derived from Goethe)
of the universe; a secret which is closed to all but the seer, the
prophet, the great man with the superhuman powers of insight
and comprehension, who must therefore be obeyed by all lesser
mortals. Like Calvinist salvation, the "revelation" in the 'symbol' is given only to a few; for most, the symbol is a concealment; the secret, however "open" it may seem to some, remains
a secret to most; the symbol is opaque rather than translucent.

The term "embodiment" has, likewise, a particular
emphasis in Carlyle's thought, which becomes apparent when
considered in relation to the intention and structure of *Sartor
Resartus* as a whole. Of these, the title itself is an indication
since, as G. B. Tennyson puts it, "the meaning with which
Carlyle began *Sartor* appears as the clothes metaphor itself; just
as clothing covers the body, which in turn houses the soul, so
the visible world covers an invisible one, which has as its
animating spirit the mind of God". (*Sartor called Resartus*,
p. 166.) The "Philosophy of Clothes", central to the book and
expanded in subject, imagery and even structure (as Tennyson
neatly diagrams) is summarized by Carlyle thus:

It is written, the Heavens and the Earth shall fade away like a
Vesture; which indeed they are: the Time-vesture of the Eternal.
Whatsoever sensibly exists, whatsoever represents Spirit to Spirit, is
properly a Clothing, a suit of Raiment, put on for a season, and to be
laid off. Thus in this one pregnant subject of CLOTHES, rightly understood, is included all that men have thought, dreamed, done, and
been: the whole External Universe and what it holds is but Clothing;
and the essence of all Science lies in the PHILOSOPHY OF CLOTHES.
(*SR*, 1, XI, p. 58.)

The image, then, which governs the relationship Carlyle
envisaged between the invisible and the visible (whether this
was between God and the world; soul and body; or thought and
expression) is that of clothes, and not that of "embodiment".

Or rather it is of "embodiment" in the sense of clothes: the body considered not as an integral part of an indissoluble body/soul complex , but as a dispensable though sadly necessary covering for what is, by itself, the real and the important.

That Carlyle did think of "embodiment" and "vesture" as thus synonymous is clearly seen in a passage from 'The Hero as Poet'. The heroes it is who have understood "That divine mystery, which lies everywhere in all Beings, 'the Divine Idea of the World, that which lies at the bottom of Appearance,' as Fichte styles it; of which all Appearance, from the starry sky to the grass of the field, but especially the Appearance of Man and his work, is but the *vesture*, the embodiment that renders it visible." (*HH*,. p. 80.) This vesture image is in fact the one Carlyle has in mind even when explicitly speaking of symbol as embodiment. That is evident in the conclusion he brings to the reader's notice, asking, towards the end of *Sartor Resartus*, "art not thou too perhaps by this time made aware that all Symbols are properly Clothes; that all Forms whereby Spirit manifests itself to sense, whether outwardly or in the imagination, are Clothes?" (*SR*, 3, ix, p. 215.)

The synonymity of the terms "embodiment" and "vesture" evident in Carlyle's thought, evacuates the term "blends" (in his definition of symbol as that in which the "Infinite is made to blend itself with the Finite") of any meaning, for clothes do not "blend" with that which they cover in any sense of a real – intrinsic, to use a Carlylean word, – fusion such as is envisaged in Coleridge's concept. In spite, then, of the terminology, the Carlylean 'symbol' is not one with that which it symbolizes. In other words, the immanence of God in the world, the relationship in which God and the world are seen to stand, is apprehended differently by Coleridge and Carlyle. Differently, in spite of the fact that each could, and did, speak of the universe as a symbol of God. The description of the relationship appears to be the same for each; it is only if we consider it closely that the differences in the envisaged reality of that relationship become obvious.

That the meaning of the term 'symbol' is not fundamentally the same for Carlyle and Coleridge is evident in other ways. Thus, Carlyle frequently uses the term as an alternative to "emblem", "hieroglyph", "device", which indicates that, in spite of his observations about the intrinsic and extrinsic values of symbols, it is the latter which most easily come to his mind. Again, Carlyle often uses the terms "Allegory" and "Symbol" interchangeably, unlike Coleridge, for whom they differed *toto genere*. Thus, Carlyle considers that "Pagan Religion is indeed an Allegory, a Symbol of what man felt and knew about the Universe . . ." and further in the same passage he says that "To get beautiful allegories, a perfect poetic symbol, was not the want of men, but to know what they were to believe about this Universe". ('The Hero as Divinity', *HH*, p. 6.)

This not only indicates the merging of allegory and symbol, but shows that Carlyle thought of both as constructions which do not reflect the essential qualities of the universe they represented, but only what men believed, or felt, about it. This is true even in the one instance where Carlyle does distinguish between allegory and symbol. Here, in his lecture on 'The Hero as Poet', Carlyle writes that "Dante's Hell, Purgatory and Paradise are a symbol", and "the future Critic . . . who considers this of Dante to have been all got-up as an Allegory, will commit one sore mistake!" (*HH*, p. 97.) But if we ask why, Carlyle's answer is that "Men do not believe in Allegory" (*ibid.*) whilst Dante, and all his contemporaries, believed in hell, purgatory and paradise, and did not present these consciously as emblems, but as representations of reality. Obviously, it is not what the relationship between the referent and its counterpart *is*, which is important in distinguishing between 'symbol' and allegory here, but what the author *thought* it to be that makes the difference. Again, the 'symbol' which Dante creates is called "an emblematic representation of his *Belief* about this Universe", and "it expresses . . . how the Christian Dante *felt* Good and Evil to be the two polar elements of this creation". ('The Hero as Poet', *HH*, p. 97, italics mine.) Thus, even if not allegory the symbol is not, as in Coleridge, the representation of what creation is 'really' like (the point at which the subjective and objective coincide); but a reflection only of a – possibly mistaken – belief and feeling about it: the projection of a suspect, subjective consciousness only.

Carlyle's concept of symbol, particularly different from Coleridge's because the relationship envisaged between symbol and referent is an extrinsic and not an intrinsic one (embodiment as clothing, and not as incarnation) has this very important consequence for theology: symbols, like clothes, become outworn, are changeable, are expendable – as frequently re-iterated by Carlyle. This means that nothing which is a symbol has any lasting quality: it always can be, and often should be, superseded. About this, indeed, Carlyle is quite explicit, and by suggesting that all forms of worship, all dogmas, all religions are 'symbols', he is drawing attention to what he considers their essential mutability and temporary value.[21] This is not an intention which can be associated with the use of the term by Coleridge, and the difference between them on this matter is consistent with a further distinction: Coleridge's much more reverent attitude towards traditional formulas and institutions. The theological difficulty (if it is a difficulty) in Coleridge's use of the term of all 'isms' as well as of Christianity, is that he thereby seems to assign to all an equal validity; conversely, Carlyle's application of the term to all religions, Christianity included, suggests that all are equally inadequate, none definitive.[22] But it is interesting also to note here that, just as Coleridge did not use the term 'symbol' of the church or its dogmas, so Carlyle nowhere applies it to the Bible. The Bible is not a symbol for Carlyle for the same reason that it is a symbol for Coleridge: it *is* the Word of God.

However, although Carlyle does not call the Bible a symbol (or symbolical) he does use the term, as I have suggested above, in connection with Christianity and Christ. And the passage will serve to illustrate, finally, Carlyle's typical ambivalence but essential bias, as well as its theological consequence. In the Chapter on 'Symbols', already mentioned, Carlyle writes:

Highest of all Symbols are those wherein the Artist or Poet has risen into Prophet, and all men can recognise a present God, and worship the same: I mean religious Symbols. Various enough have been such religious Symbols, what we call *Religions*; as men stood in this stage of culture or the other, and could worse or better body forth the Godlike: some Symbols with a transient intrinsic worth; many with only an extrinsic. If thou ask to what height man has carried it in this manner, look on our divinest Symbol: on Jesus of Nazareth, and his Life, and his Biography, and what followed therefrom. Higher has the human Thought not yet reached: this is Christianity and Christendom; a Symbol of quite perennial, infinite character; whose significance will ever demand to be anew inquired into, and anew made manifest. (*SR*, 3, III, pp. 178–9.)

There are several things here which demand notice. Firstly,

Carlyle speaks even of those symbols with intrinsic value as of but transient worth. Then, he appears to place Christianity and Christendom in a special class – as symbols of perennial character. But the final sentence makes it clear that it is not the symbol which has such a lasting character, but its significance; not, then, Christianity and Christendom in its totality, the thing it is, but its 'essence', which can eventually be presented in some new – and better – form.

Likewise, the life of Jesus of Nazareth is only our "divinest Symbol" as yet; there is nothing definitive about it; it may yet be improved upon. There is no suggestion here that Christ is a symbol of God, because he is God incarnate, God made visible to man because he is both God and man. There is, instead, the contrary suggestion that his biography is the work purely of "human thought": all idea of the 'symbol' as essentially a creation of a – hypostatic – union between God and man, something which is both of God and of man, is lost. In view of this, it is not surprising that when writing of heroes Carlyle should pay only lip-service to Christ, and that his Great Men are god-like after a very different pattern.

Carlyle's thought, like his prose, is complex, and not easy to summarize. But it can be said that from his early idea of true literature – such as that of Goethe and Shakespeare – being an insight into, and presentation of, the "open secret" lying at the heart of the Universe, Carlyle came to consider that it is only history (as he conceived it) which can reveal to men God's dealings with his creation; only history is "true poetry", and only the historian is the true prophet.[23] Very early Carlyle had come to realize that history was a many-dimensional affair, and that attempts to present events as a linear series of causes and effects was a falsification of its complexity.[24] He repudiated those histories which were based on preconceived notions of the Universe as a mechanism, or on theories of association, no less than Coleridge did in his exclamation on the subject in *The Statesman's Manual*. If Carlyle himself chose the form of dramatic narrative as the best vehicle of true history, it was not, however, because he thought history should be literary at the expense of being true to facts. Of these he was as careful a gleaner as even Mr Gradgrind might have wished. He chose dramatic narrative because he thought that the important facts were not necessarily, or at all, those large events recorded of prominent figures upon which most histories concentrated and therefore could be presented in their proper complexity and perspective only in this form, and not in the cataloguing methods of "Dryasdust".[25] Only that history which attempted to show, and to deal with, the complex relations of what might at first sight seem like inconsequential trivia could be a presentation of the Divine workings of Providence, which it was the historian's task to reveal.

All this is, in some ways, not unlike Coleridge's theory of the Bible, which, as we have seen, he thought of both as history and symbol. And indeed, just as Coleridge thought of Nature (and possibly literature) as also the "Word" of God, so Carlyle thought of secular history as also a kind of Bible. But, in the later Carlyle, it is not "insight", conceived as a God-given power, which matters, and which alone will reveal the true patterning of events; rather, it is the collection – though always with the proper collation – of 'facts' which will allow the pattern to be revealed (though for this too the historian must dwell at length upon his subject matter). And the knowledge which is then given us is not so much a knowledge of *God* "as he is" but a knowledge of how God acts; God himself remaining outside and beyond that which he thus moves, rather than, as in Coleridge, himself within, if also without, it.

In any case, the similarities and differences notwithstanding, the relevant point to notice is that, whereas to his early theory of literature Carlyle did attach the term 'symbol', he does not link his later concept of history with this word. Even had he done so, and thus, to some extent, had he used the term in a sense similar to Coleridge's, this further difference – which I have also already alluded to – would have remained: even a true history was not, for Carlyle, absolute and definitive; he believed, even here, in the necessity of continual re-interpretation which could make what had once been written obsolete. The possible obsolescence of symbols, however, is not only hardly compatible with that crucial element of Coleridge's definition, that symbols "partake" of that which they symbolize. It is also – if the term is applied to creeds and Christ as well as to cowls and candles – a vital one for theology. And the way the word is used by Carlyle, when compared with Coleridge, shows that, even where there are similarities, coincidence of meaning in this important respect cannot be assumed, and the comparison therefore underlines once again the theological importance of the enquiry: what *did* such and such a writer mean by the term?

In the following chapter, therefore, I shall turn to consider how the term 'symbol' and its cognates was used by Newman, himself an important nineteenth century theologian, who, not only – like Carlyle – might have been influenced by Coleridge, but who has also been claimed as the progenitor of Modernism.

4

NEWMAN

Some Confusions

The extent to which Coleridge's thought influenced Newman remains an open question, but there has never been any doubt that, in some respects, their ideas were very similar.[1] This Newman himself recognised on first reading Coleridge in 1835, admitting (in a chronological note to his correspondence) that "During this spring I for the first time read parts of Coleridge's works; and I am surprised how much I thought mine, is to be found there". (*LC*, 2, p. 35.) Four years later, in *The British Critic*, while criticizing Coleridge for indulging in "a liberty of speculation which no Christian can tolerate", Newman also allowed that Coleridge had, to some extent, prepared the way for the Oxford Movement.[2] More particularly, in a footnote to the 1871 edition of the *University Sermons*,[3] Newman pointed to a passage in *Biographia Literaria* which, he said, anticipated "several portions" of his own sermon, 'The Influence of Natural and Revealed Religion Respectively', preached in 1830; whilst in the *Essay in Aid of a Grammar of Assent*[4] he himself quotes from Coleridge's *Aids to Reflection* (a work which he certainly possessed) in support of his own argument.

Nor, of course, have these affinities between Newman and Coleridge remained unnoticed. It was Thomas Acland, a friend of Newman's, who first suggested the coincidence to him in 1834 (*LC*, 2, p. 35), and recently John Coulson has investigated the common elements of some of their most fundamental ideas in his book on *Newman and the Common Tradition*. In the intervening years some, like D. G. James,[5] have tried to draw close parallels between them, whilst others, as for instance H. F.

Davis,[6] while admitting the likeness, have sought to counter-balance this by indicating differences.

Carlyle's name has also been linked with Newman's, mostly in contrast, as two men who fought the same foe but with very different weapons, yet not only so.[7] In 1905 an article in *The Atlantic Monthly* explored what the author called "an unrecognised affinity" between the two, and the resemblance of some of Carlyle's tenets to "the bases of Newman's theory of belief".[8] That Newman and Carlyle differed widely on a number of crucial issues, indeed in the whole fabric of their acknowledged faith, does not necessarily invalidate such a claim, and some of the areas of resemblance have been indicated more recently by George Levine in his comparison of the writings of Carlyle, Macaulay and Newman.[9]

These links between Coleridge, Carlyle, and Newman, whether of contrast or similarity, and tenuous and disputed though some may be, give point to a comparison of Newman's use of the term 'symbol' with those of the other two. But such a comparison is rendered even more apposite when one feature of nineteenth century thought shared by all three is remembered: the concept of organic development, of growth, of evolution. We have seen that both Coleridge's and Carlyle's concepts of 'symbol', different though they are, appear alike because, for each, the term describes a concrete presentation of an idea; the idea being the principle of such organic evolution. Their difference lies in the relationship envisaged between the idea and its presentational symbol.

Newman was also concerned, in a theological context, with the development of ideas. Born in 1801 into a moderately evangelical family; deeply touched by Calvinist influence at school; briefly allying himself with the latitudinarians of Oriel College where he became a fellow in 1822; ordained priest in the Anglican communion a year later, and appointed vicar of the University Church in 1828, Newman's studies took him back to the Fathers of the early church, and he came to see in them the true exponents of Christian doctrine. This perception led him to the High Church Anglicanism of the Oxford Movement of which he became the leader. But having been an ardent exponent of the Via Media during the 1830s he became convinced that the road he was on must lead him to the Roman Catholic church, into which he was received in 1845, and in which – having been something of a controversial figure – he died a Cardinal in 1890.

Newman combined in his thinking and writing the power of close argument with a fundamental mistrust of ratiocination; evinced a curious blend of empiricism and Platonism; and showed a sensuous delight in the beauty of this world, shot through with a suspicion that this world was no more than an appearance of a more spiritual reality elsewhere. Travelling the theological road he did during nearly the whole of that particular century it was inevitable that he should address himself to the question of how the nineteenth century church he recognised as true, with its proliferation – so it might seem – of doctrine and dogma, which were absent from those early fathers whom he so much revered, could be the same with that original which they professed. His book *An Essay on the Development of Christian Doctrine*, first published in the year of his conversion to Roman Catholicism, is central to this preoccupation. But being a nineteenth century thinker Newman saw development not as a purely deductive process, but as accommodating the current concepts of an inner dynamism which, as we have seen, were evident also in the thought of Coleridge and Carlyle.[10] Thus, what Newman meant by 'symbol' in relation to the idea of Christianity is of especial interest.

All the more so, since Newman's theory[11] was later invoked by some Modernists in justification of their own, more radical, positions on the question of the mutability of dogmas.[12] This connection has since been repeatedly denied and repudiated.[13] Indeed, whatever the strength of the connection, when Modernism was condemned in the encyclical *Pascendi Gregis* of July 1907, the possibility of Newman's involvement was keenly felt. Wilfred Ward, a strong partisan of Newman's and at the time editor of the *Dublin Review*, considered that Newman's vindication must lie, partly at least, in distinguishing the meaning with which he used the phrase "dogmas are symbols" from that which was implied in the condemnation.[14]

Again, some forms of Modernism may be seen, not unfairly perhaps, as the application of theologically unacceptable theories of evolution, symbolism, and vital immanence,[15] to faith and the historical content of Christianity. Clearly it is important, therefore, to determine what Newman meant by the term 'symbol' in the context of growth and the development of ideas, and how this relates to the question of God's immanence and transcendence – precisely the areas which define the differences between Coleridge and Carlyle. And this remains true even though Newman did not pay that attention to a definition of the term 'symbol' which, given the area of his concern, we might be expected to think he would.

That insufficient heed has so far been paid to Newman's actual use or uses of the term 'symbol' and its cognates will become apparent in what follows, although this neglect is not altogether surprising since the word is not one he often uses, and never with that particular attention that it receives in Coleridge, where, even if appearing less frequently than might be supposed, it has undoubted importance. Nevertheless, some of the instances of Newman's employment of the term are sufficiently interesting and problematic to merit consideration, in view of the connections between Newman's thought and that of Coleridge, Carlyle and Modernism which have been mentioned above.

The first such instance of the term 'symbol' in Newman's writing which I wish to note, furnishes yet another example of the failure to consider thoroughly the meaning of Coleridge's terminology. Writing to R. H. Froude in January 1836, Newman refers to his first meeting with James Stephens, of whom he says: "I could not in my first talk with him make out to my satisfaction that he was not too much of a philosopher, looking (in Coleridge's way) at the Church, sacraments and doctrines, (etc.) rather as symbols of a philosophy than as *truths* – as the mere accidental types of principles". (*LC*, 2, p. 138.)

Clearly, the implied equation here between "symbols" and "accidental types of principles", and the opposition of "symbols" and "truths", is un-Coleridgean. And if, indeed, Coleridge did not think of the existing, institutional Church and its doctrine, as "consubstantial with the truth" which they attempted to embody, it is highly ambiguous to imply that he therefore looked at them as 'symbols' – since the term 'symbol', for Coleridge, has precisely the connotation which is here denied. Moreover, as we have seen, Coleridge did consider at least the sacraments of marriage and of the eucharist as much more than "accidental types of principles": he thought of them, in fact, as 'symbols' in his own sense and not that implied here. This remark of Newman's, then, even if it does not show us which part of Coleridge's work he had read in 1835, does indicate what he had not read to date with any attention.

Such a casual use of the term 'symbol', however, even if its reference to Coleridge is curiously misleading, would be of no particular consequence were it not for two other factors. The first is that its misleading nature continues to be perpetuated; the second, that its use in this sense by Newman, puts a query against his own application of the term to the Church and sacraments.

To substantiate my first claim, I wish briefly to consider a passage in Coulson's *Newman and the Common Tradition*. Here, in discussing Newman's and Coleridge's notions of 'the Church', and having outlined some similarities, Coulson continues:

Where Newman and Coleridge differ is over the extent to which this Church of Christ is a tangible, visible, and identifiable empirical entity or, to use Newman's term, polity. When Coleridge speaks of the idea of the Church he seems to do so in order to distinguish the Church of Christ from its empirical polity as the Church-Establishment, or *Enclesia*. (p. 62.)

True: and, using his own terminology, Coleridge might have added that it was precisely because he did distinguish totally between the idea of the Church and its empirical presence, that he would not call that empirical presence a 'symbol'. As the tenor of his writing about the Church Establishment sufficiently indicates, he did not think that the empirical Church bore that relation to the idea of the Church which would make the former a 'symbol' of the latter.

But, in expanding upon this difference, Coulson quotes Newman's criticism of Coleridge, given above, and further adds that Coleridge "seems content" to "identify the Church ... with an idea or symbol" which, he considers, "is to have nothing more substantial than a paper Church; since to start from an idea is – as it were – to start in mid-air; we must begin and end with what the *idea* or symbol is *of*". (*Newman and the Common Tradition*, p. 64.)

The argument in this whole passage (pp. 62–5) shows certain confusions: it suggests, for instance, that Coleridge thought of the visible church as a 'symbol' – a suggestion which only makes sense given a definition of this term which is not Coleridge's and which has precisely the opposite implications in Coleridge's terminology from those given it here; and it suggests that an idea for Coleridge is synonymous with 'symbol', a misleading equation, when one remembers Coleridge's own attempt to define the nature of each, and the relationship between them. The whole clearly illustrates the need for a firm grasp of Coleridge's – admittedly slippery – concepts of 'idea' and 'symbol' and their relationship, and an equally clear definition of Newman's use of the terms if this kind of comparison and contrast is to be sustained unambiguously, and with equal justice to each. In this Coulson fails. For, though he begins the comparison between Coleridge and Newman with the statement that "In speaking of the Christian *idea*, of the *idea* of the Church, or of the Trinity, Newman is using the term in a way which is strikingly similar to Coleridge's use of it as a realizing principle ..." (p. 61), his eventual criticism of Coleridge's concept of "the Church of Christ" in relation to Newman's rests on a definition of 'idea' (viz. "not reality at its most real but an image of what acts upon us in the manner of objects of sense-perception" (p. 64)) which in its empiricist assumptions is wholly at variance with Coleridge's own terminology. Since a comparison of Newman and Coleridge necessitates that we bear in mind Newman's and Coleridge's use of words, such inadvertence to distinctions in key terms, such as 'idea' and 'symbol', is irritating to say the least.[16]

Not only irritating, however, for it also leads Coulson to surmise (incorrectly, as I shall indicate) that Newman, in his *University Sermon* on 'The Theory of Developments in Religious Doctrine' (1843) "seems to be specifically refuting Coleridge's doctrine of symbolism" (p. 64, n. 4). If this is so, then, in view of Newman's own use of the term 'symbol' in the letter cited above (where he appears to criticize Coleridge for thinking the church and sacraments symbols and not truths), what can we make of Newman's own statement in the same sermon that "Catholic dogmas are, after all, but symbols of a Divine fact" (para. 23, p. 332), or, indeed, of the later assertion that "Holy Church in her sacraments and her hierarchical appointments, will remain even to the end of the world, after all but a symbol of those heavenly facts which fill eternity"? (*Apologia*, p. 25.) For do not Newman's "after alls" and "buts" here seem to point to the same disjunction between symbol and truth? This then is the second reason which makes it necessary to ask the question

XVth University Sermon

(reminiscent of Kingsley's though it be), what *did* Newman mean when he himself thus used the term 'symbol' in such contexts?

The Use of the Term 'Symbol' in the XVth University Sermon

If then we look at the actual context of Newman's reference to dogmas as "symbols of Divine fact", a certain similarity between the meaning of the term here, and the Coleridgean sense will become apparent – notwithstanding Newman's earlier use of the word (in the letter to Froude). For the latter half of the paragraph of Sermon xv where it occurs runs as follows:

Creeds and dogmas live in the one idea which they are designed to express, and which alone is substantive; and are necessary only because the human mind cannot reflect upon that idea, except piecemeal, cannot use it in its oneness and entireness, nor without resolving it into a series of aspects and relations. And in matter of fact these expressions are never equivalent to it; we are able, indeed, to define the creations of our own minds, for they are what we make them and nothing else; but it were as easy to create what is real as to define it; and thus the Catholic dogmas are, after all, but symbols of a Divine fact, which, far from being compassed by those very propositions, would not be exhausted, nor fathomed, by a thousand. (para. 23, pp. 331–2.)

Here, the thought that creeds and dogmas – symbols – "live" in the "one idea" which in some measure they express, is reminiscent of Coleridge's definition of symbols as "consubstantial with the truth of which they are the conductors", and as "partaking in" the idea which they present. For Coleridge they *present* that truth to the Understanding, which for its functions of analysis and reflection needs such a concrete (even if verbal) embodiment of what the (Coleridgean) Reason apprehends intuitively. Likewise here, in Newman, the expression of the one idea in various ways is necessary because the human mind cannot otherwise reflect upon it. It is evident, too, that the term 'idea' is used similarly by both (in this particular context) as the 'living image' (to use purposely a somewhat ambiguous phrase) of the Divine. We might, therefore, be led to suppose that Newman's use of the term 'symbol' here is entirely coincidental with Coleridge's – the main difference being that

Newman designates only dogmas and creeds as such symbols, whilst Coleridge applies the term primarily to the Bible.

But this difference in application is, I think, significant of other differences which render the coincidence of Newman's use of the term 'symbol' with Coleridge's far from complete. The disparity is, indeed, already indicated here, in the suggestion that dogmas, creeds, (symbols therefore) are a "piecemeal" resolution of the "idea" into "a series of aspects and relations". But to substantiate this it is necessary to outline the argument of the sermon, and to explore further the terminology Newman uses with reference to dogmas, and the relationship he envisages between them and the "one idea" in which they "live".

The purpose of the sermon is

to investigate the connexion between Faith and Dogmatic Confession, as far as it relates to . . . [the doctrines of the Trinity and the Incarnation]. . . and to show the office of the Reason in reference to it. (para. 9, p. 319.)

To use Walgrave's words in *Newman the Theologian*, Newman does this as against "the liberal view denying any real correspondence between interior faith and the formulas of dogma, the latter being a kind of disguise, indispensable indeed, but variable according to places and seasons, whereas the view of faith is ever unchangeable". (p. 139.)

Both the terms "Faith" and "Reason" are susceptible of many interpretations, and as Newman himself spent some time in discussing these terms in his preface to the 1871 edition of the sermons, it is well to indicate what he meant by them in this instance. By Faith in this context, he does not mean that "assent without doubt" which he singles out in the preface as its proper definition; rather it is, as Walgrave terms it: "a real knowledge of supernatural realities". (*Newman the Theologian*, p. 124.)

At the outset of the sermon such a knowledge is simply assumed. But it is important to notice what this assumption, and the terminology used, hides: namely, that in the investigation of the relationship between Faith, so defined, and dogmas there are three, and not only two, notions involved, and therefore not one but at least two possible relationships: the supernatural realities (or "Divine Fact" of para. 23); the knowledge we humans have of these; and the expression or statement of that knowledge. In the first half of the sermon, however, Newman is concerned only with the relationship of dogma to Faith. He here tacitly works on the assumption that the first two terms: the Divine Fact, and our knowledge of it, the Divine Idea and the impression it makes on our minds, are equivalents, and he refers to them indiscriminately as "Fact", "Revelation", "Idea", "Impression", etc.[17]

The word "Reason", as Newman himself notes in the preface, is used by him in at least three particular senses, which can be summarized as (i) skill in logical argument; (ii) the ability to set out arguments from history; (iii) the process of deciding questions of religious truth apart from serious personal experience. But the general meaning of the term is any act or process of knowing which is not immediate but discursive.[18] In many respects it is like Coleridge's use of the term Understanding, a not unimportant fact to note in determining Newman's concept of 'symbol' *vis-à-vis* Coleridge's, as will be seen.

There is no important confusion inherent in the phrases "Dogmatic Confession" or "creeds and dogmas" which would render it necessary to define Newman's terms here; but it is to the purpose to note other terminology associated with them. First, dogmas, whether they are "expressive of the judgments which the mind forms, or the impressions which it receives, of Revealed Truth", are "propositions" (para. 10). Further (para. 20) dogmas are referred to as a series of statements, a system. Then (para. 23) they are said to express "portions" of the "idea vouchsafed to us" and are likened to "definitions", as well as – as has already been noted – being resolutions of the idea into "a series of aspects and relations". All these expressions are frequently repeated, and at least in one instance (para. 28) the connections between such dogmatic "propositions" (the links in the system) are said to be those of implication. Such – and this is all I want to note for the moment – is the vocabulary used by Newman of what he also calls "symbols". The direction it points in, and the matrix it springs from, are logico-mathematical. Coleridge's "symbol" keeps very different company.

What, then, is the "connexion" between "Faith" (under its various synonyms) and "Dogmatic Confession", as seen by Newman? Or, in other words, what is the nature of the relationship he envisaged between "the one idea" (or our knowledge of it, the impression it makes on our minds) and the 'symbols' which express it? Coleridge's notion of "partaking", and "consubstantiality" between the "idea" and its "symbols" is explicable partly at least in terms of his theories of creativity and imitation. A symbol, for him, is a symbol when, and only when, it is created in a particular way: when it is the product of the Imagination "incorporating the Reason in images of sense". It is symbol because the creative process involved is an echo of the creativity of God, and all that that implies for Coleridge. Newman's explanation of the "connexion" is given in terms of "development". Are the two processes at all similar, at least according to Newman's concept of "development" in this sermon?

The first intimation of the nature of the connection is given after the definition of dogmas cited above. Here Newman says that Revelation sets before the mind "certain supernatural facts and actions, beings and principles; these make a certain impression or image upon it; and this impression spontaneously, or even necessarily, becomes the subject of reflection on the part of the mind itself, which proceeds to investigate it, and to draw it forth in successive and distinct sentences". (para. 10, p. 320.) The connection, then, is one of "reflection", "investigation", "drawing forth". Further (para. 14) ideas which animate and form the Christian mind are said to be "elicited" and "defined"; or again, and here explicitly, "development" is said to be "but the carrying out of the idea into its consequences" (para. 21, pp. 329–30).

Newman also gives two illustrations of the connection between "idea" and the statements in which it is expressed. In paragraph 11 he compares it with the relationship which may be said to obtain between an analysis of poetry, the "philosophy of poetry", and what a given poet "might have in his mind in certain compositions and characters": in paragraph 18 the development of Christian ideas is likened to a "scientific analysis" of the principles of philosophy, physics, ethics, politics or taste.

Before more can be said, it is necessary to observe that the term "development" which, so far, has been descriptive of the relation between the idea and its statements, is also used to describe the relationship between the various propositions, the particular statements which express the idea. What must be noticed in such instances – as in the case of the vocabulary used of dogmas – is the recurrence of terms like "analysis", "investigation", "deduction": all processes associated with what Newman calls Reason, which, as has been observed, is close to what Coleridge meant by Understanding. Development for Newman is, then, largely, the function of that kind of Reason, and as such, hardly like the creative process as described by Coleridge. Can, then, the results of two such dissimilar processes be the same, even though they may both be termed 'symbols'? And if Coleridge reserves the term predominantly for the Bible, and for works of art, while Newman uses it in the realm of dogma, is this not a reflection of the difference?

There is, however, another element apparent even in the predominantly fractional vocabulary Newman uses of dogmas as representations of the ideas. For even while Newman speaks of dogmas as "part by part" correspondences of ideas, he also calls them "projections" (para. 16); and though a "projection" is also a mathematical concept, it involves the notion of a presentation of the whole, as a whole, rather than the serial nature of representation suggested by such words as parts or portions. To parts and portions other parts and portions can, and must, be added if the whole is to be represented; a projection, on the other hand, allows of no such additions. Thus the relationship between dogma, symbol, and idea is here not quite that of the step-by-step discursive kind which is attained by Newman's Reason. And another, perhaps Newman's favourite, term used in this connection re-emphasizes this non-discursive bias: dogmatic propositions express not only portions but "aspects" of an "impression" or "idea" (paras. 23, 28).[19] "Aspects" will involve a certain partiality, as being from a certain point of view, but this partiality is not of a serial kind, or at least, if a series, one in which the components bear a different relation to one another than is implied in a part by part series. But if the presentation of "aspects" is also a function of Reason, (since Reason is so widely defined) it is Reason functioning in a very different way from that suggested by deduction.

Perhaps the emphasis on the other-than-logical and mathematical or serial element of "development" (using this word to denote the connection envisaged between "Faith" and

"Dogmatic Confession", "idea" and "symbol"), is most force-fully made in paragraph 26. Here Newman observes that

> though the Christian mind reasons out a series of dogmatic state-ments, one from another, this it has ever done, and always must do, not from those statements taken in themselves, as logical propo-sitions, but as being itself enlightened and (as if) inhabited by that sacred impression which is prior to them, which acts as a regulating principle, ever present, upon the reasoning; and without which no one has any right to reason at all. . . . For though the development of an idea is a deduction of proposition from proposition, these propositions are ever formed in and round the idea itself (so to speak), and are in fact one and all only aspects of it. (p. 334.)

The idea (or its sacred impression) is here seen as itself active in the process of reasoning, rather as Coleridge's Understand-ing, in its fully human functioning, is interpenetrated by the higher Reason (in his sense). And perhaps this insistence on the inner activity of the idea itself in development has even some resemblance to the nature of true creativity as understood by Coleridge. In so far as there is such a resemblance (and the sense in which the Reason is understood to be enlightened by the idea is relevant to this); and in so far as, as a result, each dogma (or symbol) is an "aspect" of the idea, seen and pre-sented by the aid of its own light, so far Newman's use of the term 'symbol', as a description of "dogma" here coincides with Coleridge's. But in saying this, Newman's predominant emphasis on the more analytic functioning of Reason, which enters into the theory of development, and hence affects the nature of the connection envisaged between idea and 'symbol', must not be disregarded. For 'symbols' which are connected both to each other and to the central idea not only as aspects but by deduction or implication, must be very different from that "system of symbols harmonious in themselves" which Coleridge attempts to describe (*SM*, p. 436). Certainly, if it is possible, as Newman would have us believe, that a develop-ment can be both deductive, logical, mathematical, and also – and that in no supererogatory fashion – something other than this, at one and the same time, then there is an overlap between the ways Newman and Coleridge use the term 'symbol'. But the extent of the disparity cannot be ignored. The areas of coinci-dence and distinction stand to each other, I would suggest, as mathematics to poetry, and if the imaginative content of each is only now being accepted more widely, few would fail to recognise the difference.

So far, however, only one instance of Newman's use of the term 'symbol' has been considered, and there are two others in this sermon alone. How do these relate to that already examined? Since both these further instances occur in the latter half of the sermon, more must now be said about Newman's general argument there.

In the first half of the sermon, as I have pointed out, Newman by and large assumed the complete correspondence between the "Divine fact" and the impression it made on our minds; between the "Divine Idea" and that "Idea" as known by us; and he was concentrating on investigating the relationship between that "Idea" (in both, or either, of its senses) and the verbal statements we make about it. Nevertheless Newman is well aware, even here, of the possible discrepancy between such an "Idea" or "fact" and our knowledge of it, and he attempts to deal with this on an analogy with the discrepancy there may be between the impression(s) that material objects make on our senses, and the consequent idea we have of such objects (para. 22). But he also notices that in such a parallel there is a difference: whereas the senses receive their impressions of objects directly, we have no like faculties for such a direct perception of the Object(s) of Faith (para. 25). Newman says this explicitly here in spite of the way in which he has been speaking previously, in a phraseology which might lead one to suppose that he held the opposite view.

Be that as it may, his point here is that the impression of "Revealed Truth" which we receive is, partly at least, mediated; partly at least, it originates from "the habitual and devout perusal of Scripture . . . the gradual influence of intercourse with those who are in themselves in possession of sacred ideas; . . . the study of Dogmatic Theology . . ." (para. 25, p. 333.) We obtain, that is to say, the impression which develops in the mind and whose development results and consists in language statements, from the language statements themselves. But if so, then Newman has to face the question: how can we obtain a Divine idea through an essentially *human* idiom? The ideas which we will obtain from language can be commensurate only with that language and nothing more; and our ideas of the Divine will therefore be not the Divine idea as it is, but our human concepts of it, the relationship between the two remaining problematic. If our "ideas of Divine things" originate from no other source but the language we use of them, so the objection runs, then they are but

co-extensive with the figures by which we express them, neither more nor less, and without them are not; and when we draw inferences from those figures, we are not illustrating one existing idea, but drawing mere logical inferences. . . . It follows that our anathemas, our controversies, our struggles, our sufferings, are merely about the poor ideas conveyed to us in certain figures of speech. (para. 31, pp. 338–9.)

It is this objection which Newman tries to counter in the succeeding paragraphs of his sermon. His main effort is directed towards demolishing the assumption upon which the objection rests, namely, that language can give us ideas which are equivalent only to the words used, and nothing more; and he marshals a number of examples which, he maintains, show that the opposite is the case. With the cogency of Newman's argument I am not concerned: it depends to a large extent on the aptness of the examples to the question in hand, and on the validity of extending these to what is, in the end, the special case of language about a supra-natural entity.

Such, however, is the context in which Newman again uses the term 'symbol'. Here, in paragraph 38, Newman indicates that there is a distinction between, on the one hand, the "supernatural and eternal laws" which are discovered through, and analysed in, mathematical language; and, on the other, the various attempts which such a language makes to represent them. Yet, he maintains, we are able to know the former in spite of the inadequacies of the latter. Newman holds that the "immutable principles and dispositions of which this science [mathematics] treats" are really independent of any methods or calculi which men may have adopted to embody them, yet those laws can neither be contemplated nor pursued without one or other of such methods. All such "calculi" – as the geometrical or the differential – are, moreover, very different one from the other, "yet they are, one and all, analyses, more or less perfect, of those same necessary truths, for which we have not a name, of which we have no idea, except in the terms of such economical representations". (para. 38, p. 345.)

And, continues Newman, "They are all developments of one and the same range of ideas", as well as "all instruments of discovery as to those ideas". Moreover, "They stand for real things, and we can reason with them, though they be but symbols, as if they were the things themselves, for which they stand." (*ibid.*) This is so, even though each such "method", "calculus", "symbol" will, if taken too far, issue in some "great impossibility or contradiction". This shows indeed that none is "a true analysis or adequate image of those recondite laws which are investigated by means of it". (*ibid.*) Nevertheless, because each, or all, act as reliable "instruments of discovery" up to a point, each and all must have a real relationship to the laws which they both disclose and analyse: otherwise how could they lead us to discover the laws, as they certainly do?

The entities here called "symbols", then, are particular kinds of language structures[20] which lead us to a knowledge of Ideas understood not simply as the mental counterparts of the statements forming the structure, but as having some existence independent of them. Thus, again, Newman uses the term 'symbol' in a way similar to Coleridge's: as embodiments of extra-mental Ideas in which the Ideas are made manifest, and through which they become known. But the difference already noted can be seen here also: for, although for Coleridge a 'symbol' (or symbol system) is the means of the discovery of such an Idea, as well as its presentation, it is never its *analysis*. The Coleridgean 'symbol' is the product of the Reason-impregnated-Imagination (as he understands these words); analysis, on the other hand, is the work of the Understanding and is (when appropriate) directed towards the symbol, and not the Idea, which in itself cannot be subject to such analysis. Or again, one could say, 'symbols' for Coleridge, are products of the Imagination, and are therefore not 'analyses', since the work of the Imagination is that of fusion. Or, that if, for both Coleridge and Newman, 'symbols' are the products of Reason widely defined, Reason for each has a different meaning.

What Coleridge and Newman are certainly agreed upon is that at least some forms or uses of language can be sources of, or can produce, quasi-experiential knowledge. Such forms or uses of language not only tell us about, not only describe, that to which they refer (and allow us to 'know' it in this way): they also give us what approximates to a direct acquaintance with the referent, so that the statements we can subsequently make about the referent are not mere deductions from the language structures which were the sources of our knowledge. Both Newman and Coleridge call such language structures "symbols", and hence agree upon one, very important, common quality. But, of the various examples Newman gives to illustrate his thesis, it is the mathematical one only in which he uses the term 'symbol' with reference to such structures. However suspicious Newman may have been of mere logic, however much he insisted that deduction, or the formal processes of reasoning, were not enough for a knowledge which was fully human, which could give direction and certainty to the fundamental issues of life; yet the bias given to his mind in his early Oriel days, chiefly by Whately,[21] whose *Logic* Newman helped to write, was never eradicated, and it is predominantly this logic which, for him, determines the structure of a 'symbol'. And in this it is distinguished from the similar concept in Coleridge's thought.

Distinguished – but certainly not entirely distinct. For Newman was aware, as the thrust of his argument shows, that mathematics was not to be equated with a mechanical process involving nothing more than a sequence of substitutions from self-evident premises to an implied conclusion. He saw that mathematical science is more than a technique, a mechanical skill, a proficiency which depends simply on learning the rules. Without actually saying as much, his arguments and illustrations here are all expositions of his belief (and appeals for the recognition of this belief) that imaginative insight (in a sufficiently Coleridgean sense) is an indispensable part of all fruitful human activity, even that which possesses the most purely logical (in the strict sense) surface. Nor was Coleridge unaware of this same fact, as we have seen. But if truly creative science, like art, has its imaginative element; and if art, like science, may be considered as an articulation of the world as known – and both, therefore, symbols – yet art and science remain, in an important sense, differently related to that world. To say both are symbols, and to leave it at that, is to ignore this difference of relationship; and to say that Newman and Coleridge gave the term 'symbol' an identical meaning is a failure of discrimination of precisely the same kind. Certainly, there is some basis, even in this sermon, for maintaining that both Newman and Coleridge held the same concept of 'symbol'. For the position Newman had to maintain in the second half of his sermon is the opposite of that which he attributes to the objectors whose views he sketches in paragraph 31. And these, Newman says, hold that "there is no such inward view" of the doctrines of the Trinity and the Incarnation "distinct from the dogmatic language used to express them", contrary to what he himself had so far been supposing. For, the objectors maintain, the metaphors by which such doctrines are signified "are not mere symbols of ideas which exist independently of them, but their meaning is coincident and identical with the ideas". If this is the view of his supposed objectors, then, in the terminology of this paragraph, Newman himself must hold that metaphors are symbols of Ideas which exist independently of them, and that they do give us an "inward view" of such independently existing Ideas (or doctrines: the terms are again conflated). And, as D. G. James rightly observes, this is precisely what Coleridge himself maintained of the language structures he called 'symbols'.[22] So far, then, there is agreement, and it is a careless confusion on Coulson's part that he surmises that Coleridge is the objector Newman here has in mind.[23] But – and this is the point James fails to observe – Coleridge did not call *dogmas* symbols in this sense. Newman, on the other hand, whilst certainly implying by his examples, that language functions thus symbolically in various instances, uses the term 'symbol' itself in this sermon only in his mathematical illustration, and speaks of dogmas as symbols in language which is more appropriate to deductive sciences than to (even the logic of) poetry. Thus, though Newman and Coleridge appear to agree in what they mean by the symbolic functioning of language, they part company in their notions of what kinds of language structures can best perform such a function.[24] This polarization of their thought renders the initial resemblance more problematic than a simple affirmation or denial of coincidence would suggest, as some other instances of Newman's use of the term 'symbol', as well as some indication of his general trend of thought, will serve to show.

Some Further Instances of the Term 'Symbol' in Newman's Writing

Newman's tendency, referred to above, of using the term 'symbol' within a vocabulary, and hence with connotations appropriate to mathematics, is quite explicit in at least one instance. In the *Essay in Aid of a Grammar of Assent*, published in 1870, Newman, discussing "formal inference", says that: ". . . no process of argument is so perfect as that which is conducted by means of symbols". (*Grammar*, ch. VIII, p. 258.) This is because symbols have a constant and unequivocal meaning, as in Arithmetic, where "1 is 1, and just 1, and never anything else but 1; it is never 2; it has no tendency to change its meaning and become 2; it has no portion, quality, admixture of 2 in its meaning". (*ibid.*) The term "symbol" in this passage is being used to denote such arithmetical cyphers, and a contrast is drawn between these and words, which are a "constant trouble to syllogistic reasoning" having "innumerable implications" (p. 260). Thus, if words are to serve in formal inference (i.e. if they are to act as symbols) they must be drained "of that depth and breadth of associations which constitute their poetry, their rhetoric and their historical life", till each stands "for just one unreal aspect of the concrete thing to which it properly belongs, for a relation, a generalization, or other abstraction, for a notion neatly turned out of the laboratory of the mind, and sufficiently tame and subdued because existing only in a definition". (p. 260.) In syllogistic method, that is to say, words can be used only in so far as they can be made to resemble and to function like cypher-symbols of arithmetic; and words become 'symbols' in this sense only when their import is "stinted" and "circumscribed" (Newman's terms) in the manner outlined.

Such a use of the term 'symbol', which, when applied to words, intends that we should consider them stripped of their evocative nuances, and their concrete particularity, is obviously quite different from that use of the term – which might be called 'poetical' – which focuses our attention on the richness and associations of the particular things so designated. Many, perhaps all, words or phrases can, of course, be termed 'symbols' in either sense, and the sense intended is usually quite clear from the context, as indeed is the case in this example from the *Grammar*. Nor is the use of the term 'symbol' to mean a cypher an innovation; and this use with reference to words need not mean that a writer cannot use it with a poetical sense in a different context without the charge of inconsistency, since the two senses of the term 'symbol' are not necessarily ambiguous. But, if these two senses are so clearly disparate, a comparison between them is of no interest: we can simply conclude that Newman's use of the term 'symbol' in this instance of the *Grammar* is of no relevance to the previous discussion on the relationship of his use of the term to Coleridge's.

This is, indeed, to some extent true, and this example primarily serves to show just what differing implications the term 'symbol' can have in differing contexts. But precisely in so far as this example indicates the difference in the meaning of the term 'symbol' in mathematical, and poetical contexts, it also serves to throw light on the nature of the incipient polarization of the term already noticed in Newman's University Sermon, and as a consequence of this, its uncertain resemblance there to Coleridge's employment of the word.

Another instance in which Newman uses the term 'symbol' somewhat similarly to that cited from the *Grammar*, but in fact more ambiguously (so that it may be seen as a kind of transition between this, and the earlier examples from the University Sermon), occurs in a letter to William Froude, written from Rome on April 29th, 1879.[25] This is no casual or hasty note, but an attempt by Newman to lay bare the convictions he shared with Froude, as well as to clarify the precise area of their disagreement. Newman felt that Froude had misunderstood the nature of both, and this in spite of their long acquaintance, correspondence, and Froude's knowledge of Newman's work. As in the University Sermon already considered, Newman here attempts to liken, as well as differentiate between, the methods of theologians and scientists, drawing an explicit parallel between the development of "the laws of motion and the first principles of geometry" and the development of Catholic doctrine, and again shows his consciousness that the work of such men as Newton is not achieved merely by "syllogism and other logical procedure". Thus the context, and the serious attempt at self-explanation within which the term 'symbol' is here used, give this instance a particular interest. Newman writes:

Our teaching, as well as yours, requires the preparation and the exercise of long thought and thorough imbuing with religious ideas. Even were those ideas not true, still a long study would be necessary for understanding them. . . . What you call the random reasonings of theologians will be found to have as clear a right to be treated with respect as those proceedings of mechanical philosophers who you say are so microscopic in their painstaking. Words are but the symbols of ideas, and the microscopic reasoner, who is not only painstaking but so justly successful in his mechanics, is simply an untaught child in questions of theology. (Ward: *Life of John Henry, Cardinal Newman*, p. 590.)

Much more clearly than in the Sermon, the obvious stress here is on the futility in theological questions, of reasoning from "words which are but symbols'. Symbols, so it is suggested here, are merely counters by the manipulation of which no idea which exists independently of them can be arrived at. It is, then, not only that reasoning by itself is an insufficient instrument for arriving at those truths with which theology is concerned, but that what are called 'symbols' in such a process can have, of themselves, no translucent qualities whereby the idea can be perceived in them, a connotation central to Coleridge's concept of 'symbol', and one which seemed to form some part of Newman's own earlier argument. The emphasis is not on a 'symbol' as a focal point of insight, but rather on the inadequacy of symbol-structures in conveying ideas. This note had already been sounded in the xvth Sermon,[26] but there it was coupled with an apparent insistence that, nevertheless, through "symbols" we could arrive at and have knowledge of, independently existing Ideas. Here, that seems to be excluded. Nor could one say that, in the argument of the Sermon, the quality of "translucence" belonged to some symbols, and not to others, or that the term "symbol" was being used in entirely disparate senses; "translucence" being the quality of 'poetical' symbols, and not of 'mathematical' ones. No such clear division can be made. Rather, there is even there a greater hesitation about the knowledge that we can receive through "symbols", a greater awareness of their ultimate inadequacy, than is compatible with the Coleridgean concept, and which, in this letter, is brought clearly to the fore. And it is the difference in respect of the "knowledge" that "symbols" can give us of "Ideas" which, again, separates Newman's concept of 'symbol' from Coleridge's.

Some further instances of the term 'Symbol'

The minimization of the knowledge-giving (revelatory in a secular sense) or translucent character of symbols is, indeed, part and parcel of Newman's general tendency towards scepticism, in respect of what a man could be said to know without the help of a special revelation from God. This was perhaps partly engendered in him by the Empiricist Tradition, in the terms of which he so often expressed himself; and with it he struggled as late as the 'Letter on Matter and Spirit' of 1861.[27] But in Newman this potential scepticism is balanced by a serene acceptance of a world which is not susceptible to sense-perception, and which, as J. M. Cameron points out,[28] is itself an extension of the empirical assumption that our thoughts are more immediate than our sensations, and hence that man's 'soul' is more to be taken for granted than the existence of his material body. So Newman, in the 'Letter on Matter and Spirit', while being "disposed to take for granted that the existence of matter as distinct from the impressions upon our senses can in no possible way be proved to us by reason", or by demonstration, and that it is revelation which teaches us the existence of such substances, can also seriously surmise that the cause of the effects which we feel and call a rose may be an Angel or the soul of a child.[29]

The empiricist strain of Newman's thought thus also served to strengthen what seems to have been his tendency even as a child, when he thought that "life might be a dream, or I an Angel, and all this world a deception, my fellow-angels by a playful device concealing themselves from me, and deceiving me with the semblance of a material world". (*Apologia*, pp. 1–2.)

The – however brief – period of Calvinist influence of his late boyhood,[30] is traceable in his cautious approach to the world of the senses, which, however beautiful he felt it to be, was seen by Newman as a temptation away from God, or at best a 'veil' behind which he was hidden.[31] Later, the Platonism he encountered in the Alexandrine Fathers served to confirm his belief in the greater reality of the spiritual world as against the world of matter, which, in any case, his Christianity would have already nurtured. This Platonic cast of mind did more than lead Newman to "underestimate the 'literary' nature of Scriptural statements, and provided support for a Christological perspective which hardly does justice to the humanity of Christ"

(Lash, p. 61), important as this is in the present discussion. Newman in fact went even further. Curiously intertwining with his empiricism and early religious influences, his Platonism led him, in his search for truth, to reject "the idea that one could find an ultimate truth in nature, or any symbol of truth in the human mind apart from revelation". (Beer, 'Newman and the Romantic Sensibility', p. 218.) The world, then, was not something in which God was made present to man,[32] and it is significant that, in the 'Letter on Matter and Spirit' it is only to the extent that Newman is sceptical that a rose is what it appears to be, that he thinks it may be a presence of God. The rose becomes an 'effect' of a cause (God's presence) rather than the 'cause' of our awareness of him, and thus what it is in itself, as rose, becomes unimportant. (*PN*, 2, p. 208.)

This is the background of thought against which Newman's apprehension of the material world as "sacramentally connected" to the spiritual world, must be seen. The "sacramental principle" he found in Butler, in Keble, and again in the Alexandrine Fathers.[33] It was "the doctrine that material phenomena are both the types and the instruments of real things unseen" (*Apologia*, p. 16), and Newman understood it to mean that "the exterior world, physical and historical, was but the manifestation to our senses of realities greater than itself". (*ibid.* p. 24.) If one remembers only Newman's distrust of abstract reasoning, his insistence on the concrete way of knowing, his affirmation that knowledge comes primarily through experience, such expressions could lead one to think that, in giving this recognition to the material and historical world, Newman accorded it the status of a Coleridgean 'symbol'.[34] But this would be to disregard that bias in Newman's thought which made his sister compare him to Berkeley,[35] and which, though he affirmed the existence of matter, allowed him to say: "the very idea of an analogy between the separate works of God leads to the conclusion that the system which is of less importance is economically or sacramentally connected with the more momentous system, and of this conclusion the theory, to which I was inclined as a boy, viz. the unreality of material phenomena, is an ultimate resolution". (*ibid.* p. 9.)

The "analogy"[36] between God and the world which Newman maintained, and which was the basis of his "sacramental principle" did not, then, involve such an affirmation of the presence of God *within* that world, as would enhance its own proper being, making it a 'symbol' translucent of that presence. If both the theories of analogy and symbol are concerned with the way in which God is manifested in or through the world of created beings (or the relationship in which God stands to the world and can be spoken of in human language) that of analogy insists more on the transcendent God allowing himself to be glimpsed through, but beyond, the phenomenal world, this recognition needing his interpretative help. The theory of symbol, on the other hand, without denying the transcendence, leans towards the opposite pole: that of God's immanence *in* the world, and the consequent capacity of that world to be, in itself, revelatory.

So, though the world for Newman is certainly a manifestation of God, in some sense, it nevertheless "still remains without its divine interpretation", and "what is visible . . . does but shadow out at most, and sometimes obscures and disguises, what is invisible". For Newman this is true of all things which have their being here, and it is in this context that he says: "Holy Church in her sacraments and her hierarchical appointments, will remain even to the end of the world, after all but a symbol of those heavenly facts which fill eternity." (*ibid.* p. 25.) He does not think of symbols here as "accidental types of principles" as he supposed Coleridge did in like context (see p. 96). The connection between the Church and God is not "accidental", the sacraments are not conventional signs. But, though he did say more of the Church and the sacraments than this,[37] in so far as they are here called 'symbols' they are shadows,[38] rather than embodiments of God's presence. As in the case of language structures which, as 'symbols' are, after all, but very faint and incomplete indications of an Idea beyond them, so those concrete presences, whether of the sacred or secular order, which are 'symbols' are no more than its shadows. In the theory of 'analogy' contrasted with the theory of 'symbol', and in the concept of 'symbol' in Coleridge and (so far as he can be said to have used this term significantly) in Newman, there is a common ground, but the crucial emphases are different. And, though like Coleridge, Newman thought of the 'symbols' of dogma, of Church, of sacrament, as having a permanent place in Divine dispensation, so long as this world lasted, yet, in the measure that his greater emphasis on this world's transience, and on the beyondness of the world of reality, separates his use of the term 'symbol' from Coleridge's, in that measure it brings it closer to – though never makes it coincident with – Carlyle's.

It should be remembered in conclusion that Newman, though he thought that "half the controversies in the world are verbal ones" (*University Sermons*, p. 200), and that much could be done to clarify the issues involved by definitions, was no more, and perhaps rather less, adept than Coleridge, at using a word with a consistent sense, even within one argument.[39] Moreover, the word 'symbol' itself, was not one with which he was much concerned. But the very casualness of Newman's usage of the term, in varying but related contexts, indicates the manifold ramifications of meaning the concept can carry. The complex relationships these bear one to another, preclude a simple identification or differentiation of these various senses of the term. What emerges is that the context, and even the writer's *Weltanschauung*, can shift the meaning in theologically significant directions which are obscured because the word used remains the same. If it is true that Newman, Coleridge and Carlyle, all saw "the universe as fact and symbol"[40] – and this can easily be claimed – we should not be misled into thinking that the phrase is indicative of any significant consensus of theological opinion. Neither does their designation of language (or certain language structures) as 'symbols' or 'symbolical' indicate a similarity of thought on its nature and function either as literature or as theology.

5

DEAN INGE, GEORGE TYRRELL AND GEORGE MACDONALD

Coleridge died in 1832; Carlyle in 1881; Newman in 1890. The century during which they lived and wrote saw many changes, political, social, scientific; changes which profoundly affected religious thought. The theological problems presented by the developments in the secular sciences were, if not more evident, perhaps more fundamental than the problems of organization and evangelization occasioned by the movement of people from the country to the rapidly growing industrial towns. The effect of Darwin's *The Origin of Species* published in 1859 was only the highest wave of a series breaking upon the beaches of what had seemed the biblical paradise of secure knowledge, and encroaching further and further upon the rocks of dogmatic certainty. The latter half of the century, as we now see, was as much an age of doubt and uncertainty as it was a proclamation of faith in imperialism and progress. The works of such writers as Arthur Clough, Edmund Gosse, Samuel Butler and Matthew Arnold attest this. And there was no dearth, either, of religious controversy – from the furore created by the appointment of Hampden, suspected of unorthodoxy, as Regius Professor of Divinity at Oxford in 1836, and Bishop of Hereford in 1847; through the prosecution by the church authorities of two contributors to the 1860 *Essays and Reviews*; to the suspicions raised by the publication of *Lux Mundi* in 1889.[1] But, in spite of the fact that it would seem to us now that the vocabulary of symbolization was inescapable in many of the discussions thus generated; and in spite of Coleridge's, and perhaps even more, Carlyle's, use of the term 'symbol' in moving similar problems, the terms, as I have already said, were not adopted as in any sense significantly appropriate till the very end of the century. It is to three writers of this later period, who did use the relevant terms with some emphasis, that I wish now to draw attention. George MacDonald, who was born in 1824, is by far the earliest of the three, and he might in some ways be considered as more of a contemporary of Newman. But I leave him till last because, more than either Inge or Tyrrell, he seems to be re-entering the sphere of discussion on the borderlines of theology and literature, and is therefore acquiring a new, if perhaps not very great (or greatly deserved) status.[2]

Dean Inge

Inge's formative influences were those of Oxbridge. He was born in 1860, and educated at Eton and Cambridge, returning to the former as a master in 1884, before being appointed to a Lectureship at Hertford College Oxford in 1888. There he stayed till 1904, and, after four years in London as the virtual Rector of All Saints in Ennismore Gardens, and much preaching in well-known churches (including Westminster Abbey), he was appointed Lady Margaret Professor of Divinity at Cambridge in 1907. In 1911 he was offered and accepted the Deanery of St Paul's, from which he retired in 1934, though he continued writing almost until his death in 1954.

But while his life seems thus to be one of continuing professional success, he, too, was suspected of unorthodoxy. His Paddock Lectures of 1906, on 'Personal Idealism and Mysticism', gave rise to some unease among those selecting the candidate for the Lady Margaret Professorship, on account of his attitude regarding miracles. Apprised of this by the Master of Magdalene, Inge noted in his diary: "I wrote a letter to him to show them, explaining (in part) my views about the Virgin Birth and the Resurrection". (Adam Fox: *Dean Inge*, p. 92.) The explanation must have been satisfactory, since Inge was appointed, but the "in part" is both interesting and significant, and it is a pity that the letter referred to seems to be missing. What his views on these subjects were, and what the hesitations of the electors may have been, may perhaps become clear in the attempt to clarify what he meant by the term 'symbol', not only in these lectures, but in the various places

Dean Inge

where he used the term or its cognates in his many published works.

At the very outset of his Bampton Lectures of 1899 on 'Christian Mysticism', W. R. Inge shows his awareness that the term 'mysticism' is used loosely, and that in his day it was "sometimes . . . used as an equivalent for symbolism . . . sometimes for theosophy or occult science" (*CM*, 1, p. 3), and he is careful, therefore, to indicate what he himself means by it. For him,

> Mysticism has its origin in that which is the raw material of all religion, and perhaps of all philosophy and art as well, namely that dim consciousness of the *beyond*, which is part of our nature as human beings. (*ibid*. p. 5.)

It arises when

> we try to bring this higher consciousness into relation with the other contents of our minds. (*ibid*.)

Incomplete as these quotations are, they nevertheless already reveal some important fundamentals of Inge's thought: an unquestioned assumption that there *is* a "beyond" of which men are naturally (and not only supernaturally) aware; and that not only religion, but art and philosophy as well, are attempts to give our "dim consciousness" of such a "beyond" some precision. At the same time Inge acknowledges the part which "symbols" must play in any such attempt, for since our consciousness of this beyond is formless, "it cannot be brought directly into relation with the forms of our thought. Accordingly, it has to express itself by symbols, which are as it were the flesh and bones of ideas". (*ibid*.) This, though hardly a definition of what a symbol is, at least indicates the context within which the term functions in Inge's work: it is to be seen as some kind of correlative of our apprehension of the transcendent. Inge, however, was also aware, as Symons was not, that "The word 'symbol' . . . has an ill-defined connotation, which produces confusion and contradictory statement." (*CM*, 7, p. 250.) He recognizes that sometimes at least symbolism affirms only an "accidental or subjective" connection between a symbol and its referent, which distinguishes it from mysticism which is "based on a positive belief in the existence of . . . deep correspondences and affinities, not less real than those to which

119

the common superficial consciousness of mankind bears witness". (*CM*, 7, p. 251.) But he himself prefers "to use the word symbol of that which has a real, and not merely a conventional affinity to the thing symbolised" (*ibid.*), which he considers to be Kant's use of the word.[3] For him, therefore, mysticism and symbolism are at least closely related terms, both depending upon an affirmation of ontological inter-relatedness, which can be, on the one hand, apprehended, on the other, expressed.

Such an affirmation, and the definition of 'symbol' as that which exhibits "a real, and not a conventional affinity", shows Inge to be, here, closer in thought to Coleridge than to Symons, or indeed to Carlyle, whose theory of symbols he explicitly repudiates as hardly compatible with Christianity. (*CM*, 8, p. 320.) To what extent, then, is Inge's concept of 'symbol' like that of Coleridge?

There is no doubt but that Inge's concept of the transcendent, and its relationship to man and the world he inhabits is, in many ways, like that of Coleridge. For Inge, as for Coleridge, the transcendent is, ultimately, the Christian God, who is not (as he seems to be for Yeats) a projection of man's psyche, and thus his creation. Like Coleridge, Inge insists that man has the power to discern spiritual truth,[4] to know God, in some sense directly, if inchoately. Like Coleridge, he maintains that "since we can only know what is akin to ourselves, *man, in order to know God, must be a partaker of the Divine nature*". (*CM*, 1, 6.)

In a later series of lectures, *Truth and Falsehood in Religion*,[5] he expresses this conviction thus: "We must, I think, believe, as a necessary postulate or act of faith, that our higher reason is in vital ontological communion with the Power which lives and moves in all things, and most chiefly in the spirit of man" (*TFR*, p. 108), and by the "higher reason" Inge intends what Coleridge had meant, since he explicitly says in this context that "the distinction, much insisted on by Coleridge, between the understanding and the higher reason, should be maintained". (*ibid.*) This particular point is, however, probably the only one for which Inge is directly indebted to Coleridge. Though as this and other instances show, he was conversant with Coleridge's work,[6] he was, in general, wary of Coleridge's theology, thinking him too much of a voluntarist.[7] And the coincidence in thought can easily be ascribed to common sources of influence, predominantly to Plato and Plotinus, but also to Boehme and

the Cambridge Platonists, all of whom (together with Wordsworth) figure largely in Inge's pantheon.

But, if the influence of Coleridge himself can be discounted,
there are still other points of resemblance between them. Thus
the "Power" with which we are in "ontological communion" is
by Inge, as by Coleridge, identified with Christ, referred to in
the Johannine terms of "Logos" and "light", and, as in St Paul,
thought to be indwelling in man.[8] And, as the Trinitarian
concept of God, and the bond which exists between God, so
conceived, and man, and which enables man to know God, are
expressed by both Inge and Coleridge in similar terms, so also
is the presence of God within Nature, and the possibility of
man's recognizing God therein, emphasized by both.[9] True
Inge has no theory comparable to that which may be discerned
in Coleridge, of the way in which God is "immanent" within
nature, and perceivable therein. He is content, when he treats
of the subject, to relate the way others have thought of it.[10]
Nevertheless Inge did think that "the Divine in Nature has
hitherto been discerned more fully by the poet than by the
theologian" (*CM*, 8, p. 301), and among these pre-eminently
by Wordsworth[11] – sentiments with which Coleridge would
have agreed.

Important, too, in this context (and a consequence of the
previous point) is Inge's total rejection of any form of dualism
between mind and matter, or of the usually consequent consideration of either one as the mere epiphenomenon of the other.[12]
He held that "The reciprocal action of spirit and matter is the
one great mystery which, to all appearance, must remain
impenetrable to the finite intelligence. We do not ask whether
the soul is the cause of the body, or the body of the soul; we only
know that the two are found, in experience, always united."
(*CM*, 7, p. 258.) Hence, though he upheld the necessity of
discipline, of holiness of life, for the knowledge of God,[13] he
condemned that kind of asceticism which (apparently) strives
to be independent of the world of the senses,[14] considering that
world to be a source of temptation, or an illusion: an appearance as opposed to reality. And, in the final analysis, Inge
repudiated even that Mysticism in which "the return to God
was envisaged as a return from the unreal to the real" (*CV*,
p. 79), as "resting on a half-truth", and on "an abstract view of
the universe".

With this insistence on the fundamental inseparability of the seen and the unseen, the material and the spiritual, nature and God, it is not surprising that the function of symbols for Inge, as for Coleridge, should be one of "mediating between the seen and unseen worlds". (*FK*, p. 289.) As with Coleridge, to perform this function, symbols must be rooted in "the world which the understanding interprets to us" (*ibid.*), that is, the world of natural objects and events. But equally, in order to be symbols, such natural objects and events must be integrally related to the unseen, spiritual world, apprehendable only by the "higher reason". Thus Inge explicitly says that "the symbolic value of natural objects is not that they remind us of something they are not, but that they help us to understand something that they in part are" (*CM*, 8, p. 309), an assertion which is reminiscent of Coleridge's insistence that a symbol is an actual and essential part of that, the whole of which it represents. In one instance, also, Inge says that things are properly symbols when they exemplify "the same law which operates through all that God has made" (*CM*, 7, p. 251). This, again, could be taken as explaining the relation which exists between a symbol and its referent in Coleridgean terms.

Like Coleridge, too, Inge can insist on the revelatory character of symbols. In the *Bamptons* he approvingly quotes Goethe's (very Coleridge-like) definition of 'true symbolism' as that

where the more particular represents the more general, not as a dream or a shade, but as a vivid, instantaneous revelation of the inscrutable (*ibid.* p. 251);

and in the later *Contentio Veritatis* he goes further to say that he who considers "symbols . . . of the Deity as so many veils which hide His face" and, in order to know God, attempts to cast them aside can reach only an "empty Infinite". (p. 79.) The suggestion here is clear: it is only in symbols that we can obtain true knowledge.

In the same context Inge also hints at the nature of the "real affinity" which, in the *Bamptons*, he had said must exist between symbol proper and its referent (cf. above). This is contained in what he here writes of the Incarnation, which, he says, "is more than the husk of a higher truth; . . . it is a symbol which has an integral connexion with the thing symbolised, and which as springing from the constitution of the human mind, which is itself based in the primal ground of all being, might claim objective truth even in the absence of external evidence". (*CV*, p. 80.)

When we realize that, in this passage, both "the thing symbolised" and "the primal ground of all being" are references to God, the pattern which emerges of the role and nature of a 'symbol' is clearly like that in Coleridge. Jesus Christ is a 'symbol' because he is God Incarnate; he is 'symbol' because he is one with the referent of whom he is also the visible, tangible, counterpart in historical time; he is 'ontologically' a symbol, because this is his nature. But he is also 'symbol' for us, we can recognise him as symbol, and know God in Him, because the power of our human apprehension, our human mind, is one with, patterned on, that which is symbolized: the God who also dwells in us, and is both "Logos" and "light".

It might be objected that, since the Incarnation is a unique event, the account of Christ as symbol throws no light on the character of symbols in general. But it is clear from all that Inge says of the Logos doctrine[15] that whatever is a 'symbol' of God is so by virtue of the same immanent presence therein as is, however uniquely, incarnate in Christ. This assimilation he makes plain, for instance, when, again in the same context, he says that the attempt to dispense with symbols is "in the last resort, to dispense with our Divine-Human mediator". (p. 79.) At the same time he makes what is also a further significant point about the knowledge which we gain through symbols. He suggests that a belief in the essential importance of "our Divine-Human mediator" for our knowledge of God is incompatible with the assumption "that knowledge which is *immediate* must be higher than knowledge which is mediated through something else". (*CV*, p. 79.) In other words, the Christian must believe that those things which are 'symbols' of God are not only indispensable, but also give him a knowledge of God which is in no way inferior to that which he might gain by direct acquaintance – were this possible. As in the Incarnate Christ, though he is human, it is also God whom we meet, so in those things which are 'symbols' of God it is God himself whom we know. Knowledge of, and not only about, the referent is given us in symbols.

All these instances, like the general context of thought in which they occur, provide striking parallels between Inge's concept of 'symbol' and Coleridge's. For both, the term is linked to, and gains its particular meaning from, a similar Trinitarian concept of God, indwelling in man, present in nature, and incarnate in Christ. For both, symbols are sensuous presentations of ideas, apprehensible by a similarly conceived "higher reason", but needing concrete form to be available to man's understanding. For both, the symbol *embodies* a dynamic power or law, and not a static concept: and it is never an abstraction. Both see the symbol as, in a similar sense, "part of" that which it represents, and the link between symbol and referent cannot therefore be conventional or arbitrary for either: it is always intrinsic, but nevertheless perceptible, and based on a likeness which is not an external resemblance of parts but the externalization of an indwelling force. Hence each considers the symbol to be knowledge-giving: for Coleridge symbols are "translucent", for Inge they are "instantaneous revelations", and as such they must be self-authenticating. Though holiness of life may be a necessary prerequisite for our appreciation of symbols for what they are, that appreciation, and the consequent knowledge gained, do not depend on additional interpretation. For both, the knowledge "mediated" by symbols is not inferior to "immediate" knowledge. Knowledge of the symbol is knowledge of the thing symbolized at the same time.

But extensive though the similarity between Inge and Coleridge in their respective account of 'symbols' appears to be, it must be noted that – as in the case of his general *Weltanschauung* – Inge is not indebted to Coleridge either for his views, or their expression. In defining 'symbols', in speaking of 'symbolism', Inge quotes, or refers to, numerous writers: to Kant and Goethe, as we have already seen; to Harnack's *History of Dogma* (*CM*, p. 253n.); to a little know article in the *Edinburgh Review*;[16] to numerous mystics, indeed to a great variety of sources.[17] But, though he is obviously conversant with Carlyle on this topic, and even with Emerson (*CM*, 8. p. 320), nowhere in this connection does he mention Coleridge. Although the *Biographia* appeared in two editions about the turn of the century, once with the 'Two Lay Sermons' included, and though Coleridge's letters and some of his jottings were edited and published by E. H. Coleridge[18] at about this time, these were obviously not considered as relevant to Inge's discussion of symbols. How-

ever remarkable they may appear, resemblances must therefore be traced to their sharing a number of older traditions,
particularly perhaps the Platonism of Plotinus.

Inge's failure to appreciate and take account of Coleridge's
concept of 'symbol' is evident, however, not only in the absence
of reference, but also in this: that, although in the contexts
indicated, Inge stresses the revelatory knowledge-giving and
essentially participatory character of symbols, the paradigm of
which is the Incarnate Christ, he can, in other equally significant contexts, use the term 'symbol' in ways which are not
easily compatible with such a view, without any awareness of
the difficulties involved. Thus, for instance, commenting on the
Epistle to the Hebrews, he can say: "Systems of laws and
ordinances, of which the Jewish Law is the chief example . . .
rightly claim obedience . . . until the higher truths which they
conceal under the protecting husk of symbolism can be
apprehended without disguise" (*CM*, 2, p. 73), which is in
direct contrast to his later statement that the Incarnation is not
"the husk of a higher truth . . . it is a symbol". If the different
concept of 'symbol' implied by these two examples can be
explained by a lapse of time, this cannot be said of the juxtaposition of two similarly dichotomous definitions of symbolism to
be found in footnotes to the same Bampton Lecture. I have
already referred to Inge's approving quotation of Goethe's
definition of "true symbolism" as "a *vivid, instantaneous revelation*
of the inscrutable" (italics mine). Only a page earlier, however,
Inge had also quoted from Ludhart,[19] with equal approval, to
the effect that

Nature is a world of symbolism, a rich hieroglyphic book: everything
visible *conceals* an invisible mystery, and the last mystery of all is God.
(*CM*, 7, p. 250n.) (italics mine.)

Inge's two sources, as he quotes them, single out one or other
of the two characteristics of revelation on the one hand, and
concealment on the other; but Inge himself – like Carlyle before
him – brings both together as definitive of a symbol, saying:
"Nature half conceals and half reveals the Deity; and it is in this
sense that it may be called a symbol of him." (*ibid*. p. 250.) To
say this is to say more than, and something different from,
saying that a symbol is a partial, or an inadequate revelation of
its referent; or even that it is revelatory only to those who have

the capacity to perceive. In Inge's definition of Nature as symbol an antithesis is suggested (even if unintentionally) which goes beyond the Scriptural basis which he tries to give it, namely that, according to St Paul,[20] "the invisible things of God from the creation of the world may be clearly seen and understood from the things that are made; while at the same time it is equally true that here we see through a glass darkly, and know only in part" (*ibid.*), which in fact indicates only that nature, though revealing, is so only partially, incompletely, inadequately, in some sense. But even if some meaning of the term "conceal" can be compatible with some meaning of the term "reveal" in such a way that the dichotomy disappears, the statement, as it stands, is difficult to reconcile with the 'Coleridgean' stress on translucence of referent in symbol, and with the kind of knowledge of the referent in the symbol (in no way inferior to direct knowledge) which such a concept implies, and towards which, as we have seen, Inge appears to incline. Had Inge, then, seriously considered what Coleridge had to say on this matter, he could not, I suggest, have failed to indicate that, for instance, Ludhart's and Goethe's definitions *are* different, to note his preference for one or the other, or to suggest how they might be reconciled. He was, after all, quite aware, as I have already said, that the term 'symbol' was used in a confusing variety of ways, and in a somewhat similar case of the definition of 'symbol' as arbitrarily or intrinsically connected to its referent, he had so recognized the difference, and clearly showed his preference for the latter.

Nevertheless – and this, too, shows how little alive he was to the purport of Coleridge's concept – Inge does not always use the term 'symbol' in a way consonant with his stated preference, or at least not with the Coleridgean meaning which he sometimes seems to approach. Thus, for Inge, the connection between 'symbol' and 'referent', though described as real may, at some stage, cease to operate. Not only, that is, can symbols acquire a conventional relationship (though already possessing a real one), they can also cease to be symbols altogether and become "bare fact or bare fable". (*CV*, p. 87.) Indeed, according to Inge, it is "the tendency of all symbols to petrify and evaporate". (*CM*, 1, p. 5.) Inge's emphasis here (and its singularly Carlylean turn of phrase) is to be noted: it is not that for some reason (e.g. lack of 'holiness' on our part) we cease to perceive symbols as such and are therefore unable to recognize God in Nature, or even in Christ; it is that the symbols themselves cease to be symbols. The point is this: if the primary characteristic of a 'symbol' is its effect on us (e.g. a symbol is that which suggests or conveys) then that which may have been a symbol ceases to be such when it no longer performs that function. In this case if or when a symbol is not perceived as a symbol, it is not a symbol. On the other hand, if a symbol is described primarily in terms of what it is, independent of our perception of it as such (as, for example, in terms of the relationship which obtains between it and its referent which, if not conventional, at least may be thus independent), then a symbol will remain a symbol whether we perceive it as such or not.[21] The difference between Coleridge and Inge is this: that though both see the symbol in terms of "real" relationship, that reality for Coleridge is more "objective", less dependent on the perceiver, than it is for Inge. We have seen that, for Coleridge, the form in which an idea finds embodiment is its organic expression: in nature, as symbol, the relationship between idea and form is there for us to perceive, and also to imitate, when we will recreate the relationship in symbols of our own making. Inge, too, speaks of symbols in terms of the form in which an idea is expressed; but the sense in which "symbols are . . . the natural form of ideas" he explains thus: "the connexion between form and idea is subjective in the sense that it rests on individual feeling; but the connexion is real to us . . ." (*CV*, p. 85.) The "to us" is significant.

Something of the same difference of emphasis can be seen in another context. Coleridge, it will be remembered, insisted on distinguishing symbols *toto genere* from both metaphors and allegories. Moreover, the language of 'symbol' was, for him, a "medium between literal and metaphorical". Its aim was not, as with literal language, to give an account of events in which the element of interpretation is supposedly non-existent; nor was it, on the other hand, an account in which a pattern was imposed upon 'the facts' on the basis of some subjective preconception, or of merely superficial resemblances. 'Symbolical' language, as has been said, was the proper rendering of a *perceived* relationship which was really there, but needed insight (imagination) to be perceived, and imagination (in Coleridge's sense) to be thus rendered. Inge also made some apparently similar distinctions. We have already seen that he thought of symbols as "mediating" between the seen and the unseen, and that symbols are the forms of ideas. These he also distinguishes both from "philosophical speculation" and from "conscious allegory", as well as from "bare fact" (*CV*, pp. 86–7). And in his high regard for the insight of a poet such as Wordsworth, and his claim that it is the poet rather than the theologian who has both perceived and rendered the 'symbolical' quality of Nature, he seems to come near to the Coleridgean claim that it is by "imagination" and not "speculation" or "fancy"[22] that we can arrive at, and present, the truth as it really is. Nevertheless, when speaking of language, Inge, unlike Coleridge, assimilates 'symbol' and 'metaphor', making no distinction between them;[23] and, what is perhaps more important, he tends to contrast the "literally true" with the "symbolical". Thus he writes:

The basis of the belief in future judgment is that deep conviction of the rationality of the world-order, or, in religious language, of the wisdom and justice of God. . . . This conviction, like other mystical intuitions, is formless: the forms or symbols under which we represent it are the best that we can get. . . . We may use them freely, as if they were literally true, only remembering their symbolical character when they bring us into conflict with natural science, or when they tempt us to regard the world of experience as something undivine or unreal. (*CM*, 2, pp. 54–5.)

In Coleridge's theory, symbolical language, when seen as symbolical, could not have such consequences.

There is, then, I suggest, an incompatible and never resolved duality about Inge's use of the term 'symbol'. On the one hand the term means for him something which reveals, which gives self-authenticating knowledge, because it is essentially "one with" that which it stands for. The paradigm in this case is the Incarnate Christ, who is the visible, tangible, revelation of the Father, because he and the Father are one, and who, by his indwelling Spirit, is also the light whereby men can recognise him (and other symbols) for what they are. On the other hand a symbol is – not only in some undefined sense an 'imperfect' presentation of the referent (incompatible as *that* itself is with the idea of Christ as symbol) but – that which "conceals". At best, in this case, the referent can only be made known by the symbol if the relation which obtains between the symbol and the referent is understood (and therefore only *to* those 'already in the know'); an understanding which must be separately given, since the "connexion" is conventional, arbitrary, secret. If "real" the connection between symbol and referent is still only "real" in so far as we think it is, and not because it is there for our recognition. Hence a 'symbol' may be a fiction, an illusion, not representative of the way things really are, but, at most, of the way we think them to be. This ambivalence, of which Inge is not aware, stems from one traditional definition of symbol as "that which reveals and conceals at one and the same time", which he unquestioningly accepts. His is not the only use of the term which exhibits it: Coleridge, too, was quite capable of using the word 'symbol' casually, in a way which did not accord with his own definition. But the ambiguity is more radical in Inge's work, as can, I think, be seen in his treatment of the historicity of scripture, and the importance of its historical component for Christianity.

Coleridge, as we have seen, wished to say that the Bible was both "symbol and history". By this he meant – roughly – that the historical narratives of the Bible were presentations of actual events, in a way which made their inner meaning visible: they presented the pattern of salvation (grasped by man's Reason) to man's Understanding. It was a presentation of things as they really are, and not only as men may think them to be: 'as they really are' because seen by the light of the in-dwelling presence of God in man. It was consequently a presentation which was equally the result of man's (subjective) experience of the events, and of the events as they happened objectively. The two are one because God's presence and work in man is contiguous with (and the same as) his presence and work in things and events, in such a way that the events are themselves but the externalization of God's work in man. Hence "symbol" and "history" are one, and depend equally on events having actually taken place.

Inge also insists that our recognition of God in the objects and events around us depends on the presence of God within us; and he also speaks of the "essential connection between spiritual fact and its temporal manifestation", saying that religion assumes that "there is a phenomenal and a spiritual side to all experience, and regards the former as symbolic of the latter". (*CV*, p. 85.) Frequently, however, his turn of phrase shows that the primacy in the symbolical unity here suggested belongs quite definitely to the inward, spiritual, and even subjective element of the partnership. Thus he writes that the normal form of religious faith (i.e. its symbol) "is an event, or a series of events, which is *conceived* as having actually taken place, and which is *valued* as the symbol or sacrament. . .". (*ibid*. p. 84.) Or again:

We must face the fact that no religion has found any difficulty in *manufacturing* symbols to supply its needs. The creation of religious symbols has taken place in perfectly good faith, and, it must be added, by perfectly good logic. So long as men are convinced that a spiritual revelation, the truth of which is certain to them, must have, as its inseparable concomitant, certain events in the visible order, they are justified in stating positively that those events actually occurred. (*ibid*. pp. 85–6.)

The italics are mine. But the words I emphasize inevitably raise the question: what is the historical status of such "events" or "symbols"? Inge's words here are not dissimilar from those of Newman to which Kingsley took exception, that if certain alleged miracles in the life of a saint did not actually happen, they are such as should have happened, and hence that the hagiographer is justified in including them in his biography. The consequence for the historicity of narratives so constructed is obvious, and even if a defence can be elaborated, the position is not that envisaged by Coleridge.[24]

George Tyrrell

Tyrrell died in 1909; Dean Inge not till 1954. Chronologically, therefore, the latter belongs to the present century rather than the last, and in a partly historical survey it might seem that a consideration of Tyrrell's work should precede that of Inge. But this impression, based on the date of death, is misleading. Tyrrell was, in fact, slightly the younger of the two. He was born in 1861, a year later than Inge, and though this is itself of little moment there are more cogent reasons why he should be considered after the long-lived Dean.

The first of these is that Tyrrell's theology, much more than Inge's, was shaped by thought contemporary with his own. Not that Inge was unaware of, or indifferent to, the trends in philosophy, in science, and in historical method which affected the theology of the turn of the century (when both men, it should be remembered, were in their forties); but his thought was moulded primarily in, and by, an established tradition: Eton and Cambridge, the Classics and an established Church; Plato and Plotinus and the whole current of neo-Platonism which it was his over-riding interest to exhibit as a Christian philosophy best suited to the modern situation. Tyrrell had no such roots. His conversion, at the age of eighteen, to Roman Catholicism was from an Irish Protestantism he had never wholly accepted. But it was for him still much more of a search for faith, than the acceptance of patterns of thought which he had explored, found enriching and satisfying, and could call his own. Although he admits that he was always at first swayed towards the thought of those with whom he came into contact – whether in books, or more often (significantly) in person – there is little evidence in his writing of identification with any thinker or system, past or present.[25] He is not, like Inge, chiefly an expositor who comments in agreement or criticism, but a man struggling with problems as they exist for him and for those whom he meets NOW, to which past solutions seem scarcely relevant. It is this keenly felt response to the dilemmas of his own day, in all their urgency, which makes Tyrrell seem so much more contemporary a figure than Inge.

But also, just as Tyrrell's theology was elaborated more as a response to the contemporary situation (and very often to a particular problem within it) than was Inge's, so too it is less settled, less monolithic, more mercurial (like himself), than Inge's. If Inge extends his basic principles to meet what he sees as the current difficulties, Tyrrell only discovers what these principles are for him when facing the issues to hand. And therefore – since, however interesting this would be in itself, the compass of this book will not allow me to analyse the movement of Tyrrell's thought in detail – I shall be here concerned chiefly with the way the term 'symbol' functions in the latest exposition of his theology, namely, the posthumously published *Christianity at the Crossroads*, his "last word on Modernism". This work was partly an answer to Inge's criticism of the Modernist position in the *Quarterly Review* of April 1909, itself a response to, and an element in, the discussion of that controversial subject which had been given a more than theological *éclat* by the condemnatory encyclical *Pascendi Gregis* of October 1907.

Finally, critic of Modernism that he was and remained, Inge could later write "George Tyrrell once said that some day nothing might be left of Christianity except the Pauline Christ-mysticism and the law of love – I have been moving in this direction . . .",[26] an admission which itself gives some justification for considering Tyrrell's work after Inge's, in spite of the latter's much longer life.

Tyrrell's background was very different from Inge's. Born in 1861 two months after his father's death, he spent the first 18 years of his life in his native Dublin, in impoverished circumstances, and as a practising member of the Church of Ireland. He was attracted to England by the High Church Anglicanism of Richard Dolling, whom he assisted in his social work in London, but before long he thought of joining the Church of Rome, and, after a series of perfunctory sessions of instruction by the Jesuits of Farm Street, he became a Roman Catholic within months of his arrival in England. Scarcely a year later, in the autumn of 1880, he entered the Jesuit novitiate, and after the usual spiritual training, philosophical and theological studies, and some parish work – which he enjoyed and did well – he was appointed to the professorship of philosophy at the Jesuit house of studies in Stonyhurst. Here for the first time he crossed swords with the authorities, since his interpretation of St Thomas Aquinas was more liberal than that which was currently accepted by his Jesuit confrères. Partly because of this he was transferred to Farm Street, and more parochial duties in 1896. Increasing friction between himself and his superiors over his theological views and writing led to his retirement from the London house in 1905, and to his final severance with the Jesuits a year later. The last four years of his life, till his death of Parkinson's disease in 1909, were spent in Storrington, with hopes at first that his position as a secular priest would be regularized, but with actual increasing conflict between himself and the church authorities who even penalized his friend, Henri Bremond, for assisting at his death, and giving him a Catholic burial, since he had been excommunicated soon after the promulgation of the encyclical, *Pascendi Gregis*, which condemned Modernism as a heresy. In spite of this, Tyrrell did not cease to think of himself as a true member of the Church of

Rome and wished to die supported by its sacraments, though he was not prepared to renounce his views. How far these views are now accepted and acceptable is still a question of considerable emotive force.

Tyrrell's first ventures into print were articles for the Jesuit periodical *The Month*. The earliest appeared in 1886, six years after he first entered the Society of Jesus, the last in 1904, shortly before his final rupture with it, and the majority in the later 1890s; and many of these, together with those from other sources, were later reprinted in book form. His first books – *Nova et Vetera*, *Hard Sayings* and *External Religion* – appeared in the last three years of the nineteenth century, the last-mentioned being a series of sermons preached to Catholic undergraduates at Oxford University in the Hilary Term of 1899 – about the time, then, that Inge was delivering his Bampton Lectures in the same city. Here, as in some of the earlier articles, the terms 'symbol' and 'symbolism' do occur with some frequency and emphasis, and therefore, before considering what the terms meant for Tyrrell in the latest period of his life, I want to glance at his use of them in this earlier period, including here a somewhat later book, i.e. *Lex Orandi* (1903).

As the full title – *External Religion: Its use and abuse* – of the Oxford Sermons to Catholic undergraduates suggests, and as the topics of the individual sermons confirm, Tyrrell's interest here, as in all his writing, is the relation which exists between the external forms of religion, most particularly the language in which it is expressed, and both the object of religion, and its internal apprehension. It is the question "How can we, finite and conditioned, speak of the infinite and unconditioned?" which, in one form or another,[27] Tyrrell continued to ask himself, and sought to answer, and it is obvious, therefore, that the term 'symbol' could be very relevant to his discussion of the problems involved.

Tyrrell's earliest attempt to define 'symbol', occurs in a review of de la Barre's book, *La Vie du Dogme, Autorité – Évolution*, which was published in *The Month* of May, 1899, and later reprinted in *The Faith of the Millions*. In this article, while outlining the position held by Auguste Sabatier with regard to the nature of theological (and dogmatic) language, Tyrrell writes:

In this a symbol differs from an analogue or metaphor. The latter results from a comparison between the object and something else that in part resembles it; within limits, we may increase our knowledge of the original by studying its imperfect representation. But a symbol as we here use the term is simply a fanciful or poetical cause for a known unaccountable effect. It does [not] pretend to resemble the cause.[28] Given certain devout feelings, they might have a thousand hypothetical explanations; and of these, a personal God is one. The Ptolemaic system of *radius-vectors*, the electric fluid or current, the corpuscular, and even the undulatory theory of light, are all symbolic so far as they stand for, but in no way profess to resemble the unknown causes of the phenomena whose sequence and nature they summarize. (*FM*, pp. 144–5.)

Whatever the confusions inherent in this assimilation of scientific hypotheses and all other kinds of "fanciful or poetical" causes under the one term 'symbolic', as all 'explanations' of the same kind, it is clear that Tyrrell wishes to distinguish between analogous and metaphorical language on the one hand, and 'symbolic' language on the other. The former is a *representation* of an object, event, or state of affairs, based on *resemblance* and it gives us at least some further knowledge of that which it represents. To call language "analogous" or "metaphorical", therefore, is also to imply that though we do have only such language as a source of knowledge, we will, from it, gain knowledge of the object represented. Symbolic language, on the other hand, being only an – apparently somewhat haphazard – attempt at explaining a state of affairs observed or otherwise experienced, can give us no "knowledge" of the "cause" – conceived as objectively existing – which such an explanation may presuppose. Symbolic, explanatory, language – as Tyrrell goes on to say, extending the distinction, and in doing so casting further doubts as to the applicability of the term, so understood, to scientific hypotheses – is arbitrary and of "our own poetic making", dependent, apparently, only on our whims; whilst analogous language is an affirmation of (and is therefore based on, and presupposes) "a Reality which, addressing itself to our finite mind through the broken language of creation, *necessarily* (italics mine) begets in us notions answering to these terms" (*FM*, p. 146), and which, however inadequate and imperfect they may be, must (since they are based on resemblance) give us some knowledge of the Reality itself. Analogous language is "determined from without as well as from within" as are "the impressions we receive through our senses" (*ibid.*), and, while symbols "can be altered and substantiated at will", "true analogies, whose representative value is real" must, presumably, be permanent.

Though it is perhaps not surprising, since Tyrrell had not read Coleridge, it is nevertheless worthwhile remarking that the distinction Tyrrell here attempts to make between 'analogy' and 'symbolism' is by no means identical with that which Coleridge makes between the same terms.[29] Symbolic language (or 'symbol') as defined by Coleridge, bears some resemblance to both Tyrrell's categories, but is coincident with neither. However, Tyrrell himself can hardly be said to adhere strictly to the distinction he proposes in this instance, even within the compass of the same review. Thus, contrasting the Protestant and Catholic positions regarding Scripture he can write:

To the rationalistic Protestant, even Scripture is but a provisional attempt to give symbolic utterance to the felt but unknown object of our religious instinct. . . . But to the Catholic, the language and symbolism in which Christ clothed His revelation was divinely chosen and approved, not as equating our minds to what necessarily transcends its exact apprehension and expression, but as conveying as much of the truths of eternity as we are capable of receiving in our present embryonic state of intellectual development. (*FM*, pp. 141–2.)

The term 'symbolic' is here used as a description of language which gives expression to a *felt* but unknown object. This, if not absolutely incompatible with the use of the term to mean that which gives a "fanciful or poetical cause for a known unaccountable effect", does give it a connotation which makes the term particularly inept as a designation of scientific explanation. Moreover, the 'symbolism' here ascribed to Christ does not fit easily into the framework of the distinction Tyrrell was about to make between "symbol" and "analogue or metaphor". In that distinction he insisted that "symbols can be altered and substituted at will". (*FM*, p. 146.) Here, the symbolism is not dependent solely on arbitrary human choice, but has divine sanction, and, additionally, gives us some knowledge of the Divine. Even in this one article, then, and in spite of the attempt at definition, a certain fuzziness in the use of the terms is evident.

From an earlier essay on what was virtually the same subject (a review of Sabatier's short study on *The Vitality of Christian Dogmas*), it is, indeed, clear that Tyrrell does not confine the term 'symbolic' to the rather narrow use his definition implies, namely language which has an arbitrary connection to its referent. Referring to the credal phrases "ascended into Heaven" and "sitteth at the right hand of God the Father", Tyrrell says:

Sabatier thinks that because in both cases the truth symbolized is the important point, it is quite unnecessary to believe that in the former case the symbolism was real and objective; and similarly he would treat the record of the miraculous Birth of Christ and of His Resurrection. We, however, believe not merely in the truths signified by sacred history but in the correspondence between record and fact; in real as well as verbal symbolism. (*FM*, p. 128.)

If "verbal symbolism" is here compatible with the definition given later, Tyrrell's application of the phrase "real symbolism" to "the correspondence between record and fact" indicates an extension of the term 'symbolism', used on its own, beyond the limits the definition would allow; it appears to be a much more general term which can embrace both arbitrary and real connections between symbol and referent.

The same tendency to use the term 'symbol' and its cognates in this ambivalent manner, with both a more general and a more particular meaning, can be seen also in the instances where Tyrrell links the words with sacraments. Thus he can at one time speak of Christ having "lived and acted the truth in his life, and this not merely in the sense that He fulfilled the Divine Will in all his conduct . . . but in the sense that every deed and event of his mortal life was . . . as it were a sacrament or symbol of the mysteries of the kingdom of God" (*ER*, pp. 30–1), where there is no apparent distinction made between the relevant terms. On the other hand, he can also claim that "the organised unity of the hierarchic visible Church is itself in some way a sacrament, the outward and effectual sign of that invisible union in Christ of all souls in Heaven and earth, in whom the love of Divine goodness holds the first place", adding "Of this mysterious unity the outward unity of the visible Church is at once the symbol and the effectual instrument" (*ER*, p. 56), where it seems that a 'symbol' is but a component of a "sacrament", the outward sign, lacking the sacrament's "effectual instrumentality".

Similarly, in the later *Lex Orandi* Tyrrell speaks of the "visible Church" being "the effective sacrament and symbol of the spiritual Church" (p. 40), whilst maintaining that "the sacred humanity of Christ is the sacrament of sacraments; for there the subjugation of the natural to the spiritual is absolute as in no other; His manhood is no mere finite symbol of the divinity, but is divine" (pp. 161–2), where an absolute distinction is made between "sacrament" and "finite symbol" on the grounds, it appears, that a "sacrament" allows for Christ being divine, which possibly the designation "finite symbol" excludes. He continues, however, that it is through Christ "and in union with Him" that "the visible order becomes the sacrament, the effective symbol, of the invisible" (*LO*, p. 162), a statement in which an "effective symbol" is synonymous with "sacrament", and is presumably both "outward ... sign" and "effective instrument", as well as being inextricably linked to the referent (the Divine). To confuse the issue further, Tyrrell contrasts this view of the "visible order" of things, dependent on a proper appreciation of Christ as "the sacrament of sacraments", because not only human but also divine, with what he considers (at this stage) as an only partially correct apprehension of "Nature", namely "the 'sacramentarian' view of Nature as a symbolic expression or sign of the spiritual order, as of something separate and distinct, with which it has no causal connection except so far as by enlightening man's intelligence it may occasion some movement of his will and affections". (*LO*, p. 161.)

This variety in the use of the term 'symbol' in relation to "sacrament" makes it very difficult, if not impossible, to know whether, in any given instance, the term 'symbol' is being used as synonymous with the term "sacrament" in its traditional and fairly well-defined meaning (as given above), or in some narrower, or broader, sense. And this can well leave us puzzled to know what Tyrrell might mean when he refers to certain events or objects, particularly the person and life of Christ, as "symbols" of the Divine.

What is central in this confusion is – as always – the lack of clarity, the indecision, about the nature of the relationship which a symbol is supposed to have to its referent, and hence what knowledge of the referent the apprehension of a symbol as symbol can give us. If the connection is arbitrary, or conventional, and therefore the symbol and the referent are conceived as two distinct and essentially unrelated things, then the knowledge we gain of the referent by acquaintance with the symbol must depend on some extraneous explanation or other source of information: the symbol will only be a revelation of the referent (even in a rudimentary way) when we are acquainted with something (e.g. a set of transformational rules) which is not the symbol itself. If, however, a symbol is intrinsically connected with the referent then, at least in some cases if not all, we may know the referent by and in knowing the symbol and independently of any other source. Tyrrell's early work, however, is imprecise also in this respect. We have already seen that he uses the term 'symbol' where the relationship between it and its referent is explicitly stated as arbitrary. In other instances he can imply an apparently equally total (if different) distinction between the symbol and the symbolized. Thus writing of Newman in an article published in *The Catholic World* of 1905[30] he says: "the whole Essay of 1845 assumes the presupposition of the Tractarians, namely: the conception of the *depositum fidei* as being the communicable record and symbolic reconstruction of a revelation accorded to the Apostles alone. The subject-matter of the development there discussed is not an object revealed but the symbol of that object, the primitive *Credo*". (*TSC*, p. 147.) Here, there is no indication of what the relation between the "object revealed" and its 'symbol' is (to say that it is a record and a 'symbolic reconstruction" is unhelpful); but that the one is quite distinct from the other is clear.

On the other hand, when used in conjuction with the term "sacrament" the term 'symbol' (and more especially "effectual symbol") may imply the assertion of even more than casual relationship to the referent: the kind of relationship said to exist between God and man in Christ by those who can insist that Christ is truly God and truly man. And Tyrrell can also speak of 'symbols' in a manner which seems to indicate a position midway between these two extremes of absolute distinction, and absolute identification, where a symbol is something other than its referent and yet does, of itself, give us knowledge of that referent. He can say: "Once grasp the notion that the universe is God's book, or rather his very utterance in the natural order whereby he communicates with his rational creatures, and it is seen to be, not the end of knowledge, but the beginning, not the substance but the symbol; not permanent, but as evanescent as the words which pass our own lips . . .".[31] The relation between 'symbol' and referent (word and speaker) is tenuous, and yet the former, Tyrrell suggests, does give us some knowledge of the latter. Unlike Coleridge, however, he gives no indication of how or why this should be so in this particular case where the speaker is God, and his words the universe.

In *Lex Orandi* Tyrrell admits that "The precise relation of reality to appearance, of inward to outward, of the spirit to the flesh, is one of the persistent problems of the soul." (p. 160.) He could have added that there are equally persistent problems appertaining to the relationship which obtains between words and ideas, language and thought, cause and effect. But that he thinks of the relation of reality to appearance, of inward to outward, of spirit to flesh as *one* problem is symptomatic of the general difficulty of Tyrrell's use of the terms 'symbol' and 'symbolic' in his early writing. For he uses these, as we have seen, without sufficient discrimination and explanation, with reference to a variety of such problematic relationships. Thus used, the terms neither help to distinguish between the relationships to which they refer (suggesting, rather, that all such relationships have some fundamental and important quality in common – a questionable assumption); nor do they themselves acquire a precise definition. This indeterminate use of the word 'symbol' and its cognates is but a reflection of the fact that Tyrrell had no established view of the relationships in question at this time. He says quite specifically that "We are vague . . . as to the relationship of body to soul; and still more as to the relation of creature to Creator" (p. 162), and it is not altogether surprising, therefore, that, in relevant contexts, his use of the term 'symbol' is equally vague.

The question then remains: what precision, if any, did the term 'symbol' acquire in what was Tyrrell's final statement of his position, and in such other expositions of his views as belong to roughly the same time? The questions to which the term and its precise connotation was relevant (such as the relationship between Biblical record and historical fact, the question of Christ's divinity, the relationship between dogma and scripture) had been made a theological storm-centre by the Encyclical *Pascendi Gregis*, whilst its consequences for Tyrrell had freed him from the last constraints which he might still have felt upon his freedom to write without dissimulation. It is, then, to *Christianity at the Crossroads* that I finally wish to give some attention.

Christianity at the Crossroads – the General Context
The manuscript of *Christianity at the Crossroads* was not quite finished at the time of Tyrrell's death in July 1909, but it was published posthumously as it stood. Although the book would have benefited from the revision which Tyrrell might have given it had he lived (it is, for example, repetitive in some instances) it is, nevertheless, his clearest exposition of his Modernism and sets out to distinguish this both from Liberal Protestantism, and from Liberal Catholicism, whilst also trying to establish its essential continuity with traditional Catholicism. Some account of Tyrrell's views must be given if the force with which he – very frequently – uses the terms 'symbolical', 'symbolism', etc. in this book is to be understood.

Within the history of Catholicism, Tyrrell sees two kinds of 'orthodoxy' with regard to the content of belief, revelation, and dogma. According to what he calls the old orthodoxy, there was, Tyrrell maintained, no theory of any development of dogma; the whole content of revelation had been given to the Apostles, and was preserved by the Church. In face of heresy, which was essentially innovation, the Church, in Council, stated what the Church believed, and had always believed, about the question raised. The bishops simply bore witness to the constant and universal belief of their flocks, and thus exhibited any different position to be an innovation, and hence heretical.

But because of the obvious difficulties of this theory, a new orthodoxy was developed, in which the original revelation could be considered as a series of propositions, which, being propositional, were patient of logical development. The validity of the deductions made was decided on by the councils of the Church, and the valid deductions became also part of revelation. In this case, when bishops met in council, they did not do so only to witness to what was universally held, but to debate an open question, to decide which of the various, all apparently equally possible, conclusions which were being drawn from already established positions was the proper consequent of faith already held, and most consonant with the already explicit content of revelation. In deciding this they defined all other conclusions as heretical. According to the new orthodoxy, which Tyrrell saw as allied to scholasticism, revelation is essentially conceptual, and its development an explication of what is implied by a given proposition – such conclusions, the dogmas of the Church, being equally part of what was revealed.

From both the new and the old orthodoxy Tyrrell distinguishes what he understands as Newman's theory. This, he thinks, has been confused with the new orthodoxy because both speak in terms of the development of ideas. He points out, however, that whereas in the new, neo-scholastic, theory the term 'idea' is taken in the sense of 'concept', which can be formulated as a proposition, for Newman the term meant a spiritual force or impetus, whose development therefore cannot be the logical development proper to the former. In effect, then, while the new orthodoxy considers revelation as an idea which is capable of logical development or explication, Tyrrell thinks that, according to Newman, revelation as an idea or spiritual force or impetus does not itself develop, but manifests itself variously in forms some of which are capable of development (whether logical, as with formulas, or perhaps organic, as with institutions) but none of which can be complete manifestations of the original idea.

While absolving Newman from any Modernist intentions, Tyrrell claims that it is this theory of revelation as an idea in the sense of a still active force or impetus, with its different developing manifestations, that Modernists have accepted, and that it is this which basically distinguishes their theories from the previous Catholic orthodoxies. From the old orthodoxy, because revelation is seen not as a specific and closed content of beliefs, but as a force or impetus; from the new orthodoxy, because revelation, as such a force, is always the same, though its manifestations may be different; and because revelation is not thought of as capable of syllogistic development since it is not conceptual in content.

The understanding of revelation as a force or impetus which

manifests itself in various ways has several important consequences. In the first place, on such a theory, a sharp distinction
must be made between revelation and dogma. Dogmatic
statements cannot be simply the promulgation of a revelation
already known, if not, so far, explicitly stated; nor can they be
part of that revelation in the sense that what is implicit in the
premises of an argument is part of those premises, even
though it may not be made explicit in a conclusion, and
remains part of the original position when the conclusion has
been explicitly drawn. The relationship between revelation
conceived as an idea or force, and its manifestations including
dogmas, needs some other explanation. Secondly, the concept
of revelation as such an idea, at least in Tyrrell's view, implied
that the manifestations of the idea would be necessarily
couched in the terms suited to the particular time, place, and
culture of the peoples to whom it was made. But in this case, on
what grounds could any one such manifestation of an idea
claim pre-eminence or uniqueness, as Christianity certainly
(still) did; and within Christianity itself what place, and status,
was to be accorded to the manifestation of the idea as given
through and by Jesus himself? That is to say, such a view of
revelation as Tyrrell proposed raises the question of the status
of Christianity among other religions, and of the relationship of
the Scriptures, and particularly the New Testament, to other,
and subsequent, manifestations of the idea.

It is in the answer they give to this last question that Tyrrell
thinks that Modernists differ from Liberal Protestants, who
also think of revelation in terms of an idea which must be
manifested differently in different times and places. Their mistake, Tyrrell suggests, is in interpreting the idea which was
presented by Christ and is recorded in the Scriptures in purely
moral terms, dismissing the transcendental and apocalyptic
imagery in which it is couched as irrelevant and incidental.
They see, therefore, the development of that idea in a development of morality, its evolution in terms of the progress of
civilization, and its future culmination in the perfection of that
moral development. For the Liberal Protestant, Christ is the
moral teacher who was constrained to suit his message to the
more barbaric times in which he lived, the essence of which,
however, is now at last clear, thanks to modern biblical criticism, and principally to the astuteness of German theologians,

and can be restated in the more sophisticated terms suited to the nineteenth century.

While agreeing with Liberal Protestants in their insistence that Christ had to couch his message in the thought-patterns of his own culture, Tyrrell disclaims their interpretation of it. He insists that the distinction between an essential moral content, and an incidental transcendental imagery cannot be made, and that, moreover, the emphasis in Christ's teaching is not on a new morality, but on the nature and nearness of the kingdom of God, which is presented as "not of this world". This, Tyrrell claims, Catholicism has always understood, and in maintaining the emphasis it has remained closer to the idea which Christ came to announce, than have Liberal Protestants who wish to evacuate the gospels of their essentially transcendent content. He claims that "The notion that Good was to triumph by an immanent process of evolution never entered into the 'idea' of Jesus or of the Church" (p. 63); and that the notion that "the natural world could grow into the transcendental Kingdom of God", or that "the natural man, by a process of moral development . . . [could] . . . grow into a son of God" (p. 65), was quite foreign to the thought of Christ, and has rightly remained alien to the thought of the Church. If all Christians take the message of Christ as central to their beliefs, it is, nevertheless, "not between Jesus and Catholicism, but between Jesus and Liberal Protestantism that no bridge, but only a great gulf, is fixed". (p. 65.)

In emphasizing, with the Catholic Church, the essentially transcendental nature of Christ's message, Modernists, then, are opposed to Liberal Protestants and remain within the Catholic tradition.

Nevertheless, the mistake in the Catholic position, Tyrrell insists, though perhaps not as radical as that of the Liberal Protestants, is as serious. For it ignores what both Protestants and Modernists recognise: that the form in which Christ gave us his message is a presentation of the truth conditioned by the culture, expectations, and thought patterns, of the times in which he lives and the people to whom he belonged. Catholicism is wrong in taking the terms in which the gospel message is couched as literal; or in trying to distinguish between the literal and the non-literal; or in thinking that, if the imagery is translated into conceptual terms, into a body of doctrine, such a translation will be literal. What Modernists maintain while rejecting the Protestant interpretation is that, classical and normative as Christ's presentation of the religious "idea" as preserved in the gospels is for all Christians, like all and every attempt to convey that idea, it cannot be literal, since the idea which is being presented is essentially transcendent. And this Tyrrell calls the recognition of the "principle of symbolism". (p. 81.)

In this context, and in a general sense, it is obvious that what Tyrrell means by "symbolism" is *any* presentation of an idea which (like the idea of God and the kingdom of God) is supra-human, and extra-terrestrial in *any* language possible for man. As thus used, the term 'symbol' means little more than 'inadequate presentation' of whatever sort, and whatever (other) relation it may bear to the referent. If, in using it thus, Tyrrell was trying to emphasize an important, and perhaps neglected, truth, that *no* language about, or representation of, God can ever be satisfactory,[32] he was doing so by evacuating the term 'symbolical' of any specific meaning. Did he, then, ever give it a more precise function? Did the term, for him, ever denote a more determinate relationship between a language or other presentation and its referent than that conveyed by the word 'inadequate'?

To this – or similar – questions it is difficult to give any answer to which some exception might not be found, since in *Christianity at the Crossroads* the relevant terms occur much more frequently than in any work so far considered, and – I wish to state at the outset – in ways which defy succinct analysis or easy categorization. I can, therefore, only indicate some of the confusions which emerge, as I shall show, when any attempt is made to determine more precisely the sense in which Tyrrell used them.

I have already indicated that, in one of his early articles, Tyrrell considers that 'symbols' (and hence symbolic statements) are different from both analogues and metaphors (and hence analogical or metaphorical language) because the latter are comparisons between two things built upon a supposed resemblance, whilst the former, though they stand for an unknown cause, "do not profess to resemble it". (*FM*, p. 144.) Although, as I have pointed out, even in the earlier period of writing, Tyrrell did not always keep this distinction in mind, in

Christianity at the Crossroads he appears to discard it altogether. Having said that all expressions of the transcendent are necessarily symbolic, including the one given us by Christ, and yet wishing to maintain that "what each age has to do is to interpret the apocalyptic symbolism into terms of its own symbolism" (p. 82), he has to tackle the question: how can we know when our symbolic presentations of the idea are not misleading, but accord with the normative presentation recorded in the gospels? He answers, not as Coleridge might have done, that the identity is preserved when the creative process involved in both is the same (both the work of the 'Spirit'; Christ in history, Christ indwelling in us) but that such presentations are not misleading only in so far as the various symbolisms "yield the same control over experience". (p. 82.) Realizing, however, that this leaves him open to the charges of agnosticism or pragmatism (which he wants to deny) he adds:

To say they are but symbolic of the transcendent is not agnosticism; since symbols may be representative. Nor is it pure pragmatism, since the degree of practical utility is just that of their correspondence to reality. Were nature not in some way like a mechanism, the determinist hypothesis of science would be fruitless. Because the likeness is imperfect, the fruitfulness is imperfect. (p. 82.)

In other words, what Tyrrell is here suggesting is that at least a 'proper' symbolic presentation of the transcendent *does* imply some kind of correspondence between that transcendent referent and the 'symbol' which expresses it, and that this correspondence is not mere fancy but, after all, likeness.

This change would be of little account if, in *Christianity at the Crossroads*, Tyrrell was consistent in his use of the term 'symbol' in this respect. It would then be possible to say that his latter use was different from the earlier; that at this later stage a 'symbol' for him was synonymous with an "analogue" as he had defined it in the Sabatier article. This, if not entirely satisfactory, would at least narrow the range of queries to be dealt with. But the difficulty is that Tyrrell does not always think of the possible relationship between the transcendent (or the referent) and its presentation (or symbol) simply in terms of a correspondence or likeness (vague as these terms are in any case). He can also refer to 'symbols' as the "spontaneous or deliberate representations of the transcendent cause or source of the experience" (p. 85), and of a cause, in this case, not as "a group of antecedent phenomena", but rather as a dynamic agent. Such a concept of a cause, represented by symbols suggests that the relationship is not one of resemblance but of some form of presence, of a dynamic continuity between referent and symbol. But Tyrrell pays no heed to the difference of relationship implied by resemblance on the one hand, and causality on the other, and hence the terms 'symbolic' which does duty in both cases remains unclear.

Again, though in this passage he is aware of the different concept of cause applicable to God, and as used "in the modern scientific sense" (p. 85), he does not, therefore, question the legitimacy of comparing scientific hypotheses and the representations of such a "transcendent cause or source of the experience" as he takes God to be. Both, he insists, are "fictions based on fact" – the phrase he here uses most frequently in conjunction with 'symbol' (e.g. p. 100). But this assimilation, as I have already intimated, disregards crucial differences. The most important, in this context, is this: the fiction which is a scientific hypothesis is, basically, a patterning of observed phenomena – the facts. Such a patterning may involve reference to some other, supposed but yet unobserved, phenomena (either as antecedent cause or some other way) something as yet unknown, but knowable as all other phenomena are knowable. It does not, however, involve a reference to, does not permit as an element in such a patterning, any unknown, intrinsically such because of its fundamentally transcendent nature. Moreover, even when a scientific explanation involves the claim that our experience of the world is such that some principle – such as the conservation of energy – must be operative within it, this is by no means the same kind of claim as is made by those who would maintain that our experience of the world suggests the existence of God. For the appeal to a principle operative within the phenomenal world does not involve the existence of such a principle or law in the sense in which theological discourse asserts that God exists. However formulated, scientific hypotheses remain essentially this-worldly, and must by almost universal agreement disregard all possibility of any extra-phenomenal world. But this is not so with fictions which are based on the facts of religious experience. Even if these facts, though necessarily subjectively apprehended, are

Tyrrell

sufficiently universal to be classed with scientific phenomena, and even if they are simply patternings of such experience, they do – as Tyrrell realizes – necessarily involve a reference (as cause for instance) to that kind of transcendent and unknowable world which science deliberately excludes. And hence to call the relations of both kinds of fictions to the facts which they pattern 'symbolic' begs the question of their similarity.

The same ambiguity in the use of the term 'symbolic' is evident in other instances, as a comparison of some of Tyrrell's statements will show. Thus in some cases Tyrrell speaks as if the referent of the symbolic presentation (sometimes spoken of as a vision, and sometimes as the expression or proclamation of such a vision) is "transcendent life", or a "reality" (e.g. pp. 97 and 100); but sometimes the referent of such a presentation is not the transcendent itself, but our experience of it (e.g. p. 86). Sometimes, then, a symbolic presentation is in the nature of an organization of *experience*, which, even if it is an experience of the transcendent, cannot itself be transcendent; while sometimes the symbolic presentation seems to be some kind of a representation of the transcendent itself. But precisely because the referents in these two cases are of an entirely different order, the relationship in which they stand to that which represents them cannot be assumed to be the same. To call the presentation of each a symbol, or the relationship of referent and presentation symbolic, is only to suggest that the relationship *is* the same: it is not to explain how this might be so. Since Tyrrell never furnishes such an explanation, his use of the term 'symbolic' remains unhelpful.

Similarly it is sometimes very difficult to determine what – or who – engenders the symbol, and by what process this is achieved, in those frequent cases when the context suggests that a symbol or symbolic presentment *is* the result of some activity (as, e.g., p. 85). We have already seen that Tyrrell speaks of symbols as – indifferently – the "spontaneous or deliberate representations of the transcendent cause or source of the experience". (p. 86.) At other times he can say, more decidedly, that it is "the spiritual experience" which "tends to translate *itself* into symbolic ideas and images". (p. 125, my italics.) He can also insist that "what each age has to do is to *interpret* the apocalyptic symbolism into terms of its own symbolism" (p. 82, my italics), which suggests the conscious activity of persons, and not the spontaneous effect of an experience. To this there is the following corollary: symbols sometimes seem to be something given us – independent of our own volition, or own creativity of any kind, as if their source were quite independent of ourselves, and all we had to do was to guard against the mistake of thinking they were the reality of which they are only a translation into our own terms. At other times, however, symbols seem to be definitely something we fashion ourselves, they are not only couched in human terms but are of human and conscious origin. Why two such different activities should both be called 'symbolic', and their results both 'symbols', again remains unexplained. Tyrrell has no theory of man's creativity as a microcosm of the creativity of God, no theory of imitation such as Coleridge proposes and which in his case – whether it is acceptable or not – does provide some answer to a similar problem.

The lack of coherence evident in Tyrrell's use of the term 'symbol' and its cognates, then, is due to his employment of the terms in too many disparate instances – in relation to cause and effect (p. 120) as well as to my "self" and "body" (p. 98), for example – without giving us sufficient reason for supposing all these to possess similar characteristics, which a constant nomenclature suggests, but does not, of itself, supply. This is because the whole thrust of Tyrrell's argument is directed towards the affirmation that, although some sort of relationship obtains in all these cases, in none do we have any knowledge of what that relationship is. In this respect there is no advance in the position Tyrrell took, as we have seen, in his earlier work. To speak, then, in terms of 'symbols' or 'symbolic presentments' is, for Tyrrell, primarily an affirmation of *a* relationship between the referent and the referend, and thus far symbolism may be likened to analogy which also implies such an affirmation. But – even though Tyrrell himself elides the terms – to call something a 'symbol' is to claim less than to say it is an analogue, for the latter, at least normally, also purports to involve some theory of the relationship thus affirmed, and this seems to be what Tyrrell tries to avoid by employing his vocabulary of 'symbolism'.

There is, however, one instance where it might seem that Tyrrell did envisage a particular type of relationship between referent and symbol, and that a much closer one than the relationship of resemblance or even of cause. In discussing the personality of Jesus he says that "the 'I' that speaks and acts in Jesus is the Spirit, though it speaks and acts through the limitations of a human organism. It is the Spirit made man. The Word which enlightens every man is made flesh, what works within us stands before us, to be seen and heard and handled." (p. 172.)

The two points here made, that the identity of Jesus with the Spirit (who is Divine, is God) and the indwelling of that same Spirit within each one, as a light, or a living power, is reiterated throughout the chapter, in terms reminiscent of both Coleridge and Inge. In this context the statement that "Jesus Himself was the great sacrament and effectual symbol of the Divine Life and Spirit" (p. 173), might at first suggest that, as in Coleridge, a symbol was the enfleshment, the making visible, of the transcendent and the immanent in a hypostatic union; the concrete presentation to our sense experience of the point of coincidence between the two, and, by extension, between the objective and the subjective, the thing as we see it and as it really is.

Yet, if we look closely at the context, the initial resemblance to what either Coleridge or even Inge (in similar instances) asserted of 'symbol' becomes less clear. For Tyrrell's emphasis is not so much on Jesus as a historical person, though also having, as it were, an extra-historical dimension which makes him present now; it is on Jesus as a "forceful, living, self-communicating ideal, a fire spreading itself from soul to soul". (p. 172.) The balance is shifted from Jesus as the *one* who *is*, to Jesus as a *force* which *acts*. Such a change of emphasis inevitably reflects on the concept of 'symbol' employed in the context: the stress falls not on what a symbol is in itself, but on what it does. If we compare this use with a definition of 'symbol' such as "that which is and means at the same time", or the one of Nettleship, quoted by Inge, "that which being what it is stands for something else" then the equal emphasis on both a symbol's particular kind of being, and its consequent meaning, essential also to Coleridge, is significantly transferred by Tyrrell to that of meaning only: what the symbol is in itself ceases to matter.

And further: though it might seem that in this chapter of Tyrrell's book the concept of 'symbol' includes its essential oneness with the referent (since Jesus, the symbol, is also the Spirit whom he makes both concretely present and effectual), yet Tyrrell can also say "the vehicles and sacramental symbols through which the Spirit communicates itself are no part of the Spirit. The human frame and the mind of Jesus, His local and temporal limitations of thought and knowledge, were but the sacramental elements through which the influence of his Divine Spirit was mediated." (p. 174.) Here it is not Jesus who is the 'symbol' of the Spirit, because he is "the Word made flesh", but 'symbols' are accidental instruments of the Spirit to whom they have no intrinsic relationship. Symbol and referent are discontinuous, and essentially unrelated.

Finally, since I have had occasion to compare and contrast Tyrrell's and Coleridge's concepts of 'symbol', and since the question of the symbolic *vis-à-vis* the historical is important, I want to consider an important letter of Tyrrell's relevant to both these points. Writing to Friedrich von Hügel[33] in February 1907, Tyrrell outlines what he calls his "revolutionary view of dogma", and – as would be expected – admits to distinguishing sharply between "the Christian revelation and the theology that rationalizes and explains it". The first he calls a "symbolic and imaginative construction", one which was "an idealization of a certain core of historic fact". In such a construction, however – Tyrrell goes on to say – it is impossible to distinguish between "the literal and the purely symbolic parts of the expression and the mere 'cement' or frame stuff, i.e. all that part of a parable which is merely for the sake of cohesion and is not symbolic of anything".[34]

It would seem that here there is a distinction between three categories of language, the literal, the symbolic, and neither, in what is, nevertheless, a wholly 'symbolic' construction – a confusion once again between a particular and a general meaning of the term. Theology, however, which is contrasted with revelation as not the work of "inspired imagination" but of "reflection and reasoning", and is apparently therefore not 'symbolic' in the general sense – is also a "fuller construction of the Christian revelation in just the same sense", that is, presumably as consisting of the three levels of language in the one whole. Here, then, because Tyrrell fails to distinguish between a general and a particular use of the term 'symbolic' the sharp distinction between revelation and theology with which he began is confusingly blurred – there is some sense in which both are 'symbolic' and 'not symbolic'.

It would also seem, however, that though making a distinction between 'symbolic' (in some sense) and literal language in a way which would have incurred a Coleridgean censure, Tyrrell in the first part of the letter identifies a "symbolic construction" with an "idealization of historic fact" which might bear a Coleridgean interpretation. This impression is strengthened in a later passage when Tyrrell calls such an idealization "the true inward significance" which is "concealed by the mere historic aspect", the "inward truth of history" though "not historic truth". Here, apparently, somewhat as in Coleridge, a "symbolic construction" is one which is not "history" as superficially apprehended, but a presentation of its inward truth – the real pattern of history made visible to us in a construction which depends on insight. Unfortunately, however, for the validity of such an identification between Tyrrell's concept of symbolic presentation and Coleridge's, Tyrrell also implies that such an "idealization" of history is not 'symbolism', though neither is it "literal", for symbolism seems to be, once again, something merely fanciful and untrue. As before, and as always, therefore, we are left wondering what the nature of a "symbolic construction" is in relation to the apparent fact; is it a legendary and fanciful superstructure which, though perhaps suggested by the facts as they appear, has no real connection with them but that which we ourselves misleadingly or fortuitously impose; or is it the result of insight which sees facts as they really are, and is faithful to the thus perceived inner structure because it is its organic reconstruction and visible counterpart? Because Tyrrell does not pose himself this question clearly, his use of the term 'symbolic' here also is undetermined, and lacks the necessary precision to be more than superficially comparable to that of Coleridge, or, indeed, to illuminate clearly the many problems with which, in Tyrrell's work, it is associated. It may be that, had Tyrrell lived to revise the manuscript of *Christianity at the Crossroads*, he would have recognized and dealt with some of the questions involved, but it is equally likely that he was simply not a sufficiently vigorous thinker to disentangle them successfully.

George MacDonald

Had Tyrrell's concept of symbol resembled that of Coleridge

the similarity would have been largely fortuitous since Tyrrell, as far as one can tell, was not acquainted with Coleridge's work, and it is very unlikely that he could have been indirectly influenced by his thought, especially in the area of symbolization, since this was, as has been shown, almost totally neglected. The case of George MacDonald is quite different. He had read Coleridge, whom he paraphrased and quoted in his own essays, where the context is relevant to a specific use of the term 'symbol'.[35] In such cases, while never actually quoting or directly making use of Coleridge's own definition of symbol, MacDonald, unlike other writers who were equally influenced by Coleridge's thought, does at least use the term 'symbol' himself not merely casually. This alone makes him an obvious candidate for consideration and, since he is thus singular, it is fitting that, in a work which begins with Coleridge he should be treated last, even though the bulk of his relevant writings falls rather earlier than that of either Tyrrell or Inge.

George MacDonald is now generally remembered only as a writer of a few children's books: *At the Back of the North Wind*, *The Princess and Curdie*, *The Princess and the Goblin*; by readers of C. S. Lewis he may also be known as the author of that book – *Phantastes* – whose metanoic effect Lewis describes in his autobiography.[36] That he was a Professor of Literature at Bedford College, an apparently successful and popular lecturer on scientific, theological and literary topics both in England and in America, a one-time Congregational minister, later converted to Anglicanism; known to, and highly regarded by, many eminent divines and literary men of his day, counting F. D. Maurice, Ruskin and the Rossettis among his friends; and that he has been praised by such various writers as Chesterton, C. S. Lewis and Auden nearer our own time, is not common knowledge. Most of his work is, perhaps not undeservedly, forgotten.

Like Carlyle, MacDonald was a Scot, and like him brought up in the Calvinist tradition. His education was, financially, a struggle, and his Aberdeen M.A. – in Chemistry and Physics, and not in the classics traditional in Oxbridge – was completed only after MacDonald had interrupted his studies in order to earn some money. He went down from Aberdeen in 1845, the year of Newman's conversion to Roman Catholicism, and after tutoring in a London family, enrolled for the Congregational Ministry in 1848. Two years later, having married in the meantime, he became Minister at Arundel; but here, apparently because of his theologically too liberal views, he soon ran into trouble and in 1853 was forced to resign. From then till he obtained his Bedford College professorship in 1859 he was compelled to support his growing family and to pursue his vocation by writing and preaching without even the relative security of a permanent congregation. Even after his appointment, he continued to write and lecture outside the scope of his duties, prompted partly, no doubt, by the small salary attached to his post but also by a conviction, strengthened by growing success, that he could thus fulfil his calling. Academically his achievements were recognised by his receiving, in 1868, an LL.D from his own University in consideration of "his high literary eminence as a poet and author", and the last half of his long life (he died in 1905), though shadowed by the deaths of his children and friends, and chequered by his own ill-health, were ones of growing security and continuing literary output.[37]

Like Coleridge, like Carlyle, MacDonald was well read in the German authors of his day; like Inge he shows in his writing the influence of Platonism. How comparable to Coleridge's, then, was the world-picture he evolved or subscribed to, in so far as this is relevant to the concept of symbol? The most apt general and summary statement of MacDonald's point of view can be found in his essay on Wordsworth's poetry, published in *Orts* (1882). He writes:

This world is not merely a thing which God hath made, subjecting it to laws; but it is an expression of the thought, the feeling, the heart, of God himself. And so it must be; because, if man be the child of God, would he not feel to be out of his element if he lived in a world which came, not from the heart of God, but only from his hand? (p. 246.)

Here there is some adumbration of the way in which MacDonald considered the relationship of the world to God; man to the world; and even, in the distinction between thought and heart which both enter into the making of the world (though here spoken of in relation to God), a suggestion of the way he speaks elsewhere of the faculties of men. Since it is a general statement, however, these elements must be pursued further if we are to understand the particular direction of MacDonald's thought.

What kind of an expression of the thought and the feeling

heart of God is the world? MacDonald calls this philosophy explicitly a "Christian pantheism" and stresses the indwelling of God in all things. This emphasis, that God is to be found in, and not only through and beyond, natural forms is a persistent one. Though he does, at least on one occasion, speak of all that exists as "only shadows, lovely shadows of him" who is "the great one life than whom there is no other" (*US*, 2, p. 155) which as has been said, could imply that God himself is elsewhere, it is obvious from the tenor of his thought (as it is not with either Carlyle or Newman), that the impression of a certain distance between God and his created world is not what MacDonald wishes to convey. While he is in no danger of taking God as merely the sum total of natural forms, for he does not fail to point to what might be called God's "otherness", yet it is the awareness of God *in* the world which is the dominant theme. Coupled with this insistence on God's presence in things created is his repeated assertion that in such created forms God is not concealed but revealed. Thus, he states:

I believe that every fact of nature is a revelation of God, is there such as it is because God is such as he is . . . from the moment when we first come into contact with the world, it is to us a revelation of God, his things seen, by which we come to know the things unseen. (*US*, 3, pp. 60–1.)

Earlier he had written: "I believe . . . (God) . . . is ever destroying concealment, ever giving all that he can, all that men can receive at his hands, that he does not want to conceal anything, but to reveal everything." (*US*, 1, pp. 42–3.) It is an emphasis much more unequivocal in MacDonald than it is in either Carlyle or Inge. There is, likewise, an apprehension of the "oneness of the universe ever reappearing through the vapours of question", so that "To find, for instance, the law of the relation of the arrangements of the leaves on differing plants, correspond to the law of the relative distances of the planets in approach to their central sun, wakes . . . [in the developing individual] . . . that hope of a central Will." ('Individual Development', *Orts*, pp. 57–8.) Without such a hope delight in the loveliness of the universe is unreason. In its own oneness, thus exhibited, the universe mirrors the "great one life" which is God. But within this "oneness" of "God's things" which are "his embodied thoughts" there is also "layer upon layer of ascending significance", for God "expresses the same thought in higher and higher kinds of thought". ('The Fantastic Imagination', *A Dish of Orts*, p. 320.) The insistence on "oneness" especially as apprehended in "laws", coupled with the vocabulary of a certain kind of hierarchy, cannot but be reminiscent of Coleridge, even if it stems perhaps from a more ancient common background.

The fact, too, that here, as elsewhere, MacDonald talks in terms of natural forms being *embodiments* of thought is not without significance. And the body (both in the literal sense, and as standing for all that is material, open to sensory perception) is, for MacDonald, more emphatically than it is for either Newman or Carlyle, indispensable to our knowledge of God. For

It is by the body that we come into contact with Nature, with our fellow men, with all their revelations of God to us. It is through the body that we receive all the lessons of passion, of suffering, of love, of beauty, of science. It is through the body that we are both trained outwards from ourselves and driven inwards into our deepest selves to find God. (*US*, 1, p. 238.)

Nor is this so simply because knowledge begins in sense perception. It is also because there is an essential unity between body and soul, between the outer and the inner being of a thing, the spirit informing and giving shape to the body (cf. *US*, 3, pp. 52–3) expressed for instance in such statements as "the surface [of things] is the deepest after all; for through the surface . . . we have, as it were, a window into the depths of truth" ('Imagination', *Orts*, p. 258), a sentiment often reiterated even in his fiction.

The correspondence which MacDonald sees between "God's things" and God himself, and between their inner being and their outward manifestation, is then organic and not mechanical. This is an important point to remember when discussing the way in which he uses the term 'symbol' to designate the created universe, referring, for instance, to "the symbolism of nature" (*US*, 1, p. 101). But, since even this brief discussion has touched upon the way in which MacDonald envisages the nature of man and his relation to God and his creation, it is as well to pursue this further first.

One of the more interesting points to note is the way that

MacDonald speaks of the relationship which exists between man and nature. For MacDonald the world around man is "an outward figuration of the condition of his mind" ('The Imagination', *Orts*, pp. 3–5); it is "the human being turned inside out. . . . Or, to use another more philosophical and certainly no less poetic figure, the world is a sensuous analysis of humanity, and hence an inexhaustible wardrobe for the clothing of human thought." (*ibid*. pp. 9–10.) There is suggested here a kind of congruity between man and nature, by virtue of which man can understand and interpret the world around him, which is also to be found in the thought of Coleridge; a congruity which, in Coleridge, is based on the perception that both man and nature are informed by the same spirit of God.

Such an affirmation is also present in MacDonald, who can write of "the conjunction of the mind of man and the mind of God" ('Wordsworth's Poetry', *Orts*, p. 250). In a differing terminology, yet in one that, in spite of its reference to "shadows", does carry the same conviction, MacDonald claims "Our very beings and understandings and consciousnesses, though but shadows in regard to any perfection either of outline or operation, are yet shadows of his being, his understanding, his consciousness." (*US*, 3, p. 5.) But a fuller understanding of this relationship of man to God, through or in Christ, and also to nature, can be gained from what MacDonald has to say of the constitution of man's mind, and particularly of the imagination. This, as with Coleridge, will lead also into a consideration of how the creations of man relate to the creation of God.

Unlike Coleridge, MacDonald does not elaborate upon distinctions between Reason and Understanding, though at least on one occasion he does use the latter term in what appears to be an approximation to the Coleridgean sense of that word. The distinction he makes is between Imagination and Intellect, but, as Coleridge does, he also insists that a facultative vocabulary is not meant to suggest that these powers of man's mind are separable. The Intellect for MacDonald is, by and large, the logical, the analytic faculty; the Imagination, as we shall see is, as in Coleridge, allied to both insight and creativity, and it is clear that Imagination is of greater importance. Yet, in terminology not unlike that of Coleridge, MacDonald can say:

The work of the Higher . . . [God's imagination] must be discovered by the search of the Lower in degree which is yet similar in kind. Let us not be supposed to exclude the intellect from a share in every highest office. Man is not divided when the manifestations of his life are distinguished. The intellect 'is all in every part'. There were no imagination without intellect, however much it may appear that intellect can exist without imagination. What we mean to insist upon is, that in finding out the works of God, the Intellect must labour, workman-like, under the direction of the architect, Imagination. ('The Imagination', *Orts,* p. 11.)

What the relationship is between Intellect and Imagination in understanding the work of God, MacDonald amplifies in a further passage. He writes:

It is the farseeing imagination which beholds what might be a form of things, and says to the intellect: 'Try whether this may not be the form of these things'; which beholds or invents *a* harmonious relation of parts and operations, and sends the intellect to find out whether that be not *the* harmonious relation of them – that is, the law of the phenomenon it contemplates. Nay, the poetic relations themselves in the phenomenon may suggest to the imagination the law that rules its scientific life. Yea, more than this: we dare claim for the true, child-like, humble imagination, such an inward oneness with the laws of the universe that it possesses in itself an insight into the very nature of things. (*ibid*. pp. 12–13.)

In these two passages of what is, throughout, an important essay, there is a clear statement, not only of the final insepara-bility of intellect and imagination, and their mutual inter-dependence, but also of the two other crucial points I have already noted: that the imagination in man is one both with the creative power of God, and with the nature of things, by virtue of which likeness it has the possibility of insight into their inner being. This, even if MacDonald nowhere uses the Coleridgean distinction between primary and secondary Imagination, is not unlike the theory which Coleridge propounds concerning these two aspects of the one faculty (cf. ch. 2). Moreover MacDonald sees the function of imagination, so conceived, as producing harmony, a sentiment consonant with Coleridge's.

What, then, does MacDonald say of the products of this imagination, which is both insight and a creativity resembling that of God? The first thing to note is that, having said that imagination is "that faculty in man which is likest to the prime operation of the power of God, and has, therefore, been called the *creative* faculty (*op. cit.* p. 2) he is careful to point out that there is also a "necessary unlikeness" between the two, for man does not, strictly speaking, create (out of nothing) the forms in which he embodies his thought, but uses the forms which he already finds in nature. "The meanings are in those forms already. . . . The man has but to light the lamp within the form . . . [and] the shining thought makes the form visible, and becomes itself visible through the form." (*ibid.* p. 5.) Man's imagination, as MacDonald says, is the light which makes visible both the natural form for what it is and, thereby, his own thought also, of which that form then becomes the embodiment. The image of light MacDonald often uses in a way which certainly has parallels with Coleridge's suggestion of translucence, refraction and reflection (see e.g. *US*, 3, pp. 50–1) and in a way which also underlines the conflation of man's imagination with the light which is Christ in traditional Christian terminology.

Nevertheless it is not quite the way in which Coleridge talks of the activity of the imagination in relation to its products. Certainly the oneness which the imagination is said to create out of many things is not unlike the harmony which MacDonald sees as its effect; but the process whereby this is produced has, according to Coleridge, more of creative action than MacDonald's image of light would seem to give it here. Though there is no suggestion in Coleridge any more than in MacDonald that the imagination creates out of nothing, it is for the former, if we remember, a "reconciling and mediatory power" which "incorporates the reason in images of sense", and organizes the flux of the senses "by the permanence and self-encircling energies of reason". It "reveals itself in the balance or reconciliation of opposite or discordant qualities" (cf. above p. 44), and "dissolves, diffuses, dissipates, in order to recreate". (*BL*, 1, XIII, p. 202.) While light certainly possesses energy, and, especially as envisaged by both MacDonald and Coleridge, is not merely passive, Coleridge's terminology suggests that the products of the imagination are new wholes, even if their components are originally given, to be found in the world of nature created by God. This coalescing, coadunating power, MacDonald's concept of imagination seems to lack, and hence the products which result from its action, and the relationship which they bear to the world of nature must, perforce, be different. How significant this difference is to MacDonald's concept of symbol is the question which remains to be asked. It cannot be answered without a closer look at the ways in which he used the term.

As we have seen, one of the essential constituents of Coleridge's concept of symbol was the unity which must exist between the symbol and its referent, a unity which, while sometimes suggested by the other writers who have been considered, is never consistently maintained by any of them. In his *Life* of his father, Greville MacDonald suggests that for George MacDonald

a symbol was far more than an arbitrary outward and visible sign of an abstract conception: its high virtue lay in a common *substance* with the idea presented. . . . He would allow that the algebraic symbol, which concerns only the three-dimensioned, has no *substantial* relation to the unknown quantity; nor the 'tree where it falleth' to the man unredeemed, the comparison being false. But the rose, when it gives some glimmer of the freedom for which a man hungers, does so because of its *substantial* unity with the man, each in degree being a signature of God's immanence. (*Life*, p. 482.)

This report of a conversation reinforces the view, already described, that MacDonald held of the relationship between God, man and the world of nature, and suggests a Coleridgean concept of 'symbol', whose essential relationship to the referent is made possible because the world is thus constructed. It is regrettable, therefore, that MacDonald himself seems nowhere to propound his 'laws of symbolism', not to give a definition of 'symbol' as such. His actual uses of the terms are nowhere quite so clear-cut as these remarks of his son would lead us to hope (and even in those the distinctions are not easy to understand), though in the context of thought which has been outlined, something of the tenor of these statements can be caught.

Perhaps one of the most interesting instances of MacDonald's actual use of the relevant terms occurs in his essay 'The Mirrors of the Lord' published in 1889 in the third series of *Unspoken Sermons*. Referring to St Paul he writes:

What has been called his mysticism is at one time the exercise of the power of seeing, as by any spiritual refraction, truths that had not, perhaps have not, yet risen above the human horizon; at another, the

result of a wide-eyed habit of noting the analogies and correspondences between the concentric regions of creation; it is the working of the poetic imagination divinely alive, whose part is to foresee
and welcome the approaching truth; to discover the same principle in
things that look unlike; to embody things discovered in the forms and
symbols heretofore unused, and so present to other minds the deeper
truths to which those forms and symbols owe their being. (*US*, 3,
pp. 42–3.)

Here we can clearly see that the imagination, divinely alive,
has the dual function of insight – perceiving likeness in things
apparently unlike – and of creativity; embodying what it thus
discovers in new forms and symbols; symbols which are not
only the product of such an imagination, but which are also one
with that which they attempt to convey. This is clearly much
more Coleridgean. The oneness envisaged between such a
'symbol' and the 'real' world contemplated with imaginative
insight, may seem to be best conveyed in MacDonald's fantasy
Lilith. Here the 'real' world which Mr Vane, the central character, ordinarily inhabits, is expressly shown as being but one
aspect of the total reality, so that Mr Raven who, in the 'real'
world is a librarian (though even there he appears sometimes as
the raven he is named for, or as a sexton who transforms the
worms in the graveyard into butterflies), can say that he knows
the music of the piano in the drawing-room to be also the music
of the wild hyacinths which, in the 'other' world grow where the
piano is, "among the strings of it".[38] It is not only that Mr
Raven and, because of him, Mr Vane himself, can pass from the
one world into the other, which indeed they do, as if the worlds
were contingent; but it is also that the one world and the other,
both equally 'real', are contiguous: exist coextensively. Moreover while the world of the imagination is not to be equated
with a world beyond death, it is not meant as a representation of a heaven and hell – since it has its own shortcomings as well as its own perfections – it has, in MacDonald's
intentions, an affinity with the supernatural world which
the ordinary world of Mr Vane (our real world) seems to
lack. This world of imagination can therefore teach him about,
bring him into a contact with, that further supernatural world,
as well as give him a new apprehension of his own everyday
one, and in so doing mould and change his attitudes and
behaviour.

Such a concept of the affinity which the imaginatively created symbol (in this case the world of imagination described in
the story) has with the world inhabited by men, as well as with
the world, or being, of God, has much in common with
Coleridge's concept, even though it lacks some of the latter's
complexities. One thing, however, must be noted, if the comparison with Coleridge is to be pursued. While there is an
affinity between symbol and referent expressed in the above
quotation, that quotation pertains to the mysticism of Paul,
and hence to the Pauline letters which are, by implication, the
symbols referred to. My explication of the affinity has been
drawn from an example of secular literature, an extension of the
argument which is, I think, warranted by the terms Mac-
Donald uses. But it does raise two questions: does MacDonald
make any distinction between the Bible and other literary
products? and does he ever, explicitly, call any secular work of
art a 'symbol'? Are both 'symbols' in the same sense, and if so,
has the Bible any pre-eminence in its relationship to God, such
that the knowledge we gain from it is in any way different from
the knowledge we may gain from such works as MacDonald's
own *Lilith*? These, as we have seen, were questions left unresolved by Coleridge. For while considering that the Bible was
the only 'symbolic' presentation of history, and therefore the
source which, in this respect, gave us the most complete and
penetrating knowledge of the way in which God works within
the world of men, as well as of man's own nature, Coleridge did
not establish how the knowledge gained here was different from
that which might be gained from other works of the imagination which, unlike the derided histories, were truly symbols
themselves.

In reading through MacDonald's three series of *Unspoken
Sermons* and the essays in *Orts* it becomes evident that he seems
to have used the relevant terms principally as pertaining either
to nature or to parts of the scriptures. This is true even of his
essay 'The Imagination', as also of the later 'On the Fantastic
Imagination' which forms the addition in *A Dish of Orts*. In
England's Antiphon, which is a compilation of, and a commentary on, English religious lyrics, from the thirteenth century to
his own day, MacDonald uses the terms occasionally in a sense
which suggests that poems have a more profound, as well as an
obvious meaning, the relation between the latter and the

Dean Inge, George Tyrrell and George MacDonald

former not being artificial and conventional as it is in allegory. At times he seems to use the term 'symbol' as roughly equivalent to 'device', as in talking of the "symbol of his book" by which he means that when reading it we should liken the process to walking into a church, since in both we begin with what is least important and only gradually reach the central point.[39] Nevertheless he certainly does seem to maintain that a poem, while it is "the deepest man can utter" is also "a symbol of something deeper yet, of which he can perceive only a doubtful glimmer".[40] Given his theory of imagination, one can assume here that a poem is therefore a symbol in the defined sense.

But the most interesting references to symbols in *England's Antiphon* are to be found in MacDonald's discussion of George Herbert. Since the book is not easily available, fairly extended quotation will be necessary. Having discussed and praised a number of Herbert's poems for their matter MacDonald continues:

There can hardly be a doubt that his tendency to unnatural forms was encouraged by the increase of respect to symbol and ceremony shown at this period by some of the external powers of the church – Bishop Laud in particular. Had all, however, who delight in symbols, a power, like George Herbert's, of setting even within the horn lanterns of the more arbitrary of them, such a light of poetry and devotion that their dull sides vanish in its piercing shine, and we forget the symbol utterly in the truth which it cannot obscure, then indeed our part would be to take and be thankful. But there never has been even a living true symbol which the dulness of those who will see the truth only in the symbol has not degraded into the very cockatrice-egg of sectarianism. The symbol is by such always more or less idolized, and the light within more or less patronized. If the truth, for the sake of which all symbols exist, were indeed the delight of those who claim it, the sectarianism of the church would vanish. But men on all sides call that *the truth* which is but its form or outward sign – material or verbal, true or arbitrary, it matters not which – and hence come strife and divisions. (p. 186.)

Several points in this passage are worth considering. In the first place it is not entirely clear what MacDonald is thinking of when he talks of those symbols and ceremonies to which increased respect was being shown in George Herbert's time. Did he mean rituals and statues? Did he mean the verbal forms of worship, such as the Book of Common Prayer? The phrase

162

"symbol and ceremony" leads one to suspect that he was not using the term here in any very particular way. Secondly, it is clear that MacDonald does allow the existence of arbitrary symbols, that is to say, that he seems content to call some things which have an arbitrary connection to their referent 'symbols', which Coleridge would have repudiated. This we have already seen to be the case in the quotation from Greville MacDonald's *Life*, but here there is – so far – no indication of how we may distinguish the one from the other. Both may, indeed, be equally misleading, for in both we may concentrate on the outward form without regard to the truth which that form signifies (not embodies). Thus MacDonald here suggests the possibility, even in true symbols, of a separation between the symbol and its referent such that the perception of the symbol as symbol is not, at one and the same time, the perception of the truth it presents. He states, indeed, that in perceiving the truth "we forget the symbol utterly", which at least in emphasis differs from Coleridge's understanding of the way in which symbols convey truth, though forgetting is not so radical a process of rejection as the beyondness and sometimes the simple otherwhereness implied by Newman, and the total discarding advocated by Carlyle.

But more significant than either of these points is the implication in this passage that Herbert *illuminates* symbols already given, rather than creating his own; that he allows us to see certain forms as symbols, or allows us to see the light within them, rather than that, by a new fusion of apparently disparate elements, he presents us with a truth (or truths) which we would ordinarily be incapable of discerning so palpably for ourselves. It is not so much that the poem, the thing made, is the symbol, but that the poem, the thing made, is the light by which already existing symbols (those of nature, perhaps, or scripture) can be seen or can be made to reveal their truth. This is re-emphasized in the paragraph which immediately follows that quoted above:

Although George Herbert, however, could thus *illumine* (italics mine) all with his divine inspiration, we cannot help wondering whether, if he had betaken himself yet more to vital and less to half artificial symbols, the change would not have been a breaking of the pitcher and an outshining of the lamp. For a symbol may remind us of the truth and at the same time obscure it – present it, and dull its effect. It is the temple of nature and not the temple of the church, the things made by the hand of God and not the things made by the hands of man, that afford the truest symbols of truth. (pp. 186–7.)

From this it would seem – though the passage is not entirely unambiguous – that the obscuring of truth (an aspect of symbols which, it should be noted, MacDonald does not usually stress) is removed – more or less entirely, depending both on the nature of the symbol and the quality of the poet – when seen in the light of such a poet's imaginatively constructed poem. The poem, however, does not itself seem to be a symbol; its action, indeed, seems here to be that of removing the symbol entirely (breaking the pitcher) in order that the truth may be made more visible (the lamp will shine out). Pushed a little further, it would seem that MacDonald could think that a non-symbolic form, such as a poem, could at least help us to see the truth which such symbolic forms as the Bible and nature tended to obscure, a notion which would have accorded ill with Coleridge's views on the subject. While it is certainly doubtful that MacDonald would have thought that such non-symbolic re-statements as poems could ever replace the original symbolic presentation of truth, the metaphors he uses (of a pitcher which obscures the light and must be broken if the light is to shine out) could certainly lend support to those of his contemporaries who did think that the Bible should be superseded by a modern restatement of its meaning. The whole of this passage, therefore, illustrates not only the need for a greater clarity of thought, but points to the care with which metaphors must be chosen in this problematic area.

It does certainly seem that MacDonald's concept of the imagination as a light rather than as a power which fuses disparate elements into new wholes (as in Coleridge) is dominant, if not exclusive, in his thinking and does affect the way in which the products of the imagination are viewed by him. These in MacDonald are enlighteners of symbols, rather than, as in Coleridge, symbols themselves. If[41] this is so (if the products of the imagination are not symbols, as the Bible and nature are), then this also resolves the question of the relation of the Bible (and of course of nature) to other literary constructions: the latter convey knowledge of God only in that they help us to understand, to perceive, what the Bible already contains;

MacDonald

they do not, of themselves, give us such direct knowledge. This is in many ways, neat, but it is arrived at only by restricting the term 'symbol' in a non-Coleridgean way to the Bible, nature, and – it must be added – the sacraments of the eucharist and baptism, which also are explicitly called symbols by Mac-Donald in a further passage of his chapter on Herbert. While this might account for the undoubted fact that, as I have said, the actual vocabulary of 'symbols' is most often to be found in MacDonald in relation to scripture and nature, it does not account for those instances – however few – where the term 'symbol' is used with reference to other "words" which spring from the imagination, as, for instance, in the following passage:

All words, then, belonging to the inner world of the mind, are of the imagination, are originally poetic words. The better, however, that any such word is fitted for the needs of humanity, the sooner it loses its poetic aspect by commonness of use. It ceases to be heard as a symbol, and appears only as a sign. ('The Imagination', *Orts*, p. 9.)

Nor does this begin to resolve the further question now raised: in what way is the imaginative inspiration of scripture different from that of literature? Thus there would seem to be a kind of hiatus in MacDonald's concept of symbol. There is, on the one hand, a tendency to see the Bible, nature and the imaginative works of men as 'symbols' in a sense apparently similar to that of Coleridge, and on the other hand, a tendency to accord that status only to "the works of God's hands", among which the Bible and the two sacraments must be counted. In this latter view the works of imagination are only aids to seeing the truth conveyed by these symbols, chiefly, it would seem, by throwing light on the obscurities inevitable in the symbolic presentation itself. This last seems a non-Coleridgean understanding of the term 'symbol' since Coleridge, while he did not think that symbols were necessarily easy to perceive for what they were, would not have allowed that a statement, not itself a symbol, could help us to apprehend the truth integrally involved in the symbol itself. Though MacDonald speaks of the sacraments of the eucharist and baptism in terms which accord well with the Coleridgean definition, saying that

They are in themselves symbols of the truths involved in facts they commemorate (*England's Antiphon*, p. 187),

165

there are, even in his discussion of biblical truths, certain other elements which make one wonder how firm his grasp was of Coleridge's concept. Thus, in the essay 'The Mirrors of the Lord', already quoted from above (p. 159) where there seems to be affinity between his thought and Coleridge's, Mac-Donald can also write:

Our mirroring of Christ, then, is one with the presence of his spirit in us. The idea, you see, is not the reflection, the radiating of the light of Christ on others, though that were a figure lawful enough; but the taking into, and having in us, his working in the changing of us.

That the thing signified transcends the sign, outreaches the figure, is no discovery; the thing figured always belongs to a high stratum, to which the simile serves but as a ladder; when the climber has reached it, 'he then unto the ladder turns his back'. It is but according to the law of symbol, that the thing symbolized by the mirror should have properties far beyond those of leaded glass or polished metal, seeing that it is a live soul understanding that which it takes into its deeps – holding it, and conscious of what it holds. It mirrors by its will to hold in its mirror. Unlike its symbol, it can hold not merely the outward visual resemblance, but the inward likeness of the person revealed by it. (US, 3, pp. 50–1.)

There are three points of departure here from the Coleridgean concept. There seems, in the first place, to be a willingness to speak of symbols as figurative in the same sense as similes – and one should remember here Coleridge's *toto genere* distinction. There is, further, more than a suggestion that a symbol can, after all, be dispensed with if, as seems reasonable, "simile" and "symbol" are here interchangeable. For the symbol or simile is a ladder which helps us to reach the truth, but when the climber has reached it, "he then unto the ladder turns his back" – like the man in Plato's cave turning his back on the shadow play, which, as we saw, was not Coleridge's understanding of the way symbols work. Finally Coleridge could never have written that one distinction between the living soul and the mirror which is its symbol is that the latter shows "merely the outward visual resemblance" of the former, for it is the essence of the Coleridgean symbol (as MacDonald himself, indeed, suggests elsewhere) that it should be able to present and hold within itself the inward reality of the truth it embodies. Of course a mirror presents only the outward appearance, though it might sometimes do so in ways which reveal something about a person which is not always obvious in the more animated, and less self-conscious, face directly turned to the world. But in so far as it does but the former and fails to do the latter, it is *not* a symbol in Coleridge's sense. Here MacDonald seems to misunderstand seriously the direction of Coleridge's thought, in spite of the fact that the way he speaks even here has Coleridge-like overtones.[42]

There seems, then, to be something of an ambivalence in MacDonald's concept of symbol as there was in both Carlyle's and Newman's, though his thought generally is more like that of Coleridge than theirs is. This, again, seems to me to point to a neglect of Coleridge's statements on this subject, even by those who otherwise seem to have understood and appreciated his thinking. MacDonald, indeed, like Inge, quotes Carlyle and not Coleridge when writing in a vein which sounds sufficiently Coleridgean. It is to Carlyle's *Past and Present* that he turns after saying in his essay 'The Imagination' that man

cannot look around him long without perceiving some form, aspect, or movement of nature, some relation between its forms, or between such and himself which resembles the state or motion within him. This he seizes as the symbol, as the garment or body of his invisible thought, presents it to his friend, and his friend understands him. Every word so employed with a new meaning is henceforth, in its new character, born of the spirit and not of the flesh, born of the imagination and not of the understanding, and is henceforth submitted to new laws of growth and modification. (*Orts*, p. 8.)

While explicit quotation is not necessarily the only admissible evidence of one man's influence upon another, it is a pity that MacDonald did not pay more overt attention to Coleridge's concept of 'symbol' since he often seems to echo something of his sentiments. He can insist that God's idea(s) are embodied in things: that the "idea of God is the flower; his idea is not the botany of the flower" (*US*, 3, p. 65); he can call "the water itself, that dances, and sings and slakes the wonderful thirst" a "symbol and picture of that draught for which the woman of Samaria made her prayer to Jesus" because "the water is its own self, its own truth, and is therein a truth of God". (*ibid.* pp. 67–8.) He can, at least when discussing the purport of the secret and individual name to be given to each man by God, say that this "mystic symbol has for its centre of significance the fact of the personal individual relation of every man to his God". (*US*, 1,

p. 109.) He can suggest that symbols can be seen and understood as such not by the "mere intellect" but by those who live with the life of Christ (*US*, 2, p. 41). These are all elements in the Coleridgean concept of symbol. But there seems to me much of importance that MacDonald has not apprehended and because of this I cannot, in the end, agree that, as far as the exposition of the concept of 'symbol' is concerned, MacDonald begins where Coleridge leaves off.[43] That task still remains to be accomplished.

6
SOME CONCLUSIONS

At the beginning of this book, I suggested that the uses of the term 'symbol' and its cognates were so diverse, the meanings therefore so varied, and the theological implications of the word so heterogeneous (though too often assumed to be of a particular kind), that in most cases where the term or any of its cognates occurs the first question to be asked is: what is the meaning with which it is being used by this writer and in this instance? This is rarely a simple question since the terms seem so often to be inextricably bound up with the whole *Weltanschauung* of the writer using them and one may therefore at the end ask what is to be gained from the effort involved? One obvious benefit, pertinent to theological arguments, is that those involved in discussions where the terms are apposite will be less readily accused of maintaining a position which they do not actually subscribe to just because they use the term 'symbolical' in certain contexts. But a study of the actual uses of the terms in question does do more than serve as a warning: it also uncovers areas where more clear thinking is required if present theological discussion is to profit by, and contribute to, the current interest in 'symbolization'.

If Coleridge has loomed largest in this study, it is not only because some yardstick of comparison was necessary in a confused situation. It is also because, despite his notorious weaknesses and foibles, he displayed this one hallmark of a genuine philosopher: namely, the inability to make his point about any one important issue without indicating – or claiming to indicate – its bearing upon everything else; and because, in doing so, he realized, as so many others did not, the centrality of a concept of symbol. While neither his suggestion that the order of the

universe is essentially a symbolic one, nor his conception of
Christ as the embodiment of Reason, nor his distinction between re-creative Imagination and man's other intellectual
powers, is entirely original, yet, in the way he presents them
and attempts to combine them, he does succeed in suggesting
new possible arrangements of our basic categories, metaphysical and epistemological, as well as religious; and he does show
that attention to the precise nature of symbols and how they are
created is essential in any such endeavour.

The sketchiness and fragility of the intellectual structure in
which Coleridge's bold project was embodied goes a long way
towards explaining the neglect or misunderstanding of his
actual pronouncements on the nature of the symbol by subsequent thinkers, including those who, at first sight, seem to owe
most to him. But the failure to give weight to Coleridge's ideas,
and to apply and test them methodically over a wide range of
instances, was also symptomatic of a much deeper and more
pervasive weakness in nineteenth century English thought,
both religious and philosophical. For, whatever the doubts
which we now recognise to have existed beneath the Victorian
belief in progress, the compulsion to search for the ultimate
bases of our knowledge in any sphere was, with perhaps a few
exceptions, curiously peripheral and ill-sustained. No one who
has read carefully the authors dealt with in this book can doubt
the strength of their religious needs and doubts and longings, or
can fail to appreciate the intellectual energy with which they
sought to illuminate certain aspects of spiritual and intellectual
life. But the most basic epistemological issues, including the
nature of our knowledge of God, were not at the centre of their
concern. Because of this, they and most of their contemporaries, were ill-equipped to deal effectively with the direction
of thought which Coleridge had indicated in his own incom-
parably inadequate way. Perhaps we in the twentieth century,
with our greater scepticism, are better able to see the importance of the questions raised, and have a greater need to pursue
them. Whether we have the philosophical acumen, and the
vision necessary 'only to connect' – whether, indeed, some such
connections as Coleridge indicated can be more firmly made – I
will not venture to speculate. A summary of the ways in which
Coleridge's near contemporaries and those succeeding writers
who used the terms varied from him in their concepts of

'symbol' will serve to highlight the confusions which will exist.

Carlyle, I have suggested, though originally influenced by his study of Goethe and German Romantic thought, and though reacting against much in English eighteenth century philosophy and theology, both of which were starting-points also for Coleridge, differed from Coleridge in his concept of 'symbol' in several important ways. Though, again like Coleridge, Carlyle thought of nature as a 'symbol' of God, the relationship between symbol and referent which the term designated for him here was that of shadow rather than, as in Coleridge, embodiment. Nature, as symbol, was something through and beyond which God might be apprehended, but in which he was concealed rather than revealed. This, together with Carlyle's division of symbols into "extrinsic" and "intrinsic", and the fact that he had no theory of how symbols were created, and therefore no clear criterion for distinguishing between a real and an arbitrary relationship between symbol and referent, resulted in his tendency to think of all symbols as discardable and replaceable; as serving sometimes to suggest the referent, but only for a time; while the propensity of all symbols was to grow fainter, to degenerate into riddles, to become, with time, a hindrance, rather than a help to, and indispensable mode of, knowing the referent. To retain their usefulness symbols, like clothes, must be more or less frequently changed as they are outgrown and become meaningless; symbols have no permanent value since they are not vitally connected with the referent in a way which man discovers rather than invents. This, for Carlyle, was true of theological formulations, which were also 'symbols'. These, too, must be periodically refurbished and have no intrinsic capacity to reveal to us, or to bring us into contact with, the God who is their ultimate subject. Even the Gospels, which Carlyle still thinks of in terms of "biography", though having greater permanence than most other symbolical constructions, do not entirely escape the possibility of radical replacement, whilst Jesus as a person becomes, for Carlyle, only one among a line of "heroes".

Newman, although in his concept of the relationship which obtains between nature and God, he is more like Carlyle than he is like Coleridge, and although he appears to have misunderstood Coleridge's meaning of the term 'symbol', and used it with reference to him in a quite misleading way, is yet nearer to Coleridge than to Carlyle in this: that symbols for him are language constructs which, if approached aright, are always capable of bringing us into touch with, giving us real and as if direct knowledge of, their subject, which, in the case of dogmas, is God. They have a permanent value, and give us constitutive and not only regulative knowledge; they tell us not only that a reality exists beyond them, but something about that reality which is, however inadequate and perfectible, yet not erroneous or misleading. Symbols are, for Newman as for Coleridge, vitally connected to the Idea which they present. The Idea is not only a mental entity, a mere counterpart of the language from which it may be derived, but has an existence apart from, and as it were 'larger than', the 'symbols' in which it is presented, and in which alone it can be known and explored. And Newman, like Coleridge, affirms this because he holds that language can, even in cases of quite ordinary, this-worldly, discourse, give us quasi-experiential knowledge of an extra-mental Idea. He is frequently on the verge of recognising that reflection upon how we use certain words can give us knowledge of more than their precise non-verbal counterparts.

But there is, nevertheless, an important difference in Coleridge's and in Newman's conceptions of what a symbol, even as a language construct, is; a difference which is found in the answer to the question: how are symbols created or constructed? For Coleridge, man-made symbols are the products of the Imagination (in his sense) and thus of the repetition by man of the creative act of God. Each symbol, therefore, is a thing important in itself, and whole; it is a part of that greater whole of the universe (or art) only because each is an embodiment of that same dynamic, all-pervasive, organic principle of development. But Newman, who has no concept of nature as symbolic – except as "shadow" but not as "embodiment" – has also no thought of man-made symbols as such creative parallels of nature. Imaginative creativity (however imagination is defined) does not give rise to symbols, except insofar as something more than mechanical reasoning is necessary even in what seem like purely deductive processes. A given statement, or series of statements, is, indeed, the development of an Idea, but not the embodiment of that developmental principle by which both nature and true art live and move and have their being. Newman's usual – and indeed basic – examples of development are mathematical, and not 'artistic', as the context of his use of the term 'symbol' shows. This is not to say that one symbol is connected to another merely by a process of deduction: each, Newman also wishes to maintain, is also 'somehow' connected to the Idea itself; but *that* connection remains vague; it is the deductive relation of proposition to consequent which is dominant. Hence, symbols "partake" of that which they present (the Idea) in different ways for Newman and for Coleridge; and for Newman, each 'symbol' is also essentially a part of a system, these parts being connected to each other by a process at least something like logical explication.

This, at least, is true as far as Newman's concept of dogma as symbols is concerned. When calling the Church and sacraments "symbols", Newman seemed to have in mind only that aspect of 'symbol' which he has in common with Coleridge, namely, that symbols present and reveal, and bring us into contact with, the reality which they embody. But in this case Newman has no theory of how such an embodiment occurs. The Church and sacraments are not developments of the Idea in the same way that dogmas are, and there is no indication why both should be called 'symbols': to say only that it is because both are developments is to forget what a heterogeneity of processes *that* word covers. Newman, while using the term both of language and of non-linguistic entities, provides us with less explanation than Coleridge does for designating *both* as 'symbolical'.

Inge's concept of the 'symbol', more than either Carlyle's or Newman's, was, like that of Coleridge, backed by, and attached to, a Trinitarian concept of God, who was present within all creation by his indwelling spirit, and who was also (as in Coleridge) the 'light' by which men could discern his presence therein. Sharing both Coleridge's predilection for Plato and Platonism, and the Logos doctrine found both there and in the writings of St John, Inge also shared something of Coleridge's "theory of mind". Perhaps because of this his notion of what a 'symbol' is, and how it functions, comes close to the Coleridgean concept than anyone else's. Yet Inge also speaks as if, for him, the connection between symbol and referent could, after all, be tenuous and impermanent; and, like Carlyle rather than Coleridge, he sees symbols not only as inadequate revelations of the referent, but as (more positively) concealments of it, notions quite alien to the Coleridgean theory.

Tyrrell, I have suggested, differs from Coleridge because, for him, the term 'symbolical' seems to function principally as an affirmation that a relationship so designated cannot be described. Thus in Tyrrell's work the precision which Coleridge had attempted to attribute to symbols and symbolical relationships (however complex, cumbersome and imperfectly detailed; however, even, lacking in complete consistency such a theory might be) is missing. This, though at times it seems, and probably is, due to a lack of philosophical acumen, is, in the last analysis, something more positive. While for Coleridge a symbol and a symbolical relationship is a particular kind of thing, and a particular kind of relationship: for Tyrrell, on the contrary, it would seem that a symbol is a symbol precisely by virtue of the fact that its relationship to its counterpart is unknowable.

Finally, the study of MacDonald shows affinities with Coleridge which all the other writers considered lack. But while he seems to have insisted on the substantial relationship between symbol and referent clearly evident in Coleridge, the imprecisions and obscurities of MacDonald's use of the term and the lack of any real attempt at explication show that a much more explicit attention to the concept of symbol, and to the implications of Coleridge's theory, is still necessary.

Nor is the attention to the concept of 'symbol' itself the only remaining problem. Or rather, what attention to the concept of symbol shows is that the term is associated with other concepts which themselves lack clarity and which need to be made more explicit, when used in relation with the vocabulary of symbolization. Two such are the concepts of 'history' and of 'analogy'. We have seen that, for Coleridge, a 'symbolic' presentation of events is the only one which is properly historical: that is to say, it is the only one which not only presents events which actually occurred and as they occurred, but which also exhibits the inward pattern and significance of such events – as is seen in Coleridge's extended remarks about the narrative of the fall. In doing this, 'symbols' are sources of revelation, creations in which we can apprehend the way things *are*, the way God acts and what he is. To say then, for instance, that the gospel narratives of Christ's life, death and resurrection are 'symbolical', or even that Christ himself is a 'symbol' in the Coleridgean sense, is not to deny their historicity.

Although, as I have said, the juxtaposition of 'symbol' and 'history' in Carlyle is nowhere explicit, and although 'symbols' are, for him, essentially evanescent, yet it could be said that for him, too, a narrative which is 'symbolical' is not necessarily fictitious in the sense that the events upon which it is based did not happen, or that Christ was not a historical figure. Clothes, after all, usually clothe a body, or at least hang on a peg. In so far, therefore, as Carlyle suggests that Christianity, and perhaps even the gospels themselves, are 'symbols', he does not thereby impugn their factual content, but rather suggests only that, since they are interpretations of facts, and not merely catalogues of facts, they may be replaced by other interpretations. For Carlyle all genuine history is *an* interpretation of facts, and Christianity is, in this sense, history. If Carlyle at times seemed to believe that the cataloguing of facts within any interpretation was possible (the vulgarly empiricist nineteenth century concept of what 'history' should be) he also thought that it was a futile pursuit, and he considered the Christian presentation of facts to be an altogether more noble endeavour. That the Christian interpretation of facts was not definitive and absolute was a characteristic which it shared with *all* true history, and not something which made it 'unhistorical'. There is therefore no greater opposition between Christianity as symbolical and Christianity as history in Carlyle than there is in Coleridge.

Unfortunately, such a conclusion is apt to make us oblivious to the differences in the concept of 'symbol' involved. The discussion of Coleridge and Carlyle, however, should have shown that these are not to be so easily disregarded. What must be stressed therefore – and indeed this is the crucial, but too often forgotten point in any account of 'symbol' in relation to 'history' – is that the term 'history' is as much a variable as is the term 'symbol'. Of this variability, too, a comparison of Coleridge and Carlyle would provide a good example. For while both would have subscribed to the view that all genuine history involved interpretation, only Coleridge saw some 'history' – paradigmatically the Bible which he therefore called 'symbol' – as being the *proper* interpretative presentation of events of human life. This, Coleridge claimed, could be so, for in the Bible man's essentially subjective interpretation of objective facts coincided with the inner reality and intended patterning of those facts themselves: in the Bible both the interpretative presentation, and the original creative and directive force of the events, were but two ways in which the same spirit of Christ – the Word of God – was present and active in the created world of nature, man, and his affairs. For Carlyle, however, the Bible, even though the Word of God and therefore in some sense sacrosanct, could not be history in the same definitive sense, since Carlyle, lacking Coleridge's theory of the Imagination, could not but consider all interpretations of events – however inspired – as essentially successive and supplementary. Obviously here there is a profound difference in what 'real history' amounts to. While this difference remains unexplicit and unexplored no clear account of the 'symbolical' in its relation to the 'historical' can emerge. For this, a coherent philosophy of history is as necessary as a consistent theory of symbol. It certainly could be said of both Inge and Tyrrell that one reason why it is never altogether clear whether, by their uses of the term 'symbol' in relation to creed and gospel, they intended to deny the historicity of the events there recorded is that their theories of history are as uncertain as their uses of the term 'symbol' are imprecise.

In the preceding chapters I have also referred to the relationship which may obtain for a given writer between the concepts of 'analogy' and 'symbol'. But here, again, the difficulty arises in determining whether any given concept of 'symbol' and 'symbolic language' is at variance with the theory that some of our language about God is 'analogical'. As in the case of 'history' and 'symbol', this is not only because the term 'symbolic', as descriptive of language, can vary in the ways that I have outlined. It arises also – as, again, the references to it in this book have indicated – from a failure to agree on what is meant by 'analogy', and 'analogical language', and on the assumptions underlying our uses of these terms. Into the full implications of this problem I am not equipped to enter. But, since both theories of 'symbol' and 'symbolic language', and theories of 'analogy' and 'analogical language', in so far as they are theological terms, often involve notions of man's relationship to God, and the knowledge we may be said to have of God, what I hope an exposition of the very different concepts of such relationship and such knowledge in theories of 'symbolic language' may have done is to provide some firmer basis for comparison and contrast for those who are interested in determining the theological merits and demerits of 'symbolism' as opposed to 'analogy'. I would suggest that the most one can say is that such and such a theory of 'symbolism', or such a writer's notion of 'symbolic language' is at variance with this or that theory of analogy and analogical language, whilst overall generalizations are, on close inspection, bound to appear absurd.

What is true in the cases where the term 'symbolism' is used in connection with history and analogy is true also of all the questions with regard to the meaning of the term 'symbol' raised in Chapter 1. No general answer to them is possible: not only does the meaning of the term 'symbol' vary, but the correlative terms with which it is associated are themselves loosely and indifferently used. If, therefore, we intend that our own employment of the term 'symbol' and its cognates should be precise and informative, we must not only take care that we give them a specific meaning, and use it consistently; we must also realize that we will not be able to do so unless we are equally clear as to what we mean by such terms as 'history', 'analogy', 'experience', 'knowledge', 'inadequacy' and so forth.

But such questions of definition are parts of wider problems. As we have seen again and again in the course of this book, such central epistemological questions as 'What is meant by calling some of our knowledge inadequate or imperfect?' and 'What is the connection between inadequacy and, on the one hand, incompleteness or partiality, and on the other hand, vagueness merging into sheer vacuity?'[1] constantly obtrude into any serious attempt to pin down the meanings that are being given to the term 'symbol' in particular contexts. Yet, in spite of the twentieth century preoccupation with both symbolism and epistemology, such questions as these – or, one could add, the question of the relationship between intuition and abstraction, or of what we can mean by saying that something both reveals and conceals at one and the same time – have been curiously neglected. It is to such questions that attention must be given if the term 'symbol' is to attain any useful epistemological function in religious discourse today. And to this end it would not be inappropriate to pursue further even than Coleridge did the questions why and how it is that in certain works of art, in certain language constructs, we do seem to recognize.

a translucence of the special in the individual, or of the general in the special, or of the universal in the general.

NOTES

INTRODUCTION

1 For a discussion of this point see M. H. Abrams, *The Mirror and the Lamp*.
2 See W. J. Bate, *Coleridge*, p. 64.
3 See Roger Sharrock, 'Fables and Symbols' in *New Blackfriars*, vol. 50, no. 585, p. 233.
4 I refer to John Coulson, *Newman and the Common Tradition*, which is further discussed in Chapter 4.
5 See Stephen Prickett, *Romanticism and Religion*, ch. 8.
6 See G. Egner, *Apologia Pro Charles Kingsley*.

CHAPTER 1. THE CONCEPT OF SYMBOL

Our Present Discontents

1 C. S. Peirce, *Collected Papers*, vol. 2, Book II, ch. 3, para. 307, p. 172.
2 Martin Foss, *Symbol and Metaphor*; H. H. Price, *Thinking and Experience*; S. K. Langer, 'On a new definition of symbol' in *Philosophical Sketches*, 1956; Brand Blanshard, 'Symbolism' in *Religious Experience and Truth: A Symposium*, ed. Sidney Hook; F. W. Dillistone, 'Introduction' in *Myth and Symbol*, ed. Dillistone.
3 Lyman Bryson, 'The Quest for Symbol' in *Symbols and Values: An Initial Study*, ed. Bryson *et al*.
4 Dorothy D. Lee, 'Symbolization and Value' in *Symbols and Values: An Initial Study*.
5 S. K. Langer, *Philosophical Sketches*, p. 60.
6 E. I. Watkins, *A Philosophy of Form*, p. 366 and note.
7 Philip Wheelwright, *The Burning Fountain: A Study in the Language of Symbolism*.
8 David Cox, 'Psychology and Symbolism' in *Myth and Symbol*, p. 56.

9 C. G. Jung, *Collected Works*, ed. H. Read, vol. 6, *Psychological Types* (tr. R. F. C. Hull), p. 473.

Some Examples from Literature and their Theological Relevance

10 *The Works of William Blake*, ed. E. J. Ellis and W. B. Yeats, vol. 1, p. 239.

Some Confusions in Theology

11 See for instance such books as L. F. Barmann, *Baron Friedrich von Hügel and the Modernist Crisis*; Alfred Fawkes, *Studies in Modernism*; J. J. Heaney, *The Modernist Crisis: von Hügel*; J. Lewis May, *Father Tyrrell and the Modernist Movement*; M. D. Petre, *Modernism: Its Failures and Fruits*; Paul Sabatier, *Modernism* (which includes a translation of the *Pascendi Gregis* encyclical); J. Ratté, *Three Modernists*; and particularly the work of A. R. Vidler, as well as others quoted in the text, or listed in the bibliography.

12 M. L. Cozens, *A Handbook of Heresies*. First published, London, 1928, reprinted in an abridged edition as late as 1960, where the relevant passage (pp. 98–9, ed. 1928, p. 89, ed. 1960) remains unchanged.

13 Maisie Ward, *The Wilfrid Wards and the Transition*, vol. 2: *Insurrection versus Resurrection*, Appendix B, p. 560.

14 D. G. James, *The Romantic Comedy: An Essay on English Romanticism*, p. 207.

15 *Ibid.*

16 Edwyn Bevan, *Symbolism and Belief* (The Gifford Lectures 1933–4), pp. 223ff.

17 From Marcel Hébert's *Profession de foi du Vicaire Savoyard*, written in 1894, but unpublished. See Albert Houtin, *Un Prêtre Symboliste: Marcel Hébert 1851–1916* (PaMS 1925), p. 92. I quote it in the translation given by Bevan, *Symbolism and Belief*, p. 226.

18 Francis Bacon, *The Advancement of Learning*, London (Heron Books), reprint of 1861 ed. See also L. C. Knights' essay 'Bacon and the Seventeenth Century Dissociation of Sensibility' in *Explorations*.

19 Eliot first used the phrase in his 1921 essay on 'The Metaphysical Poets' in the *Times Literary Supplement*. In his later essay on Milton, first delivered as the Henrietta Hertz Lecture to the British Academy on 26 March 1947, he recognized (with surprise) that the phrase had caught on, and that the "causes" for this "dissociation of sensibility" were much more complex than he had first envisaged. See T. S. Eliot, *Selected Prose*, Penguin Books, 1953, pp. 117 and 139.

20 See further: Thomas Silkstone, *Religion, Symbolism and Meaning*, pp. 41–7, for a discussion of Thomist criticisms of symbolism, especially those of P. M. de Munnyck and M. T-L. Penido.

CHAPTER 2. THE TERM 'SYMBOL' AND ITS COGNATES IN THE THOUGHT OF COLERIDGE

Abbreviations used:
AR   *Aids to Reflection* (*Complete Works*, ed. Shedd, 1884, vol. 1).
BL   *Biographia Literaria* (2 vols.), ed. J. Shawcross, 1967. This edition also contains the essays 'On the Principles of Genial Criticism'; 'Fragment of an Essay on Beauty'; and 'On Poesy or Art', to which reference is made in this chapter.
CL   *Collected Letters* (2 vols.), ed. E. L. Griggs, 1956.
F   *The Friend* (2 vols.), ed. B. Rooke, 1969.
N   *The Notebooks of Samuel Taylor Coleridge* (2 double vols.: text and notes), ed. K. Coburn, 1957 and 1961.
PL   *The Philosophical Lectures of Samuel Taylor Coleridge*, ed. K. Coburn, 1949.
Shedd *Complete Works* (7 vols.), ed. Shedd, 1884.
SM   *The Statesman's Manual* (*Complete Works*, ed. Shedd, vol. 1).
TT   *Table Talk*. Any edition; the date of the entry is given.
Capitalization
When referring to Coleridge's concepts of Understanding, Reason, Imagination, Ideas, I have used capital letters for these terms, although Coleridge is, in this respect, inconsistent.

The Context of Thought
1 See, for instance, Lecture 2, p. 106.
2 J. A. Appleyard, *Coleridge's Philosophy of Literature*, p. 252.
3 E.g. on the fly-leaf to a copy of 1816 edition of *The Statesman's Manual* belonging to James Gilman.
4 E.g. *F*, vol. 1, p. 112.
5 E.g. *AR*, p. 241. For a fuller discussion of the relation of Reason to Ideas see Owen Barfield, *What Coleridge Thought*, ch. 10.
6 *SM*, p. 484. See also *AR*, p. 219n.
7 The terms 'regulative' and 'constitutive' are Kantian. 'Ideas' for Kant are not objects of thought, but rather the concerns, the problems of what he calls Reason. An Idea for Kant would be constitutive if our grasp of it provided (or constituted) a sufficient ground for affirming the existence or special nature of any particular fact or feature of the world. But Ideas, even if they do not give us such sufficient grounds, do stimulate and direct, and in this sense 'regulate' our further thinking towards some comprehension of the totality of the universe, the essence of the soul and God.

Coleridge has something of Kant in mind in his own use of all these terms, but he is more affirmative than Kant. Very roughly, the term 'constitutive' for Coleridge meant 'having the power to make a thing what it is', and the term 'regulative' meant 'enunciating the laws of its being'.

8 Letter of 10 September 1802, *CL*, 2, p. 459.
9 Letter to Richard Sharp, 15 January 1804, *CL*, 2, p. 1034.
10 Quoted by Kathleen Coburn in the 'Notes' to *Philosophical Lectures*, p. 403, note 45, from MS Egerton 2826, i.e. vol. II of the *Treatise on Logic*.
11 'On Poesy or Art', *BL*, 2, p. 257.

Coleridge's Concept of 'Symbol'

12 *SM*, p. 437, cf. p. 465.
13 Punctuation here as in the Coburn edition. ⟨ ⟩ indicates an uncertain reading.
14 See *CL*, 2, p. 1034. Fancy, according to Coleridge, works by association only, and pays heed merely to outward and superficial resemblances, since it is allied not to Reason but to the Understanding.
15 For further discussion of this point see Prickett, *Coleridge and Wordsworth*.
16 'Lectures on Shakespeare and other Dramatists' 8, Shedd, 4, p. 623.
17 Mary Rahme, 'Coleridge's Concept of Symbolism', *Studies in English Literature 1500–1900*, 9: 4, 623.
18 A. S. Gerard, *English Romantic Poets: Ethos, Structure and Symbol in Coleridge, Wordsworth, Shelley and Keats*, p. 56.
19 Cf. Colossians ii. 17.

Some Final Reflections

20 Patricia Ward, 'Coleridge's Critical Theory of Symbol' in *Texas Studies in Literature and Language*, 8: 1, 15ff.
21 Norman Fruman, *The Damaged Archangel*.
22 Thomas MacFarland, *Coleridge and the Pantheist Tradition*.

CHAPTER 3. SOME CONTEMPORARIES OF COLERIDGE
– CHIEFLY CARLYLE

Hazlitt, De Quincey and Others

CW The Collected Writings of Thomas De Quincey, ed. David Masson, Edinburgh, 1889–1890.

1 The lecture was delivered in 1857. See *The Complete Prose Works of Matthew Arnold*, ed. R. H. Super, vol. 1, *On the Classical Tradition*: 'On the Modern Element in Literature', p. 22.

2 See *Coleridge: The Critical Heritage*, ed. J. R. de J. Jackson, p. 255.

3 J. S. Mill, *Collected Works*, vol. 12, *The Early Letters*, ed. F. E. Mineka; Letter 102 dated 15.4.1834 to John Pringle Nichol.

4 Mill's *Essays on Literature and Society*, ed. J. B. Schneewind; 'On Tennyson's Poems', p. 134.

5 Stephen Prickett, *Coleridge and Wordsworth: The Poetry of Growth*, ch. 1.

6 See Thomas De Quincey, *CW*, 8. Postscript to essay on 'The System of the Heavens as revealed by Lord Rose's Telescope', entitled 'On the relations of the Bible to merely human science'.

7 C. R. Sanders, *Coleridge and the Broad Church Movement*. See particularly chs. 7 and 8.

8 1842. The dedicatory letter is to H. N. C. Coleridge.

9 There was a series of exchanges between Maurice and Mansel, first on the interpretation of the phrase 'eternal punishment' (1854); and later as a result of Mansel's Bampton Lectures of 1858. Maurice's arguments against Mansel are to be found in *What is Revelation?* (1859) and *A Sequel to 'What is Revelation?'* (1860).

10 *The Claims of the Bible and Science* (1863).

11 Memoir of Mr Stephenson of Lynsham, c. 1838, in J. F. Maurice's *Life of F. D. Maurice*, vol. 1, p. 147.

12 Letter to Daniel Macmillan 22.5.1834, concerning the 2nd edition of *The Kingdom of Christ. Life*, vol. 1, p. 340.

13 See, for instance, A. R. Vidler's discussion of this in his *The Theology of F. D. Maurice*.

Carlyle

All the references to Carlyle are to the Centenary edition (1896–1899). The abbreviations used are as follows:
CME Critical and Miscellaneous Essays, vols. 1, 2, 3.
HH Heroes and Heroworship.
SR Sartor Resartus.

14 Basil Willey, *Nineteenth Century Studies*.

15 Reprinted in *CME*, 2, pp. 56–82.
16 'Characteristics' (1831), *CME*, 3, p. 4.
17 See *Life of Sterling*, ch. 8, p. 60.
18 Thomas MacFarland, *Coleridge and the Pantheist Tradition*.
19 Carlyle, like Coleridge, repudiated materialism, but he went further than Coleridge in a correspondent repudiation of *matter* itself, as a *Notebook* entry indicates:

> I think I have got rid of Materialism: Matter no longer seems to be so ancient, so unsubduable, so certain and palpable as Mind. I am Mind: whether matter or not, I know not – and care not. (Quoted by George Levine in *Boundaries of Fiction*, p. 26, from *Two Notebooks of Thomas Carlyle*, ed. Charles Eliot Norton, p. 151.)

20 See George Levine, *The Boundaries of Fiction*.
21 E.g. *SR*, 3, iii, p. 179. 'Time . . . at length defaces or even desecrates them [i.e. symbols] and symbols, like all terrestrial garments, wax old.'
22 E.g. *SR*, 3, ix, p. 215.
23 On this subject see Hill Shine, *Carlyle's Fusion of Poetry, History and Religion*.
24 See 'On History' (1830), *CME*, 2, pp. 88–9.
25 See for instance what Carlyle has to say of the writing of history in the opening pages of 'The Diamond Necklace', *CME*, 3, pp. 324–30.

CHAPTER 4. NEWMAN

Abbreviations used:

Apologia	*Apologia Pro Vita Sua*, ed. C. F. Harrold, 1947.
Grammar	*Essay in Aid of a Grammar of Assent*, ed. C. F. Harrold, 1947
LC	*Letters and Correspondence of John Henry Newman during his Life in the English Church*, ed. A. Mozley, 2 vols., 1898.
PN	*The Philosophical Notebook*, 2 vols., ed. E. Sillem, 1972, revised A. Boekraad.
University Sermons	*University Sermons: Fifteen sermons preached before the University of Oxford 1826–1843*, 3rd ed., [1872], repr. London, 1970.
Lash	N. L. A. Lash, *Newman on Development* London, 1975.

Some Confusions

1 There is no reason to doubt that Newman was not directly acquainted with Coleridge's writings before his own thought was

already developed, but Coleridge's influence was not confined to his books, and at least one friend of Newman's (H. J. Rose) was well acquainted with Coleridge's thought as early as 1816. See John Coulson, *Newman and the Common Tradition*, Appendix 'How much of Coleridge had Newman read?' pp. 254–5.

2 *The British Critic* of April 1839; an essay on 'The Prospects of the Anglican Church', reprinted in *Essays Critical and Historical* (1871), vol. 1, p. 268.

3 *University Sermons*.

4 Ed. C. F. Harrold, p. 231.

5 D. G. James, *The Romantic Comedy*.

6 H. F. Davis, 'Was Newman a Disciple of Coleridge?' *Dublin Review*, vol. 217, no. 435.

7 See H. Tristram, 'Two Leaders: Newman and Carlyle' in the *Cornhill Magazine*, vol. 65, pp. 367–82.

8 Jefferson B. Fletcher, 'Newman and Carlyle: An Unrecognised Affinity', *Atlantic Monthly*, vol. 95, pp. 669–79.

9 George Levine, *The Boundaries of Fiction*, pp. 174ff.

10 N. L. A. Lash points to the similarities between Newman's concept of an 'idea' and that of Carlyle, as expressed, for instance, in Carlyle's essay on 'Characteristics' (*CME*, 3, pp. 9–10) (Lash, p. 169). The same passage is singled out by J. H. Muirhead as having affinities with Coleridge (*The Platonic Tradition in Anglo-Saxon Philosophy*, p. 139).

This is not to claim that Newman derived his concept from either Coleridge or Carlyle, nor that it was a direct outcome of the influence of German idealist and liberal thought, nor that it is identical with any of these. But it is precisely because no such identity of meaning can be assumed even when the terminology is similar, that careful consideration of the question is necessary, as has been seen in the case of Coleridge and Carlyle. For a discussion of the relationship of Newman's thought on 'development' with that of German theologians, see W. O. Chadwick, *From Bossuet to Newman*, ch. 5, 'Newman and the Philosophy of Evolution', pp. 96ff.

11 Note that N. L. A. Lash maintains that Newman didn't have a theory of development at all.

12 For instance, George Tyrrell.

13 E.g. A. R. Vidler, *The Modernist Movement in the Roman Catholic Church*, pp. 51–2, and Philip Flanagan, *Newman: Faith and the Believer*.

14 See *Dublin Review* vol. 142, no. 284. This was a reply to the criticism of the encyclical in the *Edinburgh Review* of October, 1907. Ward had hoped to enlist the help of some notable theologian, but he was dissatisfied with the article written for him by the Bishop of Limerick (E. T. O'Dwyer), because he thought it did not make the

necessary differences clear, and hence felt he had to reply himself. See Maisie Ward, *The Wilfrid Wards and the Transition*, vol. 2, *Insurrection and Resurrection*, chs. 14 and 15 and Appendices. The distinction which Ward makes is that, for Newman, symbols are 'shadows' of 'Reality', and not 'empty' symbols. He seems to equate this with the distinction between 'analogical' and 'equivocal' language.

15 These are the three elements of Modernism as described in the encyclical which are usually emphasized. See, e.g., Charles Sarolea, *Cardinal Newman and his Influence on Religious Life and Thought*, and, after him, C. F. Harrold, *John Henry Newman*.

16 Earlier in his book (p. 34ff.) Coulson discusses the relation between idea, sacrament and symbol in Coleridge, with reference to what Coleridge thought of the Church, and the same kind of lack of clarity is apparent there. He again makes the mistake of thinking that the terms 'symbol' and 'idea' in Coleridge are synonymous, and slips between a Coleridgean and a non-Coleridgean definition of 'symbol'. His reference to Coleridge's letter of 13 October 1806 (*CL*, 2, p. 1197) in which Coleridge says that "the human race not by a bold metaphor but in a sublime reality, approach to, and might become, one body, whose Head is Christ (the Logos)" only confuses the issue, in the context, since Coulson does not distinguish here between the human race and the Church as an institution. In the letter Coleridge is talking of the former (which, by implication, is seen to be the 'symbol' of Christ) but he does not apply these terms to the Church.

For another case in which the terminology used is not sufficiently distinguished see D. G. James, *The Romantic Comedy*, in which, as already referred to in Chapter 1, he holds that for both Newman and Coleridge Christian dogma was 'symbol'. It is interesting to compare the similarities adduced here with the argument in Coulson's book. The passage which Coulson indicates as a refutation of Coleridge (*University Sermons*, XV, para. 31) and which is discussed below, James quotes as an instance of agreement between them (p. 207).

The Use of the Term 'Symbol' in the XVth University Sermon

17 Note here, as also below, the Humean terminology.

18 Walgrave, *Newman the Theologian*, p. 96.

19 Cf. here the discussion of "views" and "aspects" of an "idea" in Lash, pp. 49–50; and the related discussion on the two views of the process of development, which Lash calls the "linear" and the "episodic", and which, he says, "are neither fully elaborated nor systematically unified" (pp. 57ff.).

20 I use this term loosely, to designate not only differences of form as between, e.g., a creed and a sonnet, with the differences of the composing of each which this implies, but, e.g., a fictional character, since, e.g., both *Hamlet* the play, and Hamlet, the prince, are language creations. So, too, is a word portrait of a historical figure.

21 Richard Whately (1787–1863) was fellow of Oriel till 1822, principal of St Alban's Hall from 1825, and eventually Archbishop of Dublin. One of the more prominent of Oxford Liberals, he had a zest for ratiocination and the logical exposition of fallacies. Newman pays tribute to him in his *Apologia*. Part of his *Logic* is a closely argued refutation of Hume.

22 Cf. the comparison drawn between Coleridge and Newman in *The Romantic Comedy*, pp. 205ff.

23 If he has, then he was misunderstanding Coleridge. But it is much more likely that Newman was thinking of the position which Hampden had expounded in his Bampton Lectures on *The Scholastic Philosophy Considered in its Relation to Christian Theology* of 1832. Newman had crossed swords with him earlier, and the issues were once again in the air at the time the sermon was preached, as an attempt had just been made to repeal the statute drawn up against Hampden as a result of the 1836 controversy of which he and Newman had been the chief protagonists. Cf., e.g., Chadwick, *The Victorian Church*, vol. 1. Hampden maintained that "The scripture intimates to us certain facts concerning the Divine Being: but conveying them to us by a medium of language, it only brings them before us darkly, under signs appropriate to the thoughts of the human mind." (Bamptons, p. 54.) He concluded from this that a system of theological propositions which has scriptural language as its basis is to be compared with "starting from an inaccurate algebraic statement, and working out results by the established rules of calculation. It is like making every circumstance in an emblem or metaphor the ground of scientific deduction." (Bamptons, p. 364.) For Hampden, too, 'symbolical language' is 'inadequate', as for Newman. But it is both apposite and interesting to note here, that by 'inadequate' Hampden also seemed to mean 'probably inaccurate'. The 'inadequacy' of symbolic language for Newman was not of inaccuracy, but of incompleteness. Hampden also says that theological propositions are "a symbolical language derived from the operations of the mind about the natural world . . . [and therefore] that the conclusions drawn from these terms are nothing further than connexions of symbolical language" (pp. 363–4); they do not give us knowledge of "new facts in the Divine scheme of things". It is also this use of the term 'symbolical' that is here being attacked by Newman.

24 What Newman thought about the language of literature and that

of science, and the difficulties this creates for a comparison with Coleridge can be seen in an extract from a lecture on 'Literature and Science' delivered to the Catholics of Dublin.

> I have said Literature is one thing, and that Science is another; that Literature has to do with ideas, and Science with realities; that Literature is of a personal character, that Science treats of what is universal and external. In proportion, then, as Scripture excludes the personal colouring of its writers, and rises into the region of pure and mere inspiration, when it ceases in any sense to be the writing of man . . . then it comes to belong to science, not Literature. Then it conveys the things of heaven, unseen verities, divine manifestations, and then alone – not the ideas, the feelings, the aspirations of its human instruments.

He therefore considers that both Creeds, and the beginning of the Gospel of St John are 'Science', since they are "the mere enunciation of eternal things, without (so to say) the medium of any human mind transmitting them to us. The words used have the grandeur, the majesty, the calm, the unimpassioned beauty of Science; they are in no sense Literature, they are in no sense personal; and therefore they are easy to apprehend, and easy to translate." (*The Idea of a University*, ed. Harrold, p. 253.)

Some Further Instances of the Term 'Symbol' in Newman's Writing

25 Cf. Wilfrid Ward, *Life of John Henry, Cardinal Newman*, vol. 2, pp. 587ff. Froude died before the letter was sent.

26 *University Sermons*, XV, para. 38.

27 J. H. Newman, *The Philosophical Notebook*, ed. E. Sillem, revised by A. Boekraad, vol. 2, pp. 200ff.

28 J. M. Cameron, 'Newman and Empiricism' in *The Night Battle*, p. 227.

29 In the *Apologia* Newman also writes that he considered Angels "as the real causes of motion, light, and life, and of those elementary principles of the physical universe which, when offered in their developments to our senses, suggest to us the notion of cause and effect, and of what are called the laws of nature", and he refers also to an earlier sermon (Michaelmas Day, 1834) where he had expressed these sentiments. Cf. *Apologia*, p. 25.

30 Cf. *Apologia*. It was a Mr Mayers, a school tutor, who introduced Newman to Calvinist authors. These, Newman said, "had some influence on my opinions, in the direction of those childish imaginations which I have already mentioned, viz. in isolating me from the objects which surrounded me, in confirming me in my mistrust of the reality of material phenomena, and making me rest in

the thought of two and two only supreme and luminously self-evident beings, myself and my Creator". (pp. 4–5.)

31 Thus, writing to Jemima, his sister: "What a veil and curtain this world of sense is! Beautiful, but still a veil." This sentiment, as C. F. Harrold observes, runs as a theme throughout Newman's *Parochial and Plain Sermons* ('Newman and the Alexandrian Platonists' *Modern Philology*, vol. 37, p. 281). Cf. also Harrold's discussion of Newman's attitude to nature in his *John Henry Newman*, pp. 267ff.

32 Even of people, he says: "Here we enjoy not their presence, but the anticipation of what one day shall be; so that, after all, they vanish before the clear vision we have, first, of our own existence, next of the presence of the great God in us, and over us, as our Governor and Judge, who dwells in us by our conscience, which is His representative" (*Parochial and Plain Sermons*, vol. 1, p. 21). For Coleridge God was also to be found in our conscience, but THEREFORE he was also to be found 'outside' us. It is apposite to notice that Newman thinks we don't enjoy a person's 'presence' here, but the 'anticipation' of it. This is quite different from saying, as I think Coleridge would have done, that we DO enjoy their presence even here, and because we so enjoy it, we both experience here, and anticipate, the enjoyment we shall continue to have when there is "a new heaven and a new earth".

33 Cf. *Apologia*, pp. 16–17, 23–4.

34 Again, there is evidence for this. Thus in his essay on 'Milman's view of Christianity' (*Essays and Sketches*, ed. Harrold, vol. 2), Newman writes that "Christian history is an outward and visible sign of an inward and spiritual grace" (the catechism definition of a sacrament) and doubts that "the sign can be satisfactorily treated from the thing signified" (pp. 218–19). It has two aspects, the internal and the external, the divine and the human, and "we may feel the two to be one integral whole, differing merely in aspect, not in fact". (*ibid.*) And further "the visible world is the instrument, yet the veil, of the world invisible – the veil, yet still partially the symbol and the index". Here, certainly, the term 'symbol' is being held in contrast to 'veil', as a thing which reveals, while a veil conceals. The point, however, is that this contrast is not usually maintained, and Newman uses the word 'symbol' in a way which suggests that it has both functions, with the emphasis usually on its veiling qualities. There is something here of the 'doctrine' of the *'disciplina arcani'* dear to Keble, and to Newman in his earlier Tractarian days. Though Newman may reject this as a valid theory of 'development' in 'The Essay on Development' it seems still to play some part in his thinking.

35 Cf. *Letters and Correspondence*, 2, 40–1. Brownlow repeated the same

thirty years later. In the first instance Newman indicated he had not read Berkeley, in the second, he denied being a "Berkleien" (cf. Ward, *Life*, vol. 1, p. 653). For a discussion of Newman's resemblance to Berkeley and indeed to Kant see Harrold, *John Henry Newman*, pp. 136ff.

36 Newman is here using the term "analogy" in Butler's sense, and not in that of Aquinas, which is concerned with predication. Nevertheless there is a point at which the two may be seen to overlap.

37 Cf. e.g., *Parochial and Plain Sermons*, vol. 2, on 'Mysteries of Religion' where a "Truth Sacramental" is seen as a grace which "lodges in an outward form, a precious possession, to be piously and thankfully guarded for the sake of the heavenly reality *contained in it*". (p. 211, my italics.) But note that this is not referred to as 'symbol'.

38 Explicitly, Newman says: "At present we are in a world of shadows. What we see is not substantial" (*Parochial and Plain Sermons*, vol. 5, p. 4).

39 E.g., Lash remarks that in the 1845 version of the *Essay on Development* "the concept of the 'idea' gradually shifts in the course of the argument. In the opening passages 'ideas' are described as those 'habitual judgments' which are 'exercised' on the 'things which come before the mind'. By the end of the section, the term seems to refer to an objective entity, existing independently of, and influencing the minds of men." (Lash, p. 47.)

40 The title given to one section of Newman's selections by Collins (*Philosophical Readings in Cardinal Newman*). The selection here includes the passage from the *Apologia*, pp. 24–5, in which Newman speaks of the Alexandrian Fathers and the "sacramental principle", and refers to the Church, etc. as 'symbols'; as well as a passage from the essay on 'Milman's view of Christianity', including that cited. Curiously, the transition from the one work to the other is not marked, the whole made to appear as one connected extract.

CHAPTER 5. INGE, TYRRELL AND GEORGE MACDONALD

1 *Essays and Reviews* was the work of seven friends, six of them from Oxford and Cambridge and the Headmaster of Rugby, later to be Archbishop of Canterbury, Frederick Temple. Their avowed intention was to encourage free and honest discussion of the controversial Biblical questions of the time, and, while the book now seems innocuous, it was then sufficiently daring to provoke

widespread, and sometimes bitter, critical reaction. Two of the writers were arraigned before the Court of Arches for their unorthodox opinions. *Lux Mindi* was a similar attempt to discuss the traditional tenets of the church in the light of modern knowledge and progressive ideals. Its editor was Charles Gore (later Bishop of Oxford) and its contributors were mostly Oxford men. Though more reverent in tone than *Essays and Reviews*, it too, succeeded in giving offence since it ran counter to much received opinion.

2 See for instance Stephen Prickett's *Romanticism and Religion* and C. N. Manlove's *Modern Fantasy*.

Dean Inge

Abbreviations used:

CM *Christian Mysticism*. Bampton Lectures for 1899. Sometimes referred to as Bamptons.

CV *Contentio Veritatis: Essays in Constructive Theology* by various authors. Inge contributed two essays: 'The Person of Christ' and 'The Sacraments'.

FK *Faith and Knowledge*. Collected Sermons 1892–1904.

TFR *Truth and Falsehood in Religion*. Six lectures delivered at Cambridge to undergraduates.

3 See the footnote to *Christian Mysticism*, p. 251, where Inge quotes Bosanquet on Kant's use of the term 'symbol'. Though Kant did seem to hold that the relationship between 'symbol' and its referent was not conventional or arbitrary but perceived, we must remember that this claim is made by him within a *general* phenomenalist framework not shared by Inge.

4 See e.g. *Christian Mysticism*. "We have an organ or faculty for the discernment of spiritual truth, which, in its proper sphere, is as much to be trusted as the organs of sense." The faculty vocabulary here adopted is, however, repudiated in the later *Personal Idealism and Mysticism* (Paddock Lectures, 1906), and, as is obvious from the context of the Bamptons, cannot be taken literally even there. In *Personal Idealism* Inge says: "There is no separate organ for the apprehension of divine truth, independent of will, feeling, and thought. Our knowledge of God comes to us in the interplay of those faculties. . . ." (p. 3) and again "The organ by which we apprehend divine truth is no special faculty but the higher reason . . . that unification of our personality which is the goal of our striving and the postulate of our rational life" (p. 5). In the use of a faculty vocabulary, and in the repudiation of the division in man which it suggests, as well as in what he says here of the "higher reason", Inge is also like Coleridge.

5 Six lectures delivered to the undergraduates of Cambridge University in the Lent Term, 1906.

6 Cf. e.g., *Christian Mysticism*, pp. 27 and 36; *The Platonic Tradition in English Religious Thought* (Hulsean Lectures, 1925–6), p. 71.

7 Even as late as in *Mysticism and Religion*, (1947), p. 108.

8 E.g., *Christian Mysticism*, p. 7; *Faith and Knowledge in Religion* (1904), pp. 290–1 (Sermon delivered that year in St Mary's, Oxford, on 'Liberal Catholicism'); *Truth and Falsehood in Religion*, pp. 144–5; *Personal Idealism and Mysticism*, ch. 2.

9 Thus Inge considers that one of the things most necessary "if the Church is to take her proper place in the life and thought of the twentieth century" is that its teachers should discourage that "popular supernaturalistic dualism" namely, "the notion that God only begins where nature leaves off" (Preface to *Faith and Knowledge*, pp. vii–viii); cf. also his criticism of Tyrrell in *Personal Idealism* for thinking of nature "apart from man" rather a caricature of Divinity than its proper image. (p. 20ff.)

10 Cf. *Christian Mysticism*, chs. 7 and 8 (passim).

11 Cf., e.g., *Christian Mysticism*, p. 316.

12 Cf., e.g., *Mysticism in Religion*, 'Symbol and myth', p. 93.

13 Cf. *Christian Mysticism*, p. 7; and *The Platonic Tradition in English Religious Thought*, p. 71.

14 He says, for instance: "Monkish asceticism . . . rests on a dualistic view of the world" (*Christian Mysticism*, pp. 11–12).

15 E.g., *Christian Mysticism*, pp. 46–9; 65–6; 94–5; and *Personal Idealism and Mysticism*, particularly ch. 3.

16 *Christian Mysticism*, p. 250. The article, appearing anonymously, was by Una Taylor.

17 His favourite seems in fact to be that of R. L. Nettleship, quoted three times in *Christian Mysticism* (pp. 250 and 342, and on p. 58 without attribution). Nettleship wrote: ". . . true Mysticism is the consciousness that everything we experience is an element, and only an element, in fact, i.e. that in being what it is, it is symbolic of something more". This Inge made the basis of his own definition of symbol in *Contentio Veritatis* where he wrote: "I use the word symbol . . . of a fact or occurrence in the phenomenal world which, in being what it is, signifies something else in a higher order." (p. 85.)

18 The Bohn edition of the *Biographia* and *Two Lay Sermons* (i.e. including *The Statesman's Manual*) was published in 1898; Symons' Everyman ed. of the *Biographia* in 1906; E. H. Coleridge's ed. of Marginalia: *Anima Poetae* and of *Letters* (2 vols.) came out in 1895.

19 Christoph Ernst Ludhardt (1823–1902) was a German Lutheran theologian with a fairly prolific output. Among the books translated into English was a three-volume *Commentary on St John's*

Gospel (Edinburgh 1876), *A History of Christian Ethics* (Edinburgh 1889) and *Apologetic Lectures on the Moral Truths of Christianity* (Edinburgh 1868). He uses the terms 'symbol' and 'symbolism' in a number of instances, by no means always insisting on their concealing quality, and therefore it is all the more noteworthy that Inge should choose to quote him as he does.

20 See, e.g., I Corinthians, xiii.12.

21 An example of an entirely different nature may serve as illustration. The relationship of parenthood exists whether we recognize it or not. But that of partnership, for instance, depends on agreement and may be terminated or changed. The relationship of friendship depends, at least to some extent, on the recognition of its existence.

22 Inge does make a distinction between 'imagination' and 'fancy', and considers 'allegories' the product of the latter. But the source of his distinction is not Coleridge, but Ruskin, which, as quoted by Inge himself, is as follows:

> Fancy has to do with the outsides of things, and is content therewith. She can never *feel*, but is one of the most purely and simply intellectual of the faculties. She cannot be made serious; no edge-tool but she will play with it: whereas the imagination is in all things the reverse. She cannot but be serious; she sees too far, too darkly, too solemnly, too earnestly, ever to smile. . . . There is reciprocal action between the intensity of moral feeling and the power of imagination. Hence the powers of the imagination may always be tested by accompanying tenderness of emotion. . . . Imagination is quiet, fancy restless; fancy details, imagination suggests . . . (footnote to *Christian Mysticism*, p. 252. The quotation is from Ruskin's *Mordern Painters*, vol. 2, ch. 3).

The distinction is given largely in terms of emotive response. Yet this is also the only guide which Inge can provide between 'true symbolism' and 'false'.

23 E.g., in *Truth and Falsehood in Religion*, p. 15.

24 It would be interesting to compare what Coleridge says of the importance of the life, death and resurrection of Christ, in, e.g., his *Notes on Donne* (cf. above ch. 2) and what Inge says of the same subject in, e.g., *Personal Idealism and Mysticism*, pp. 87ff. but it would take me too far from the subject of the meaning of 'symbol', and would add little to what has already been said.

Tyrrell

Abbreviations used:
ER   *External Religion: Its Use and Abuse.*
FM   *The Faith of the Millions* (First Series).
LO   *Lex Orandi: or Prayer and Creed*

TSC Through Scylla and Charybdis: or The Old Theology and the New.

25 There is, of course, evidence of influences – such as that of Matthew Arnold or William James, for instance; and a respect for the achievement of past thinkers, pre-eminently, perhaps, Aquinas. But his comment that Aquinas is made "not greater but less for being made infallible" (*George Tyrrell's Letters*, ed. M. D. Petre, p. 299) is typical of his detachment. See *The Autobiography and Life of George Tyrrell* (passim) and also J. W. Goetz, *Analogy and Symbol: A Study in the Theology of George Tyrell*, p. 27.

26 Diary entry for 18 March 1951. See Adam Fox, *Dean Inge*, p. 264.

27 See J. W. Goetz, p. 36.

28 The 'not' is my insertion since the sense obviously demands it. The omission seems not to have been noticed by any expositors of Tyrrell's thought who have subsequently had occasion to quote this passage.

29 In fact, the wedge of distinction is driven by Coleridge between metaphor and symbol (cf. above, ch. 2). He considers analogy to be "the material or (to speak chemically) the base of symbols and symbolical expressions" (*AR*, p. 235).

30 'The Limits of the Theory of Development', vol. 81, September 1905. It was a sequel to a previous article on the same subject publised in *The Month*, vol. 103, in January 1904, and was intended for the same magazine, but was rejected by it. Both articles were subsequently reprinted in *Through Scylla and Charybdis* under the titles 'Semper Eadem' I and II.

31 'The Contents of a Pre-Adamite Skull', *The Month*, vol. 67, p. 73.

32 H. L. Mansel, whom Tyrrell had read, had tried to make the same point in his Bampton Lectures of 1858, *The Limits of Religious Thought*.

33 Friedrich von Hügel (1852–1925) was a correspondent of most of the so called 'Modernists' some of whom he introduced to one another, and in general he supported their endeavours, though he himself was never implicated in the condemnation, and has rather been shielded from any suspicion of involvement in it. He was, at the time, a friend of Tyrrell's and remained so till the latter's death, though he later had misgivings about the propriety of Tyrrell's funeral which was condemned by Roman Catholic authority.

34 *George Tyrrell's Letters*, ed. M. D. Petre, p. 57.

George MacDonald

Abbreviations used:

US Unspoken Sermons, 1, 2 and 3.

Life   George MacDonald and his wife, by Greville MacDonald.

35 See, e.g., *Orts*, pp. 15 and 52, and *England's Antiphon*, p. 307ff.
36 C. S. Lewis, *Surprised by Joy*, pp. 168–71. On reading *Phantastes*, casually picked up from a station bookstall, Lewis found himself "as if carried across the frontier, or as if [he] had died in the old country [of his childhood imagination] and could never remember how [he] came alive in the new. For in one sense the new country was exactly like the old. . . . But in another sense all was changed. He did not yet know . . . the name of the new quality, the bright shadow that rested on the travels of Anados [the hero of *Phantastes*], I do now. It was Holiness". Lewis marks this as the beginning of his return journey towards Christianity.
37 See *Life*.
38 *Lilith*, p. 27.
39 p. 176.
40 p. 257.
41 I say 'if' because MacDonald's statement that "the things made by the hand of God . . . *afford* the truest symbols of the truth" could be taken to mean that nature provides man with the materials for making symbols, and is not a symbol itself.
42 I suspect that the lack of attention to the way in which an external form can reproduce an inner meaning may have led MacDonald to underrate Herbert's poem 'Easter Wings' in which the poem's subject – man's withering to nothingness through sin, and his rising to glory through Christ's redeeming grace – is reproduced in the shape of the poem's two stanzas, which thus in a 'concrete' way re-state the thought and are integral to it. This is not the case with Herbert's 'The Altar' where, though the shape does attempt to reproduce the altar of the title, that shape itself is not – as it cannot be since sacrifice is not altar-shaped – one with the subject of the poem in quite the same essential way. Yet MacDonald does not distinguish between the merits of these two poems, and dismisses them both as 'absurd'. He is, indeed, very suspicious of Herbert's 'play' even with rhyme. It is a pity that Coleridge did not turn his attention to what I take to be an important difference between the two poems – whatever their merits on other grounds may be.
43 See Prickett, *Romanticism and Religion*, p. 230.

CHAPTER 6. SOME CONCLUSIONS

1 The writings of R. D. Hampden and H. L. Mansel furnish further examples of the confusions inherent in the concept of inadequacy. Both of them used the term 'symbolical' somewhat casually in their respective Bampton Lectures of 1832 and 1858, lectures

which, in both cases, had controversial repercussions. Details of the effects of Hampden's Bamptons *The Scholastic Philosophy Considered in its relation to Christian Theology*, and his later (1834) *Observations on Religious Dissent* can be found in Henry Christmas, *The Hampden Controversy*, and W. O. Chadwick's *The Victorian Church*, Part 1, pp. 112–20. A discussion of the criticism levelled at Mansel's *The Limits of Religious Thought* is the subject of Donald Cupitt's 'Mansel's Theory of Regulative Truth', *Journal of Theological Studies*, vol. 18, pp. 104–26. Hampden reserved the term 'symbolical' for the language of dogma, in particular as sharply distinguished from the language of scripture, and by it he seemed to mean 'inadequate' in the sense of 'inaccurate' (and therefore worthless) knowledge of the subject to which it referred, since he held what I have called a 'Baconian' theory of language, in which ideas could be commensurate only with that language itself. Hence the 'symbolical' language of dogma, whose subject was ultimately God, did not give us knowledge of God, and was therefore of little importance – too little at least to be sufficient reason for divisions among Christians. Mansel, a theologian of greater acumen than Hampden, while wishing to preserve a special place for the Bible as a source of our knowledge of God, and to distinguish it in this respect from subsequent theology, wished to emphasize that all our language about God is equally inadequate, because God is essentially unconditioned, and therefore unknowable to minds conditioned by space and time, and finite as men's minds are. His use of the term while, like Hampden's, conflating 'symbolical' with 'inadequate' does not, like Hampden's do so in the sense of 'inaccurate' since, for Mansel, the rift between language and its referent when language is 'symbolical' is so complete that neither 'accuracy' nor 'inaccuracy' (which suggests some measure of approximation) could be appropriate terms. All that 'symbolical' language can do – and the language of Scripture is also 'symbolical' – is to "indicate a further reality beyond the symbol". (Bamptons, 4th ed., p. 20.)

BIBLIOGRAPHY

Abrams, M. H., *The Mirror and the Lamp: Romantic Theory and the Critical Tradition*, Oxford, 1953.
  'Wordsworth and Coleridge on Diction and Figures' in *Coleridge (20th Century Views)*, ed. K. Coburn, New Jersey, 1967.
Appleyard, J. A., *Coleridge's Philosophy of Literature: The development of a concept of poetry 1791–1819*, Cambridge, 1965.
  'Coleridge and Criticism: I. Critical Theory' in *S. T. Coleridge*, ed. R. L. Brett, London, 1971.
Aquinas, Thomas, *Summa Theologic*, (ed. the English Dominicans, trans. H. McCabe O.P.), London, 1967, vol. 2.
Arnold, Matthew, *Complete Prose Works*, ed. R. H. Super, Ann Arbor, 1960; vol. 1, *On the Classical Tradition*; vol. 3, *Lectures and Essays in Criticism*; vol. 5, *Culture and Anarchy*; vol. 6, *Dissent and Dogma*; vol. 7, *God and the Bible*; vol. 8, *Essays Religious and Mixed*.
Aulen, Gustaf, *The Drama and the Symbols: A Book on Images of God and the Problems they Raise* (trans. Sydney Linton), London, 1970.
Bacchus, Francis, 'Newman's Oxford University Sermons', *The Month*, vol. 140, no. 697.
Bacon, Francis, *The Advancement of Learning*, London, 1861.
Baker, J. V., *The Sacred River: Coleridge's Theory of Imagination*, Baton Rouge, 1957.
Barfield, Owen, *Poetic Diction; A Study in Meaning*, London, 1952.
  Romanticism Comes of Age, London, 1969.
  What Coleridge Thought, London, 1972.
Barmann, L. F., *Baron Friedrich von Hügel and the Modernist Crisis*, Cambridge, 1972.
Barth, S. J., J. Robert, *Coleridge and Christian Doctrine*, Cambridge, Mass., 1969.
Bate, W. J., *Coleridge*, London, 1969.
  'Coleridge on the Function of Art' in *Perspectives of Criticism*, ed. H. Levin, Cambridge, Mass., 1950.

Bibliography

Beek, W. J. M., *John Keble's Literary and Religious Contribution to the Oxford Movement*, Nijmegen, 1959.

Beer, J. B., *Coleridge the Visionary*, London, 1959.

'Newman and the Romantic Sensibility' in *The English Mind*, ed. H. S. Davies and G. Watson, Cambridge, 1964.

Bell, Richard, *Carlyle's Religious Influence* (Thomas Greene Lecture delivered to the Carlyle Society), Edinburgh, 1959.

Ben-Israel, H., 'Carlyle and the French Revolution', *The Historical Journal*, vol. 1, no. 2.

Bennet, E. A., *C. G. Jung*, London, 1961.

Bevan, Edwyn, *Symbolism and Belief* (The Gifford Lectures for 1933–34), London, 1962.

Blanshard, Brand, 'Symbolism' in *Religious Experience and Truth: A Symposium*, ed. S. Hook, Edinburgh, 1962.

Boekraad, A. J., *The Personal Conquest of Truth According to Henry Newman*, Louvain, 1955.

Boulger, J. D., *Coleridge as a Religious Thinker*, New Haven, 1961.

Bowra, C. M., *The Heritage of Symbolism*, London, 1943.

Brandl, Alois, *Samuel Taylor Coleridge and the English Romantic School* (trans. Lady Eastlake), London, 1887.

Bray, J. W., *A History of English Critical Terms*, Boston, 1898.

Brett, R. L. (ed.), *S. T. Coleridge*, London, 1971.

'Coleridge's Theory of the Imagination' in *English Studies*, 1949.

Bridge, A. C., *Images of God: An Essay on the Life and Death of Symbols*, London, 1960.

Bryson, L., *et al.* (eds.), *Symbols and Values: An Initial Study* (Thirteenth Symposium of the Conference on Science, Philosophy and Religion), New York, 1954.

Symbols and Society (Fourteenth Symposium of the Conference on Science, Philosophy and Religion), New York, 1955.

Butterfield, Herbert, *Christianity and History*, London, 1957.

Cameron, J. M., *The Night Battle*, London, 1962.

Carlyle, Thomas, *The Works of Thomas Carlyle* (Centenary Edition), London, 1896–1899; vol. 1, *Sartor Resartus*; vols. 2–4, *The French Revolution*; vol. 5, *Heroes and Heroworship*; vol. 10, *Past and Present*; vol. 11, *Life of Sterling*; vols. 26–30, *Critical and Miscellaneous Essays*.

Cassirer, Ernst, *The Philosophy of Symbolic Forms* (trans. R. Manheim), New Haven, 1953, vol. 1.

Rousseau, Kant, Goethe: Two Essays (trans. Guttman Kristeller and J. H. Randall), Princeton, 1970.

Language and Myth (trans. S. K. Langer), New York, 1953.

Castle, W. R. Jr., 'Newman and Coleridge', *Sewanee Review*, vol. 17, no. 2.

Cazamian, Louis, *Carlyle* (trans. E. K. Brown), New York, 1932.

Bibliography

Chadwick, W. Owen, *From Bossuet to Newman: The Idea of Doctrinal Development*, Cambridge, 1957.

The Victorian Church, 2 vols., London, 1970.

(ed.) *The Mind of the Oxford Movement*, London, 1960.

Christmas, Henry, *A Concise History of the Hampden Controversy, with a Brief Examination of the 'Bampton Lectures' for 1882 and the 'Observations on Dissent'*, London, 1848.

Coburn, Kathleen, 'The Interpretation of Man and Nature', *Proceedings of the British Academy*, no. 49, 1963.

(ed.) *Coleridge: A Collection of Critical Essays*, Englewood Cliffs, 1967.

Coleridge, Samuel Taylor, *The Complete Works of Samuel Taylor Coleridge* (7 vols.), ed. Shedd, 2nd edition, New York, 1884; vol. 1, *Aids to Reflection* (1825), *The Statesman's Manual* (1816); vols. 4 and 5, *Literary Remains*; vol. 6, *On the Constitution of Church and State, Table Talk*.

Anima Poetae, from the Unpublished Notebooks of S. T. Coleridge, ed. E. H. Coleridge, London, 1895.

Biographia Literaria (1817) (2 vols.), ed. J. Shawcross, Oxford, 1907.

The Collected Letters of Samuel Taylor Coleridge (2 vols.), ed. E. L. Griggs, Oxford, 1956.

Confessions of an Inquiring Spirit (1840), Facsimile reprint, London, 1971.

The Friend (1809–1810) (2 vols.), ed. Barbara E. Rooke, London and Princeton, 1969.

Lectures 1795: On Politics and Religion, eds L. Patton and P. Mann, London, 1930.

The Notebooks of Samuel Taylor Coleridge (2 double vols. of Text and Notes) ed. Kathleen Coburn, New York, 1957 and 1961.

The Philosophical Lectures of Samuel Taylor Coleridge hitherto Unpublished (1818), ed. Kathleen Coburn, London, 1949.

Shakespearean Lectures (2 vols.), ed. T. M. Raysor, London, 1960.

The Watchman, ed. L. Patton, London and Princeton, 1970.

Collins, James (ed.), *Philosophical Readings in Cardinal Newman*, Chicago, 1961.

Coulson, John, *Newman and the Common Tradition*, Oxford, 1970.

and Allchin, A. M. (eds.), *The Rediscovery of Newman*, London, 1967.

with A. M. Allchin and M. Trevor, *Newman: A Portrait Restored: An Ecumenical Revaluation*, London, 1965.

Cox, David, 'Psychology and Symbolism' in *Myth and Symbol*, ed. F. W. Dillistone, London, 1966.

Cozens, M. L., *A Handbook of Heresies*, London, 1928. (Abridged edition, London, 1960.)

Cupitt, Donald, 'Mansel's Theory of Regulative Truth', *Journal of Theological Studies*, vol. 18, part 1.

D'Arcy, Martin C., *The Nature of Belief*, London, 1931.

Bibliography

Davies, H. S., and Watson, George, (eds) *The English Mind: Studies the English Moralists presented to Basil Willey*, Cambridge, 1964.

Davis, H. F., 'The Catholicism of Cardinal Newman' in *John Newman: Centenary Essays*, London, 1945.

'Is Newman's Theory of Development Catholic?', *Blackfriars*, vol. 39, nos. 460–61.

'Was Newman a Disciple of Coleridge?', *Dublin Review*, vol. 217, no. 435.

Denzinger, H. J. D., *Sources of Catholic Dogma* (trans. Roy J. Defarrari), London, 1957.

De Quincey, Thomas, *The Collected Writings of Thomas De Quincey*, ed. David Masson (14 vols.), Edinburgh, 1889–1890.

Dessain, C. S., *John Henry Newman*, London, 1966.

'Cardinal Newman on the Theory and Practice of Knowledge: The Purpose of the *Grammar of Assent*', *Downside Review*, vol. 75, no. 239.

Dilley, Frank B., *Metaphysics and Religious Language*, New York, 1964.

Dillistone, F. W., *Christianity and Symbolism*, London, 1955.

(ed.), *Myth and Symbol*, London, 1966.

'The Function of Symbols in Religious Experience' in *Metaphor and Symbol*, ed. L. C. Knights, London, 1960.

Eaton, R. M., *Symbolism and Truth: An Introduction to the Theory of Knowledge*, New York, 1964.

Egerton, Hakluyt (i.e. Arthur Boutwood), *Father Tyrrell's Modernism: an Expository Criticism of 'Through Scylla and Charybdis' in an Open Letter to Mr. Athelstan Riley*, London, 1909.

Egner, G., *Apologia Pro Charles Kingsley*, London, 1969.

Eliot, T. S., *Selected Prose*, London, 1953.

Eliot-Binns, L. E., *English Thought 1860–1900: The Theological Aspect*, London, 1956.

Religion in the Victorian Era, London, 1964.

Ellmann, Richard, *The Identity of Yeats*, London, 1954.

(ed.), *The Symbolist Movement in Literature*, by Arthur Symons (1899), London, 1958.

Emmet, D. M., *The Nature of Metaphysical Thinking*, London, 1966.

'Coleridge and Philosophy' in *S. T. Coleridge*, ed. R. L. Brett, London, 1971.

'Coleridge and the Growth of Mind', John Rylands Lecture, March, 1952.

Essays and Reviews [by F. Temple, R. Williams, B. Powell, H. B. Wilson, C. W. Goodwin, M. Pattison and B. Jowitt], London, 1860.

Fawcett, Thomas, *The Symbolic Language of Religion*, London, 1970.

Fawkes, Alfred, *Studies in Modernism*, London, 1913.

Ferguson, W., 'Carlyle as a Historian', (Lecture delivered to the Carlyle Society), Edinburgh, 1966.

Bibliography

Flanagan, Philip, *Newman: Faith and the Believer*, London, 1946.

Fletcher, Jefferson B., 'Newman and Carlyle: An Unrecognized Affinity', *Atlantic Monthly*, vol. 95, pp. 669–79.

Fogle, R. H., 'Coleridge and Criticism II: Critical Practice' in *S. T. Coleridge*, ed. R. L. Brett, London, 1971.

The Idea of Coleridge's Criticism (Perspectives in Criticism IX), Berkeley, 1962.

Foss, Martin, *Symbol and Metaphor in Human Experience*, Princeton, 1949.

Fox, Adam, *Dean Inge*, London, 1960.

Freeman, Kenneth D., *The Role of Reason in Religion: A Study of Henry Mansel*, The Hague, 1969.

Fruman, Norman, *The Damaged Archangel*, London, 1972.

Gérard, A. S., *English Romantic Poets: Ethos Structure and Symbol in Coleridge, Wordsworth, Shelley and Keats*, Berkeley, 1968.

'The Systolic Rhythm: The Structure of Coleridge's Conversation Poems' in *Coleridge* (20th Century Views), ed. K. Coburn, New Jersey, 1967.

Goetz, J. W., 'Analogy and Symbol: A study in the Theology of George Tyrrell' (Unpublished Thesis, University of Cambridge, 1969).

'Father Tyrrell and the Catholic Crisis', *New Blackfriars*, vol. 50, no. 591.

Gore, Charles (ed.), *Lux Mundi: A Series of Studies in the Religion of the Incarnation*, London, 1889.

Gottfried, Leon, *Matthew Arnold and the Romantics*, London, 1963.

Hammans, Herbert, 'Recent Catholic Views on the Development of Dogma', *Concilium*, vol. 1, no. 3.

Hampden, R. D., *An Essay on the Philosophical Evidences of Christianity or The Credibility obtained to a Scriptural Revelation from its coincidence with the facts of Nature*, London, 1827.

Parochial Sermons Illustrative of the Importance of the Revelation of God in Jesus Christ, London, 1828.

The Scholastic Philosophy considered in its relation to Christian Theology (The Bampton Lectures for 1832), Oxford, 1833.

Observations on Religious Dissent, with particular reference to the use of religious tests in the University, Oxford, 1834 (two editions).

A Postscript to Observations on Religious Dissent, London, 1835.

The Study of Moral Philosophy, 1835.

Inaugural Lecture read before the University of Oxford, London, 1836.

Introduction to the 2nd Edition of the Bampton Lectures, London, 1837.

A Lecture on Tradition read before the University in the Divinity School, Oxford (2nd edition), London, 1839.

Bibliography

The 39 Articles of the Church of England, London, 1842.

Harrison, Frederic, *Carlyle's Place in Literature*, London, 1894.

Harrold, C. F., *Carlyle and German Thought, 1819–1834*, London, 1963.

    John Henry Newman: An Expository and Critical Study of His Mind, Thought and Art, London, 1945.

    (ed.), *A Newman Treasury*, London, 1943.

    'Newman and the Alexandrian Platonists', *Modern Philology*, vol. 37.

Heaney, J. J., *The Modernist Crisis: Von Hügel*, Washington, 1968.

Hegel, G. W., *Philosophy of Mind* (1894) (translated by W. Wallace), 3rd part of the *Encyclopedia of Philosophical Sciences*, eds. A. V. Miller and J. N. Findlay, Oxford, 1971.

Hodgart, P., and Redpath, R. T. M., *Romantic Perspectives: The Work of Crabbe, Blake, Wordsworth and Coleridge as seen by their Contemporaries and by Themselves*, London, 1964.

Holloway, C. John, 'The Concept of Myth in Literature' in *Metaphor and Symbol*, ed. L. C. Knights, London, 1960.

    'English and Some Christian Traditions' in *The English Mind*, eds H. S. Davies and G. Watson, Cambridge, 1964.

Hook, Sidney (ed.), *Religious Experience and Truth: A Symposium*, Edinburgh, 1962.

Hort, F. J. A., 'Coleridge' in *Cambridge Essays*, contributed by members of the University, London, 1856.

Hough, Graham, *The Last Romantics: A Criticism of Ruskin, Rossetti, William Morris, Pater and Yeats*, London, 1949.

    'Coleridge and the Victorians' in *The English Mind*, eds. H. S. Davies and G. Watson, Cambridge, 1964.

House, A. Humphry, *Coleridge* (Clark Lectures 1951–2), London, 1953.

Houtin, Albert, *Un Prêtre Symboliste: Marcel Hébert, 1851–1916*, Paris, 1925.

Howard, C., *Coleridge's Idealism: A study of its relationship to Kant and the Cambridge Platonists*, Boston, 1924.

von Hügel, Friedrich, *Essays and Addresses on the Philosophy of Religion* (1st and 2nd Series), London, 1963.

Hutton, R. H., *Cardinal Newman: A Biography*, London, 1891.

    Criticism on Contemporary Thought and Thinkers, Selected from 'The Spectator' (2 vols.), London, 1894.

    Essays on Some Modern Guides of English Thought in Matters of Faith, London, 1887.

    Essays Theological and Literary, London, 1887.

Inge, W. R., *Christian Mysticism considered in Eight Lectures delivered before the University of Oxford* (Bampton Lectures for 1899), London, 1899.

    Faith and Knowledge (Collected Sermons 1892–1904), Edinburgh, 1904.

Bibliography

Faith and its Psychology (extension of ten lectures on the Jowett Foundation), London, 1909.

Mysticism in Religion, London, 1969.

Outspoken Essays, First Series, London, 1919; Second Series, London, 1922.

Personal Idealism and Mysticism (Paddock Lectures for 1906), London, 1907.

The Platonic Tradition in English Religious Thought (Hulsean Lectures 1925–6), London, 1926.

The Philosophy of Plotinus (Gifford Lectures 1917–18), London, 1929.

The Religious Philosophy of Plotinus and Some Modern Philosophies of Religion, London, 1914.

Truth and Falsehood in Religion, London, 1906.

'The Person of Christ' and 'The Sacraments' in *Contentio Veritatis*, London, 1902.

Isaacs, J., 'Coleridge's Critical Terminology' in *Essays and Studies*, vol. 21, Oxford, 1935.

Jackson, J. R. de J., *Method and Imagination in Coleridge's Criticism*, London, 1969.

(ed.), *Coleridge: The Critical Heritage*, London, 1970.

James, D. G., *Matthew Arnold and the Decline of English Romanticism*, Oxford, 1961.

The Romantic Comedy: An essay on English Romanticism, London, 1963.

Scepticism and Poetry: An Essay on the Poetic Imagination, London, 1937.

'The Thought of Coleridge' in *The Major Romantic Poets*, ed. C. O. Thorpe *et al.*, Carbondale, 1957.

Johnson, F. Ernest (ed.), *Religious Symbolism*, Washington, 1969.

Jung, C. G., *Psychological Types*, (translated by R. F. C. Hull), vol. 6 of *Collected Works*, ed. H. Read *et al.*, London and New York, 1953.

Contributions to Analytic Psychology, London, 1928.

Kant, Immanuel, *The Critique of Judgment* (translated by J. H. Bernard), New York, 1968.

Knights, L. C., *Explorations: Essays in Criticism, mainly on the Seventeenth Century*, London, 1964.

(ed.), *Metaphor and Symbol* (12th Symposium of the Calston Research Society), London, 1960.

Kroner, Richard, *The Religious Function of Imagination*, New Haven, 1941.

Langer, S. K., *Philosophical Sketches*, New York, 1964.

Philosophy in a New Key: A Study in the Symbolism of Reason, Rite and Art, Oxford, 1951.

Problems of Art: Ten Philosophical Lectures, London, 1957.

Lash, Nicholas L. A., *'His Presence in the World: A Study of Eucharistic Worship and Theology*, London, 1968.

Bibliography

Newman on Development: The Search for an Explanation in History, London, 1975.

'Development of Doctrine: Smokescreen or Explanation?', *New Blackfriars*, vol. 52, no. 610.

'The Notions of "Implicit" and "Explicit" Reason in Newman's *University Sermons*: A difficulty', *Heythrop Journal*, vol. 11, January, 1970.

'Second thoughts on Walgrave's *Newman*', *Downside Review*, vol. 87, no. 289.

Latourelle, R., S. J., *Theology of Revelation*, Cork, 1968.

La Valley, A. J., *Carlyle and The Idea of the Modern*, Yale, 1968.

Lawlis, M. E., 'Newman on the Imagination', *Modern Language Notes*, vol. 68, no. 2.

Leavis, F. R., 'Coleridge in Criticism', *Scrutiny*, no. 9, 1941–1942.

Lee, Dorothy D., 'Symbolization and Value' in *Symbols and Values: An Initial Study*, ed. L. Bryson *et al.*, New York, 1954.

Lehmann, A. G., *The Symbolist Aesthetic in France 1885–1895*, London, 1968.

Levin, Harry (ed.), *Perspectives of Criticism*, Cambridge, Mass., 1950.

'Notes on Convention' in *Perspectives of Criticism*.

Levine, George, *The Boundaries of Fiction: Carlyle, Macaulay, Newman*, Princeton, 1968.

Lewis, C. S., *Surprised by Joy*, London, 1955.

Le Roy, E., *Dogme et Critique*, Paris, 1907.

'Qu'est-ce-qu'un Dogme?', *Quinzaine*, 16 April 1905.

Lowes, J. Livingstone, *The Road to Xanadu*, London, 1927.

Lynch, William, 'The Evocative Symbol' in *Symbols and Society*, ed. L. Bryson *et al.*, New York, 1955.

Lyttkens, H., *The Analogy Between God and The World*, Uppsala, 1953.

MacDonald, George, *England's Antiphon*, London, 1896.

Lilith: A Romance, London, 1924.

Phantastes: A Faërie Romance, London, 1915.

Orts, London, 1882.

A Dish of Orts, London, 1893.

Unspoken Sermons, Series 1, London, 1870.

Unspoken Sermons, Series 2, London, 1902.

Unspoken Sermons, Series 3, London, 1889.

MacDonald, Greville, *George MacDonald and his Wife*, London, 1924.

McFarland, Thomas, *Coleridge and the Pantheist Tradition*, Oxford, 1969.

McKinnon, Donald M., 'Introduction' to *Newman's University Sermons*, London, 1970.

Madden, W. A., 'The Religious and Aesthetic Ideas of Matthew Arnold' (Unpublished thesis for the University of Michigan, 1955).

Bibliography

Manlove, C. N., *Modern Fantasy*, Cambridge, 1975.

Mansel, H. L., *An Examination of the Rev. F. D. Maurice's Strictures on The Bampton Lectures of 1858*, London, 1859.

Inspiration: how it is related to Revelation and Reason, London, 1859.

Letters, Lectures and Reviews, London, 1873.

The Limits of Religious Thought (Bampton Lectures 1858), 1st edition, London, 1858; 4th edition, London, 1859; 5th edition, London, 1867.

Mascall, E. L., *Existence and Analogy: A Sequel to 'He Who Is'*, London, 1949.

Maurice, F. D., *The Claims of the Bible and Science*, London, 1863.

The Epistle to the Hebrews; being the substance of three lectures with a Preface containing a Review of Mr Newman's *Theory of Development*, London, 1846.

The Kingdom of Christ (1842 edition reprinted with an introduction by A. R. Vidler), London, 1958.

Theological Essays, London, 1853.

What is Revelation?, London, 1859.

A Sequel to 'What is Revelation?', London, 1860

Towards the Recovery of Unity: the Thought of F. D. Maurice, eds. J. F. Porter and W. J. Wolf, New York, 1964.

The Word 'Eternal' and the Punishment of the Wicked (A Letter to the Rev. Dr. Jelf), Cambridge, 1854.

Maurice, J. F., *The Life of Frederick Denison Maurice, Chiefly Told in his own Letters* (2 vols.), London, 1884.

May, J. Lewis, *Father Tyrrell and the Modernist Movement*, London, 1932.

Mead, E. D., *The Philosophy of Carlyle*, London, 1881.

Michaud, G., *La Doctrine Symboliste*, Paris, 1947.

Mill, J. S., *Collected Works*, London and Toronto, 1963; vol. 10, *Essays on Ethics, Religion and Society*, ed. J. M. Robson, 1969; vols. 12 and 13, *Early Letters*, ed. F. E. Mineka, 1963.

Essays on Literature and Society, ed. J. B. Schneewind, New York, 1965.

Mondin, Battista, *Analogy in Catholic and Protestant Theology*, The Hague, 1963.

Morris, Charles W., *Signs, Language and Behavior*, New York, 1946.

Mueller, F. M., *Goethe and Carlyle*, London, 1886.

Muirhead, J. H., *Coleridge as a Philosopher*, London, 1930.

The Platonic Tradition in Anglo-Saxon Philosophy, London, 1931.

Munz, Peter, *The Problems of Religious Knowledge*, London, 1959.

Nagel, Ernest, 'Symbolism and Science' in *Symbols and Values: An Initial Study*, ed. L. Bryson *et al.*, New York, 1954.

Neff, E., *Carlyle and Mill*, New York, 1926.

Bibliography

Nettleship, R. L., *Philosophical and Literary Remains of Richard Lewis Nettleship*, ed. A. C. Bradley, London, 1901.

Newman, John Henry, *Apologia Pro Vita Sua*, ed. C. F. Harrold, London and New York, 1947.

The Arians of the Fourth Century, London, 1871.

Elucidations of Dr. Hampden's Theological Statements, Oxford, 1836.

An Essay in Aid of a Grammar of Assent, ed. C. F. Harrold, London and New York, 1947.

An Essay on the Development of Christian Doctrine, London, 1890.

Essays and Sketches (3 vols.), ed. C. F. Harrold, London and New York, 1948.

The Idea of a University, ed. C. F. Harrold, New York, 1947.

Letters and Correspondence of John Henry Newman (2 vols.), ed. Anne Mozley, London, 1898.

'Mansel's Bampton Lectures', *The Rambler*, vol. 10, part 60.

Fifteen Sermons Preached before the University of Oxford, 1826–43. (3rd ed. [1872].) Repr. with Introductory Essay by D. M. MacKinnon and J. D. Holmes, London, 1970. [Facsim.]

On the Inspiration of Scripture, eds. J. D. Holmes and R. Murray, London, 1967.

Parochial and Plain Sermons (8 vols.), London, 1868–1890.

The Philosophical Notebook of John Henry Newman (2 vols.), ed. Edward Sillem, revised by A. J. Boekraad, Louvain, 1972.

Philosophical Readings in Cardinal Newman, ed. James Collins, Chicago, 1961.

A Newman Treasury, ed. C. F. Harrold, London, 1943.

Tracts for the Times by members of the University of Oxford, London, 1834–1841.

O'Connor, F. M., 'George Tyrrell and Dogma', *Downside Review*, vol. 85, no. 278–9.

Orsini, G. N. G., *Coleridge and German Idealism: A Study in the History of Philosophy*, Carbondale, 1969.

Pailin, D. A., *The Way of Faith*, London, 1969.

Peirce, C. S., *Collected Papers* (ed. C. Hartshorne, and P. Weiss), vol. 2, Cambridge, Mass., 1932.

Penido, M. T-L., *Le rôle de l'analogie en theologie dogmatique*, Paris, 1923.

Petre, M. D., *Modernism: Its Failures and Fruits*, London, 1918.

My Way of Faith, London, 1937.

Von Hügel and Tyrrell: the Story of a Friendship, London, 1937.

(ed.), *The Autobiography and Life of George Tyrrell* (2 vols.), London, 1912.

Piper, H. W., *The Active Universe: Pantheism and the Concept of the Imagination in the English Romantic Poets*, London, 1962.

Pius X, 'Pascendi Gregis' and 'Lamentabili' in *Modernism* by Paul Sabatier, London, 1908.

Bibliography

Powell, A. E. (Mrs Dodds), *The Romantic Theory of Poetry*, London, 1926.

Price, H. H., *Belief*, London, 1969.

Thinking and Experience, London, 1969.

Prickett, Stephen, *Coleridge and Wordsworth: The Poetry of Growth*, London, 1970.

Romanticism and Religion: The Tradition of Coleridge and Wordsworth in the Victorian Church, Cambridge, 1976.

Quick, Oliver C., *Liberalism, Modernism and Tradition*, London, 1922.

Rahme, Mary, 'Coleridge's Concept of Symbolism', *Studies in English Literature 1500–1900*, vol. 9, no. 4.

Rahner, K. *et al.* (eds), *Sacramentum Mundi*, London, 1968.

Ratté, J., *Three Modernists: Alfred Loisy, George Tyrrell and W. L. Sullivan*, New York, 1968.

Reardon, B. M. G., *From Coleridge to Gore: A Century of Religious Thought in Britain*, London, 1971.

(ed.), *Religious Thought in the 19th Century*, Cambridge, 1966.

(ed.), *Roman Catholic Modernism*, London, 1970.

'Newman and the Catholic Modernist Movement', *Church Quarterly*, no. 4, 1971.

Récéjac, E., *Essay on the Bases of the Mystic Knowledge* (translated by S. C. Upton), London, 1899.

Rehder, H. (ed.), *Literary Symbolism*, Texas, 1965.

Richards, I. A., *Coleridge on Imagination*, London, 1962.

Rickaby, J., *Index to the Works of John Henry, Cardinal Newman*, London, 1914.

Rowe, W. L., *Religious Symbols and God: A Philosophical Study of Tillich's Theology*, Chicago, 1966.

Sabatier, Paul, *Modernism* (Jowett Lectures, 1908) (translated by C. A. Miles), London, 1908.

Sanday, W., *England's Debt to Newman*, Oxford, 1892.

Sanders, C. R., *Coleridge and the Broad Church Movement*, Durham, Kansas, U.S.A., 1942.

'Maurice as Commentator on Coleridge', *Publications of the Modern Language Association of America*, vol. 53, March, 1938.

Sarolea, Charles, *Cardinal Newman and his Influence on Religious Life and Thought*, Edinburgh, 1908.

Schaper, Eva, 'Art Symbol', *British Journal of Aesthetics*, vol. 4, no. 3.

Schutz, Alfred, 'Symbol, Reality and Society' in *Symbols and Society*, ed. L. Bryson, *et al.* New York, 1955.

Seynaeve, J., *Cardinal Newman's Doctrine on Holy Scripture*, Louvain, 1953.

Sharrock, Roger, 'Fables and Symbols' I and II, *New Blackfriars*, vol. 50, nos. 585 and 586.

Bibliography

Sherwood, Margaret, *Coleridge's Imaginative Concept of the Imagination*, Wellesley, Mass., 1937.

Undercurrents of Influence in English Romantic Poetry, Cambridge, Mass., 1934.

Shine, Hill, *Carlyle's Fusion of Poetry, History and Religion by 1834*, North Carolina, 1938.

Silkstone, Thomas, *Religion Symbolism and Meaning*, Oxford, 1968.

Snyder, Alice D., *Coleridge on Logic and Learning*, New Haven, 1929.

The Critical Principle of the Reconciliation of Opposites as Employed by Coleridge, Ann Arbor, 1968.

'Coleridge's Cosmogony: A note on the Poetic "World View"', *Studies in Philosophy*, 21, October, 1924.

Stole, E. E., 'Symbolism in Coleridge', *Publications of the Modern Language Association of America*, vol. 63, no. 1, part 1.

Symons, Arthur, *The Symbolist Movement in Literature*, ed. R. Ellmann, London, 1958.

Tennyson, G. B., *Sartor called Resartus*, Princeton, 1965.

Tillich, Paul, 'The Meaning and Justification of Religious Symbols' and 'The Religious Symbol' in *Religious Experience and Truth*, ed. S. Hook, Edinburgh, 1962.

Tindall, W. Y., 'The Literary Symbol' in *Symbols and Society*, ed. L. Bryson *et al.*, New York, 1955.

Traill, H. D., *Coleridge*, London, 1884.

Trilling, Lionel, *Matthew Arnold*, London, 1963.

Tyrrell, George, *Autobiography and Life of George Tyrrell*, London, 1912; vol. 1, *Autobiography of George Tyrrell 1861–1884* arranged, with supplement, by M. D. Petre; vol. 2, *Life of George Tyrrell 1884–1909* by M. D. Petre.

Christianity at the Crossroads, London, 1963.

External Religion: Its Use and Abuse, London, 1899.

The Faith of the Millions (1st and 2nd Series), London, 1901.

George Tyrrell's Letters, ed. M. D. Petre, London. 1920.

Hard Sayings: A Selection of Meditations and Studies, London, 1898.

Lex Credendi: A Sequel to Lex Orandi, London, 1907.

Lex Orandi: or, Prayer and Creed, London, 1903.

Through Scylla and Charybdis: or, The Old Theology and the New, London, 1907.

'The Contents of a Pre-Adamite Skull', *The Month*, vol. 67, September, 1889.

Translation: *The Programme of Modernism: A Reply to the Encyclical of Pius X, Pascendi Gregis*, London, 1908.

Translation: *What we Want: An Open Letter to Pius X from a Group of Priests*, London, 1907.

Urban, W. M., *Language and Reality*, London, 1951.

Bibliography

'Symbolism as a Theological Principle', *Journal of Religion*, vol. 19, no. 1.

Vargish, Thomas, *The Contemplation of Mind*, Oxford, 1970.

Vidler, A. R., *The Church in an Age of Revolution*, London, 1964.

The Modernist Movement in the Roman Church, Cambridge, 1934.

The Theology of F. D. Maurice, London, 1948.

Twentieth Century Defenders of the Faith, London, 1965.

A Variety of Catholic Modernists, Cambridge, 1970.

Walgrave, J. H., O. P., *Newman the Theologian* (translated by A. V. Littledale), London, 1960.

Walsh, William, *Coleridge: The Work and the Relevance*, London, 1967.

Ward, Maisie, *The Wilfrid Wards and the Transition*; vol. 1, *The Nineteenth Century*, London, 1934; vol. 2, *Insurrection versus Resurrection*, London, 1937.

Young Mr. Newman, London, 1948.

Ward, Patricia A., 'Coleridge's Critical Theory of Symbol', *Texas Studies in Literature and Language*, vol. 8, no. 1.

Ward, Wilfrid, *The Life of John Henry, Cardinal Newman, based on his Private Journals and Correspondence* (2 vols), London, 1913.

Last Lectures, Being the Lowell Lectures, 1914, London, 1918.

Problems and Persons, London, 1903.

Ten Personal Studies, London, 1908.

Witnesses to the Unseen and Other Essays, London, 1893.

'The Encyclical *Pascendi Gregis*', *Dublin Review*, vol. 142, no. 284.

Watkin, E. A., *A Philosophy of Form*, London, 1950.

Weigel, Gustave, S. J., 'Myth, Symbol and Analogy' in *Religion and Culture*, ed. W. Leibrech, London, 1959.

Wellek, René, *Confrontations*, Princeton, 1965.

Discriminations, Princeton, 1970.

A History of Modern Criticism 1750–1950 (3 vols.), London, 1966.

Kant in England, Princeton, 1931.

Werkmeister, Lucyle, 'Coleridge on Science, Philosophy and Poetry: Their Relation to Religion', *Harvard Theological Review*, vol. 52, no. 2.

Wheelwright, Philip, *The Burning Fountain: A Study in the Language of Symbolism*, Bloomington, 1964.

The Language of Poetry, Princeton, 1942.

'Semantics and Ontology' in *Metaphor and Symbol*, ed. L. C. Knights, London, 1960.

Whitehead, A. N., *Symbolism*, Oxford, 1928.

Willey, Basil, *Nineteenth Century Studies*, London, 1949.

More Nineteenth Century Studies, London, 1956.

'Coleridge on Imagination and Fancy', *Proceedings of the British Academy*, No. 22, 1946.

The English Moralists, London, 1964.

Bibliography

Woods, G. F., *Theological Explanation*, Welwyn, 1958.
Yeats, W. B., *Autobiographies*, London, 1955.
  Essays and Introductions, London, 1961.
  with Ellis, E. J. (eds), *The Works of William Blake: Poetic, Symbolic and Critical* (3 vols), London, 1893.

INDEX

Index

Index

93–100, 101–16 passim, 171–3; and MacDonald 154, 163; and Tyrrell, 138, 141; analogy, 114–15; Calvinism, 94, 113 & 188n30; Christ, 113; dogmas and their development, 95, 98–106 passim, 109, 172, 173; empiricism, 113; Faith, 100–4; God, and his relation to man, and to the world, 113–15, 171–2; history, 114 & 189n34; ideas and their development, 95–6, 99–109 passim, 160, 172; laws, 106, 107, 111; literature and science, 187n24; mathematics, 104, 106–8, 110; matter and spirit, 113–14; metaphors, 109; Modernism, 92, 95–6; nature, 172; Platonism, 95, 113–14; poetry, 102, 110; reality and appearance, 95; Reason, 100–1, 103, 104; sacraments, 98, 115, 173; symbols, 94–166 passim, 171–3

Peirce, C. S., 7, 11
Plato, 39, 60–3 passim, 120
Powell, A. E., 70, 72
Price, H. H., 7, 10
Prickett, S., 70

Rahme, M., 60
Ruskin, J., 152, 193n22

Sanders, C. R., 72–3, 75, 77
Schelling, F. W. J. von, 64, 70, 75
Schutz, A., 9, 11
Scripture, *see under* Bible
Symbol, passim, *but see also under authors*
Symons, A., 13–15

Tennyson, G. B., 86
Trilling, L., 18
Tyrrell, George, 3, 4, 130–50, 174; and Coleridge, 135–50 passim, 174; and Inge 130–2; and Newman, 138, 141; analogue and metaphor, 134–5, 144–5, 148; Bible, 135, 140, 142; body and soul, 139; Christ, 135–50 passim; Christianity, 142, 150; dogmas, 140, 142, 150; God, and his relation to man, and to the world, 134, 139, 146, 148; ideas and their development, 141–4; Modernism, 132–3, 141, 142–4; Nature 137, 139; reality and appearance, 139; sacraments, 136–8; symbols, 132–51 passim, 174

Walgrave, J. H., 100
Ward, W., 95 & 185n14
Watkin, E. I., 10
Wheelwright, P., 10–11

Steve [signature]

Wellcome Unit for the
History of Medicine
Manchester University

Revere Osler's bookplate which he designed and etched, 1914–15. This was taken from a boy's book given to Revere by Campbell Howard for Christmas 1904. The bookplate was inserted in the books his parents gave to Johns Hopkins University in 1919 to found The Tudor and Stuart Library in Revere's memory. In the upper right corner is an adaptation of the coat of arms of Christ College, his College at Oxford, and in the upper left are instruments for designing and woodworking. At the top center is a fishing reel with line and hooks in the lower part. Below "Ex Libris" are Edward Revere Osler's initials. They are followed by abbreviations which indicate that he was a disciple of Izaak Walton, author of The Compleat Angler, 1653. Revere's signature and the date of preparation are in small print at the base.